Russia's renewal since the collapse of communism has proved extraordinarily disturbed, marked by escalating conflict between President Yeltsin and the Congress of People's Deputies inherited from the Soviet era. This culminated in insurrection and violence on the streets, and when the main rebels were given amnesty in February 1994, the situation remained as uncertain as ever. The contributors to this book analyse a Russia which is searching for its future amid a maelstrom of complex forces – political, economic, sociocultural, and international. They examine each of these elements of Russia's situation and investigate the role that each may play in shaping Russia's fortunes into the next century. Their overall conclusion is that, whatever the exact shape of the future, it will be determined by both elements embedded over many generations and the influence of seven decades of communist rule.

Russia in Search of its Future

Russia in Search of its Future

edited by

Amin Saikal and William Maley

CAMBRIDGE
UNIVERSITY PRESS

Published by the Press Syndicate of the University of Cambridge
The Pitt Building, Trumpington Street, Cambridge CB2 1RP
40 West 20th Street, New York, NY 10011–4211, USA
10 Stamford Road, Oakleigh, Melbourne 3166, Australia

First published 1995

Printed in Great Britain at the University Press, Cambridge

A catalogue record for this book is available from the British Library

Library of Congress cataloguing in publication data applied for

ISBN 0 521 48260 7 hardback
ISBN 0 521 48387 5 paperback

In memory of
Eugene Kamenka
(1928–1994)

Contents

Culture and Society

Conclusion

Preface

This book is based on a conference of the same name which was held at the Australian National University (ANU) in Canberra in December 1993. The conference was co-sponsored by the Departments of Modern European Languages (Russian Section), History, and Political Science and the Centre for Middle Eastern and Central Asian Studies of the ANU; and by the Department of Politics, University College, University of New South Wales, Australian Defence Force Academy. The papers have all been extensively revised since the conference, but beyond asking the contributors to address particular topics, we have taken no steps to impose any particular line or argument or methodology upon their contributions.

We would like to thank the Vice-Chancellor of the ANU, Professor R. D. Terrell, and the Minister-Counsellor of the Russian Embassy in Australia, Mr Viktor Samoilenko, for opening the conference. The organisation of the conference was in the hands of a committee convened by Mr Rosh Ireland, Head of the Department of Modern European Languages, and consisting of Professor T. H. Rigby, Dr Elizabeth Waters, Mr Kyle Wilson, Dr Kevin Windle, and ourselves. We wish to register our deep appreciation of the work of the committee, and especially its convenor. The committee was supported at all times by Professor Richard Campbell, Dean of the Faculty of Arts, ANU, and by Professor Ian McAllister, Dr David Lovell, and Commander François van der Berg of the Department of Politics, University College, University of New South Wales. The committee was also fortunate to receive the unstinting help of the staff of the Australian Embassy in Moscow, especially Glenn Waller. The smooth running of the conference owed much to Sharon Merten's support.

Finally, special thanks go to Mrs Chris Kertesz of the Centre for Middle Eastern and Central Asian Studies of the ANU for her care in preparing the index, and to Mrs Beverley Lincoln of the Department of Politics, University College, University of New South Wales, who provided invaluable assistance at all times.

Canberra
June 1994

AMIN SAIKAL
WILLIAM MALEY

Note on Transliteration

Russian words and names have been transliterated according to the Library of Congress system, except in the citations of English-language works by Russian authors, where published spellings have been reproduced exactly; and in a very small number of cases where an alternative transliteration is already established in English usage.

1 Introduction

AMIN SAIKAL AND WILLIAM MALEY

In December 1993, Russian voters adopted a new constitution and elected a new Parliament. In doing so they inaugurated a further phase in Russia's turbulent march towards a constitutional political order, which had begun over a century and a half earlier with the famous Decembrist uprising against the absolute rule of the Tsar.[1] However, the outcome of the December 1993 polls has fallen far short of resolving the uncertainties which surround Russia's political future. With a significant portion of votes going to candidates of Vladimir Zhirinovskii's neo-fascist 'Liberal-Democratic Party', and the new government in January 1994 apparently abandoning any commitment to what Prime Minister Viktor Chernomyrdin labelled 'market romanticism', the future of political and economic reform in Russia remains clouded, with one prominent reformer even asserting that reform is dead.[2]

In the highly charged atmosphere which the election results produced, there has been open talk of a Weimar scenario for Russia. The combination of ineffectual government and economic crisis which prevailed in Germany in the early 1930s was widely blamed for permitting the rise of Adolf Hitler and the National Socialist German Workers' Party[3]—and some would see in the votes for Zhirinovskii a similar phenomenon. Zhirinovskii's crude nationalism, hectoring rhetoric, willingness to use racialism as a mobilising strategy, and even his publication of a bizarre autobiographical tract, are hauntingly reminiscent of various steps on Hitler's path to power.

There are, however, voices of optimism as well as pessimism in contemporary Russia, and they should not be discounted. Zhirinovskii's organisation is weak—witness the March 1994 resignation of his chief of staff Viktor Kobelev—and other Russians have the awful example of what happened in Germany as an inducement not to throw in their lot with him. Furthermore, while a prolonged phase of political struggle seems almost certain, this is not atypical in transitions from autocracy to democracy. 'What infant democracy requires', Dankwart Rustow once wrote, 'is not lukewarm struggle but a hot family feud'.[4] Indeed, so dramatic have recent events been in Russia that we can too readily forget how much has been achieved in a relatively short space of time, and how comparatively low has been the cost in terms of bloodshed—although it is clear that Russia's new Time of Troubles is far from over.

Much has changed in the mere space of a decade. When Mikhail Gorbachev was elected General Secretary of the Communist Party of the Soviet Union in March 1985, he assumed the leadership of a venerable[5] and apparently secure monocratic system[6] in which political freedoms were limited, dissident voices were routinely silenced by agents of the Committee of State Security (KGB),[7] and personal advancement largely came through cooptation into an entrenched party elite.[8] The military might of the Soviet Union made it a recognised superpower, and its conventional forces over the previous decade had been used in both nearby and far-flung parts of the world, and with comparative impunity, to advance Soviet interests as formulated in the ideology of developed socialism. While some Western observers expected generational change and elite turnover to affect the character and style of the Soviet leadership,[9] and others in the mid-1980s highlighted weaknesses as well as strengths in the Soviet system,[10] few saw a Soviet Union careering towards a terminal crisis.

A tantalising and possibly unanswerable question is whether the Soviet Union was ineluctably on such a path when Gorbachev assumed the leadership, or whether he and his associates set it on that path. Irrespective of how one might attempt to address this question, there were a number of important signs which pointed to coming troubles. The new leadership inherited problems which demanded innovative solutions. These arose in both the domestic and international spheres. Domestically, the leadership was faced with serious problems of poverty and economic inefficiency,[11] corruption,[12] and bureaucratisation on a phenomenal scale.[13] Internationally, the Soviet Union faced challenges as a consequence of the decline of *détente* in the later years of the Brezhnev era (1964-1982), which provided incentives for change in both foreign and domestic policy.[14] More significantly, the USSR was entangled in a disastrous war in Afghanistan.[15] It brought sorrow to the Soviet masses as had no other event since the Second World War,[16] and reflected the perils of closed decision-making on momentous issues. In the words of one commentator, the 'large costs of the war and the inability of the Soviet military to bring it to a successful conclusion contributed to the political liberalization Gorbachev brought to the Soviet Union'.[17]

These accumulated difficulties did not make significant reform inevitable—to argue that there were no other options open to the Soviet leadership ignores the fact that in politics there are always options—but they certainly created a climate of opinion in which a vigorous General Secretary would be more likely to secure approval for radical proposals. The classic example of a radical move accommodated by a manifest failure of the Soviet system of administration was the expansion of the policy of *glasnost'* (candour) following the Chernobyl nuclear accident in April 1986.[18] The panic which spread in the vicinity of the accident when the only source of information for locals came from rumours or foreign radio broadcasts proved sufficient to prompt a policy which was to have revolutionary effects. The selection of Gorbachev as General Secretary brought to office a man of subversive opinions who managed with unusual speed to acquire the power needed to act crypto-legislatively.[19] Yet it would be a mistake to suggest that Gorbachev alone was responsible for the change of opinion within the Soviet elite. With the benefit of hindsight, it is clear that Aleksandr Iakovlev and Eduard Shevardnadze played crucial roles in the reorientation of specific spheres of official policy; and their contributions should be recognised as well.[20]

The unanticipated consequences of Gorbachev's actions proved fatal for the integrity of the Soviet system. While the policy of *perestroika* (reconstruction) had relatively limited impact, the associated policies of *glasnost'* and *demokratizatsiia* undermined the foundations of monocratic rule. *Glasnost'* facilitated not only a cultural renaissance, but the emergence of alternative ideological positions with which the party elite was singularly ill-prepared to cope. The result was an increasingly open schism within the elite, between on the one hand, conservatives such as Egor Ligachev, and on the other, radicals such as Boris Yeltsin—between whom Gorbachev manoeuvred in an attempt to bolster his own evolving position. Furthermore, as freedom of speech and freedom of association are almost inseparable companions, *glasnost'* rapidly led to the emergence of informal political groups.[21] The decisive blow to the old system came with the endorsement in June 1988 of the principle of holding contested elections.[22] This struck at the very heart of the established system of party control by coopted elites, and linked with *glasnost'*, amounted to a shift to informal multi-party politics.[23] In turn, this had insidious effects on the cohesion of the Soviet empire, as ethnonational groups emerged in the non-Russian republics, ostensibly to defend *perestroika*, but in reality to assert the importance of national sovereignty, and, ultimately, independence.[24] This message was not lost on democratic forces in Eastern Europe, who exploited it crucially to press for release in late 1989 from the domination which the Soviet Union was no longer in a position to maintain by military means in the aftermath of its humiliating retreat from Afghanistan earlier in the year.[25] But most importantly of all, it obliterated the unique role of the party as a mechanism of organisational integration, although Gorbachev seems to have been almost the last man in Russia to realise that the party was no longer part of the solution but part of the problem.[26]

By the time those opposed to Gorbachev's views moved decisively against him, in August 1991, their own power bases had been so weakened that the counter-revolution failed.[27] The events of the previous three years had delegitimated the Communist Party, and eroded the cement which held together the principal instrumentalities of state coercion. The leaders of the State Committee on the Emergency Situation (GKChP) faced a far more formidable task than those who mounted the palace coup against Nikita Khrushchev in 1964: as a Soviet commentator observed with remarkable prescience in August 1989, the political activeness of the masses provided the most reliable protection against such a coup.[28] Furthermore, the popular election of Yeltsin as President of Russia on 12 June 1991 had established a legitimate focus of opposition to the decrees of the GKChP. Finally, the stalwart and effective resistance by citizens of Latvia and Lithuania in January 1991 to moves by similar 'National Salvation Committees' to overthrow constitutional government provided a telling precedent which the citizens of Moscow were able to follow. Whether Gorbachev should be blamed for promoting those who ultimately moved against him, or praised for adroitly preventing a conservative counterstroke until it was too late to abort the process of change which had engulfed the USSR, will remain one of the great imponderables of history. It is beyond question, however, that the failure of the coup attempt drove the last nail into the coffin of the Soviet system.

The death rattle of the USSR held out little promise of a pain-free birth for the political and economic systems which succeeded it. The post-independence experiences of the Baltic states and of the former Soviet republics which formed the Commonwealth of Independent States (CIS) in Minsk in December 1991 fall outside the scope of this book.[29] Fortunately, a study of the tumultuous experiences of post-independence Russia illustrates some of the deeper dilemmas and uncertainties which all to some extent have had to face. Russia, like all these states, had witnessed the demise of significant features of its political system, in the midst of a developing economic crisis. However, its problems were also complicated by the widespread popular perception within Russia itself that it had lost the acknowledged status as a superpower which the Soviet Union had enjoyed.

Three years after the collapse of the Soviet Union, it is time to take stock of the position in which Russia finds itself. The early years of Russia's renewal proved extraordinarily disturbed,[30] marked by escalating conflict between President Yeltsin and the Congress of People's Deputies inherited from the Soviet era. A nationwide referendum in April 1993 saw 58.7% of those who voted express confidence in Yeltsin personally, and 67.2% vote in favour of early parliamentary elections, but while this vote substantially delegitimated the legislature, it did not divert it from pursuing increasingly irresponsible fiscal policies. A direct collision between the executive and the legislature appeared unavoidable, and finally came on 21 September 1993 when Yeltsin issued a decree calling for elections in December 1993 to a new Federal Assembly. These were resisted by the legislature, but the resort to violence in the streets by its more extreme supporters on 3 October prompted Yeltsin to use force to occupy its premises and imprison the leaders of the revolt, Vice President Aleksandr Rutskoi and Parliamentary Speaker Ruslan Khasbulatov. Yet within three months of the December 1993 elections, Rutskoi and Khasbulatov were again at large, thanks to an amnesty resolution passed by the new parliament, and Rutskoi had even resumed his public demand for moves to procure the reconstitution of the Soviet Union. The future of Russia appeared as uncertain as ever.

To attempt a definitive prognosis of future developments in Russia would be an act of supreme *hubris*. Russia is not following a pre-determined ballistic path. It is in *search* of its future, and a maelstrom of complex forces—political, economic, sociocultural, and international—will determine which of its possible futures actually eventuates. What one can do is seek to investigate these forces in as much detail as can be mustered. That is the aim of this book, which examines selected developments in Russia's politics, economy, foreign relations, and culture and society which are destined to play a substantial role in shaping Russia's future into the next century.

The context of political change in Russia is outlined in the opening chapter by A.V. Obolonsky. He provides an overview of the mechanisms of power within the Soviet system, and links this in the second part of the chapter to what he calls the deep structure of Russian conservatism—the psychological constants of mass consciousness. He concludes by examining the fragile state of Russia's post-communist political system, and highlighting some of the dangers which Russia faces along the road to a more democratic political order.

These issues are taken up by Archie Brown, who concentrates on the crisis of September-October 1993 and its aftermath. In contrast to those who see 'reform' mainly in economic terms, he emphasises the importance of political consolidation and protection of the ideal of the rule of law. Pursuing this line of reasoning, he is critical of the approach to the recalcitrant legislature taken by Yeltsin, and stresses the importance for political leadership in democratic polities of bargaining and negotiation between contending political forces.

William Maley surveys the state of the Russian macroeconomy, and points to conflict between different institutional actors as a key source of difficulty in effective macroeconomic management. He suggests that this embodies a conflict of visions as to the appropriate role of macroeconomic policy, and the virtues of market as opposed to bureaucratic modes of allocation. He concludes that a retreat from the shift to a market economy is inappropriate, partly because the relative costs and benefits of transition are not adequately captured by statistics upon which officials rely, but more fundamentally because the 'non-monetary measures' upon which conservatives might wish to rely to prevent a hyperinflationary collapse are little more than items of rhetoric.

The specific problems of Russian agriculture are explored by Robert F. Miller. He highlights the complexity of the agricultural sector, and argues that a consequence of this is that an immediate shift to private family farming is not a realistic possibility. He notes that consumer demand for food has been falling, adding to the plight of emerging private farms, and concludes that in the wake of the December 1993 election, significant change in the structure of the agricultural system shaped by the Soviet collectivisation drive of the 1930s is not especially likely.

Stephen Fortescue addresses the successes, failures, and prospects of the process of privatisation of large-scale industry in Russia. While workforce ownership has thus far been the dominant form which privatisation has taken, he does not expect it to remain dominant given the need to attract outside equity. In the light of the drift of government policy since the December 1993 elections, he sees a danger that workforce ownership will be replaced by ownership structures which are hierarchical, rigid, and subsidy-oriented, but the ultimate outcome of the privatisation process still remains far from clear.

In the sphere of foreign policy, Amin Saikal and William Maley trace the implications of the replacement of 'new thinking' about international relations with intellectual underpinnings for foreign policy more directly based on diverse visions of Russia's role as a power, both in the wider world and with respect to areas of direct local interest. They explore ways in which the formulation of policy has changed with the disintegration of the Soviet Union, examining the broader institutional context of the foreign policy making process, and conclude by addressing the tensions surrounding Russian policy towards the United States, the countries of NATO, and China and Japan, as well as the Baltic States and Ukraine.

Leslie Holmes examines Russia's relations with the former external empire of Eastern Europe, arguing on the one hand that they are shaped to a significant extent by the domestic political developments in the countries concerned, but on the other that both the domestic politics and international relations of these countries are in a state of flux. In the military sphere, he notes the ambivalence of NATO about expansion of its membership, and the concerns which this ambivalence, coupled with Zhirinovskii's stronger-than-expected electoral performance, has created for Eastern European leaderships. Nonetheless, he sees economic relations as probably the single most important determinant of the climate within which relations operate, and explores the factors which have made the 'turn to the West' prove problematical.

Amin Saikal then focuses on Russia's relations with Central Asia. He argues that within a short space of time, Russian policy towards the region has come full circle, progressing from an initial phase of neglect and confusion to a stage of reassertion to fill the power vacuum which was created in the wake of the disintegration of the USSR. He suggests that two factors—fear of ethnonationalism and fear of Islamic radicalism—have underpinned this turnaround, and claims that in the process, the Yeltsin leadership has taken on board many positions originating from the ranks of the military and security apparatuses, and from his hardline parliamentary critics. As a result, what has emerged is a policy which entails support of Central Asian leaderships who publicly scorn the ideals of democratisation to which Russia is ostensibly committed. Such support is based on a crude exaggeration of the Islamic 'threat', and runs the risk of sucking Russia into a quagmire which could prove unduly costly for it.

Sergei Serebriany offers a wide-ranging exploration of different meanings of 'culture'. He sees three dimensions of a Russian identity crisis, arising from the collapse of the USSR, the openness of Russia to the rest of the world, and the ideological vacuum arising from the collapse of communism, which pose questions about the future nature and place of Russia. The future of Russia is also tied to broader questions about the texture of civilisation generally, and he quotes Fazil Iskander's ominous warning that the *Kolyma Stories* of Varlam Shalamov, with their searing depiction of life in the GULAG, can be read as a warning of the future as well as a depiction of the past. Yet Serebriany shares Iskander's optimism that a new depth of spiritual culture will emerge in the face of the abyss.

Developments in Russian literature and literary criticism are further explored by Peter Sawczak. Taking as his point of departure Chuprinin's suggestion that changed political circumstances have allowed Russian literature to assume a 'normal' form, he notes that intelligent discussion of postmodernism has been limited in Russian criticism, and that

Western studies of Russian literature also risk making assessments in terms of loaded dichotomies such as that between Slavophiles and Westernisers. Nonetheless, he detects diverse and talented responses from the literary community to the cultural problemata of the post-Soviet order.

John Miller examines four alternative visions of Russia's future—statism, reformism, Russian nationalism, and communitarianism—and delineates their strengths and weaknesses. He points to the resilience of traditional political culture, as embodied most starkly in the statist vision, and concludes that the statist tradition seems most likely to prevail. Although associated with the discredited Soviet system, it offers a solution to problems of law and order, and could be bolstered by the still-largely-intact Soviet bureaucracy. However, the nuances which surround a statist model remain significant, with both Gaullist France or theocratic Iran potentially providing parallels.

In the concluding chapter, T.H. Rigby draws together some themes which run through the volume. He argues that Russia's transformation process was essentially negative, with a *telos* defined in derivative terms, and inaugurated from above, although it then triggered lower-level chaos. By supplying a constitution, president, and parliament endorsed by popular vote, the December 1993 elections marked a great step forward in Russia's political development, ending the transition period between the Soviet and the post-Soviet phases of Russian history. However, while the exact shape of the Russian future remains indeterminate, it will surely, in his view, 'embody and transmute both elements culturally encoded over many generations, and others laid down in over seven decades of communist rule'. That, indeed, is the broader message of this book.

Notes

1 Andrzej Walicki, *A History of Russian Thought from the Enlightenment to Marxism* (Oxford: Oxford University Press, 1980) pp.57-70.

2 Yuri N. Afanasyev, 'Russian Reform Is Dead: Back to Central Planning', *Foreign Affairs*, vol.73, no.2, March-April 1994, pp.21-26.

3 For different perspectives on the rise of Nazism, see William L. Shirer, *The Rise and Fall of the Third Reich* (London: Secker & Warburg, 1960); and Karl Dietrich Bracher, *Die deutsche Diktatur: Entstehung. Struktur. Folgen des Nationalsozialismus* (Frankfurt am Main: Ullstein Materialien, 1969).

4 Dankwart A. Rustow, 'Transitions to Democracy: Toward a Dynamic Model', *Comparative Politics*, vol.2, no.3, April 1970, pp.337-363 at p.355.

5 On the history of the Soviet Union, see Michel Heller and Aleksandr Nekrich, *Utopia in Power: A History of the USSR from 1917 to the Present* (London: Hutchinson, 1985); Geoffrey Hosking, *A History of the Soviet*

Union (London: Collins, 1985); Martin Malia, *The Soviet Tragedy: A History of Socialism in Russia, 1917-1991* (New York: The Free Press, 1994).

6 For more detailed depictions of the mature Soviet system, see T.H. Rigby, 'Politics in the Mono-organizational Society', in Andrew C. Janos (ed.), *Authoritarian Politics in Communist Europe: Uniformity and Diversity in One-Party States* (Berkeley: Research Series, no.28, Institute of International Studies, University of California, 1976) pp.31-80; Seweryn Bialer, *Stalin's Successors: Leadership, stability, and change in the Soviet Union* (Cambridge: Cambridge University Press, 1980); Frederick C. Barghoorn and Thomas F. Remington, *Politics in the USSR* (Boston: Little, Brown & Co., 1986); Philip G. Roeder, *Red Sunset: The Failure of Soviet Politics* (Princeton: Princeton University Press, 1993).

7 On dissent, see Marshall S. Shatz, *Soviet Dissent in Historical Perspective* (Cambridge: Cambridge University Press, 1980); Ludmilla Alexeyeva, *Soviet Dissent: Contemporary Movements for National, Religious, and Human Rights* (Middletown: Wesleyan University Press, 1985); Peter Reddaway, 'Sovietology and Dissent: New Sources on Protest', *RFE/RL Research Report*, vol.2, no.5, 29 January 1993, pp.12-16. On the KGB, see Amy W. Knight, *The KGB: Police and Politics in the Soviet Union* (Boston: Unwin Hyman, 1988).

8 For detailed discussion of the *nomenklatura* system of elite recruitment, see Bohdan Harasymiw, '*Nomenklatura*: The Soviet Communist Party's Leadership Recruitment System', *Canadian Journal of Political Science*, vol.2, no.4, December 1969, pp.493-512; Bohdan Harasymiw, *Political Elite Recruitment in the Soviet Union* (London: Macmillan, 1984) pp.153-186; T.H. Rigby, *Political Elites in the USSR: Central leaders and local cadres from Lenin to Gorbachev* (Aldershot: Edward Elgar, 1990).

9 Jerry F. Hough, *Soviet Leadership in Transition* (Washington DC: The Brookings Institution, 1980).

10 Seweryn Bialer, *The Soviet Paradox: External Expansion, Internal Decline* (London: I.B. Tauris, 1986); Paul Dibb, *The Soviet Union: The Incomplete Superpower* (London: Macmillan, 1986).

11 See Timothy J. Colton, *The Dilemma of Reform in the Soviet Union* (New York: Council on Foreign Relations, 1986) pp.32-67; Ed A. Hewett, *Reforming the Soviet Economy: Equality versus Efficiency* (Washington DC: The Brookings Institution, 1988).

12 See Konstantin Simis, *USSR: Secrets of a Corrupt Society* (London: J.M. Dent, 1982); William A. Clark, *Crime and Punishment in Soviet Officialdom: Combating Corruption in the Political Elite 1965-1990* (New York: M.E. Sharpe, 1993); Leslie Holmes, *The End of Communist Power: Anti-Corruption Campaigns and Legitimacy Crisis* (New York: Oxford University Press, 1993).

13 According to A. Rumiantsev and Iu. Goland, 'Informatsiia k razmyshleniiu. I tol'ko?', *Trud*, 12 May 1983, 800 billion official documents were created in the Soviet Union every year.

14 See Daniel Deudney and G. John Ikenberry, 'The International Sources of Soviet Change', *International Security*, vol.16, no.3, Winter 1991-92, pp.74-118; R. Craig Nation, *Black Earth, Red Star: A History of Soviet Security Policy, 1917-1991* (Ithaca: Cornell University Press, 1992) pp.245-284.

15 For details, see Amin Saikal and William Maley, *Regime Change in Afghanistan: Foreign Intervention and the Politics of Legitimacy* (Boulder: Westview Press, 1991) pp.81-99; Anthony Arnold, *The Fateful*

Pebble: Afghanistan's Role in the Fall of the Soviet Empire (San Francisco: Presidio Press, 1993).

16 See Gennady Bocharov, *Russian Roulette: The Afghanistan War Through Russian Eyes* (London: Hamish Hamilton, 1990); Artyom Borovik, *The Hidden War: A Russian Journalist's Account of the Soviet War in Afghanistan* (London: Faber and Faber, 1990); and Svetlana Alexievich, *Zinky Boys: Soviet Voices from a Forgotten War* (London: Chatto & Windus, 1992).

17 Samuel P. Huntington, *The Third Wave: Democratization in the Late Twentieth Century* (Norman: University of Oklahoma Press, 1991) p.54.

18 See Zhores Medvedev, *The Legacy of Chernobyl* (Oxford: Basil Blackwell, 1990).

19 There is by now a vast literature on Gorbachev and the reforms which he and his colleagues attempted to engineer. See Boris Meissner, *Die Sowjetunion im Umbruch* (Stuttgart: Deutsche Verlags-Anstalt GmbH, 1988); Walter Laqueur, *The Long Road to Freedom: Russia and Glasnost'* (London: Unwin Hyman, 1989); Alec Nove, *Glasnost' in Action: Cultural Renaissance in Russia* (Boston: Unwin Hyman, 1989); Abraham Brumberg (ed.), *Chronicle of a Revolution: A Western-Soviet Inquiry into Perestroika* (New York: Pantheon Books, 1990); Geoffrey Hosking, *The Awakening of the Soviet Union* (London: Heinemann, 1990); Jerry F. Hough, *Russia and the West: Gorbachev and the Politics of Reform* (New York: Simon and Schuster, 1990); Richard Sakwa, *Gorbachev and His Reforms 1985-1990* (New York: Philip Allan, 1990); Ed A. Hewett and Victor H. Winston (eds.), *Milestones in Glasnost and Perestroyka: Politics and People* (Washington DC: The Brookings Institution, 1991); Robert G. Kaiser, *Why Gorbachev Happened: His Triumphs and His Failure* (New York: Simon & Schuster, 1991); Moshe Lewin, *The Gorbachev Phenomenon: A Historical Interpretation* (Berkeley: University of California Press, 1991); John Miller, *Mikhail Gorbachev and the End of Soviet Power* (London: Macmillan, 1993); Stephen White, *After Gorbachev* (Cambridge: Cambridge University Press, 1993).

20 See Eduard Shevardnadze, *The Future Belongs to Freedom* (New York: The Free Press, 1991); and Aleksandr Iakovlev, *Predislovie. Obval. Posleslovie* (Moscow: Novosti, 1992). The importance of their role is highlighted from an opponent's point of view in Yegor Ligachev, *Inside Gorbachev's Kremlin* (New York: Pantheon Books, 1993).

21 See Vladimir Brovkin, 'Revolution from Below: Informal Political Associations in Russia 1988-89', *Soviet Studies*, vol.42, no.2, April 1990, pp.233-257.

22 See *Materialy XIX Vsesoiuznoi konferentsii Kommunisticheskoi partii Sovetskogo Soiuza* (Moscow: Izdatel'stvo politicheskoi literatury, 1988).

23 For a detailed discussions of this stage of reform, see Michael Urban, *More Power to the Soviets: The Democratic Revolution in the USSR* (Aldershot: Edward Elgar, 1990); Brendan Kiernan, *The End of Soviet Politics: Elections, Legislatures, and the Demise of the Communist Party* (Boulder: Westview Press, 1993).

24 Nowhere was this more obvious than in the Baltic states of Latvia, Lithuania, and Estonia. See Walter C. Clemens, Jr., *Baltic Independence and Russian Empire* (New York: St Martin's Press, 1991); Anatol Lieven, *The Baltic Revolution: Estonia, Latvia, Lithuania and the Path to Independence* (New Haven: Yale University Press, 1993); Kristian Gerner and Stefan Hedlund, *The Baltic States and the End of the Soviet Empire* (London: Routledge, 1993). On ethnic reassertion more generally, see Bohdan Nahaylo and Victor Swoboda, *Soviet Disunion: A*

History of the Nationalities Problem in the USSR (New York: The Free Press, 1990); William Maley, 'Ethnonationalism and Civil Society in the USSR', in Chandran Kukathas, David W. Lovell and William Maley (eds.), *The Transition from Socialism: State and Civil Society in the USSR* (London: Longman, 1991) pp.177-197; Alexander J. Motyl (ed.), *The Post-Soviet Nations: Perspectives on the Demise of the USSR* (New York: Columbia University Press, 1992).

25 On Afghanistan, see Amin Saikal and William Maley (eds.), *The Soviet Withdrawal from Afghanistan* (Cambridge: Cambridge University Press, 1989). On the Eastern European revolutions of 1989, much of value has been written. For varying perspectives, see Charles Gati, *The Bloc That Failed: Soviet-East European Relations in Transition* (Bloomington: Indiana University Press, 1990); Misha Glenny, *The Rebirth of History: Eastern Europe in the Age of Democracy* (Harmondsworth: Penguin, 1990); J.F. Brown, *Surge to Freedom: The End of Communist Rule in Eastern Europe* (Durham: Duke University Press, 1991); Ken Jowitt, *New World Disorder: The Leninist Extinction* (Berkeley & Los Angeles: University of California Press, 1992); David S. Mason, *Revolution in East-Central Europe: The Rise and Fall of Communism and the Cold War* (Boulder: Westview Press, 1992); Vladimir Tismaneanu, *Reinventing Politics: Eastern Europe from Stalin to Havel* (New York: The Free Press, 1992); George Schöpflin, *Politics in Eastern Europe 1945-1992* (Oxford: Blackwell, 1993).

26 See Neil Robinson, 'Gorbachev and the Place of the Party in Soviet Reform, 1985-91', *Soviet Studies*, vol.44, no.3, 1992, pp.423-443.

27 On the coup, see Richard Hellie, 'Russia Before, During, and After the "Keystone Coup"', *Russian History/Histoire Russe*, vol.18, no.3, Fall 1991, pp.255-315; Martin Sixsmith, *Moscow Coup: The Death of the Soviet System* (London: Simon & Schuster, 1991); James H. Billington, *Russia Transformed: Breakthrough to Hope* (New York: The Free Press, 1992); Richard Sakwa, 'The revolution of 1991 in Russia: Interpretations of the Moscow coup', *Coexistence*, vol.29, no.4, December 1992, pp.335-375; John B. Dunlop, *The Rise of Russia and the Fall of the Soviet Empire* (Princeton: Princeton University Press, 1993) pp.186-255; David Remnick, *Lenin's Tomb: The Last Days of the Soviet Empire* (London: Viking, 1993) pp.433-490.

28 N. Mikhailov, 'Vozmozhen li segodnia Oktiabr' 1964 goda?', *Moskovskaia pravda*, 18 August 1989, p.2. On the overthrow of Khrushchev, see Sergei Khrushchev, *Pensioner soiuznogo znacheniia* (Moscow: Novosti, 1991); Fedor Burlatsky, *Khrushchev and the First Russian Spring* (London: Weidenfeld & Nicolson, 1991) pp.204-210; William J. Tompson, 'The Fall of Nikita Khrushchev', *Soviet Studies*, vol.43, no.6, 1991, pp.1101-1121.

29 For useful surveys, see Ian Bremmer and Ray Taras (eds.), *Nations and Politics in the Soviet Successor States* (Cambridge: Cambridge University Press, 1993); Karen Dawisha and Bruce Parrott, *Russia and the New States of Eurasia: The Politics of Upheaval* (Cambridge: Cambridge University Press, 1994).

30 Two works which valuably address the first phase of post-Soviet politics in Russia are Richard Sakwa, *Russian Politics and Society* (London: Routledge, 1993); Stephen White, Graeme Gill, and Darrell Slider, *The Politics of Transition: Shaping a Post-Soviet Future* (Cambridge: Cambridge University Press, 1993).

2 RUSSIAN POLITICS IN THE TIME OF TROUBLES: SOME BASIC ANTINOMIES

A.V. OBOLONSKY

We shall not be able to come to a deep understanding of Russia's political situation if we concentrate only on the processes of political games or on the formal analysis of institutions. For that reason, this chapter contains three sections—historical, socio-cultural and political in the proper sense. I open with a brief systematic outline of the mechanics of power and principles of functioning of the developed Soviet political regime which prevailed until the first half of the 1980s,[1] as experience of this system forms part of the political heritage of post-Communist Russia.

Mechanics of power: modus operandi of the Soviet regime

A mass party built on the principles of strict centralism—the Communist Party of the Soviet Union—was the only organised force in official political life. This ensured political control over all levels of society and the spread and duplication of commands issued from the single centre. Mikhail Gorbachev and part of his team made serious efforts to turn this mechanism into a force that could be an instrument for positive change, but all these attempts failed. The party mechanism acted for many decades to protect conservatism, and to preserve the old state of things. It proved to be absolutely inappropriate as a means for promoting the true modernisation of the regime. Since the time of Stalin, the post of General Secretary of the party was a key power position. Although formally the General Secretary's powers were not reflected in any law, this did not prevent the occupant from exercising awesome powers. But even this did not mean total freedom of action. The Communist Party apparatus had many diverse channels of influence and imposed curbs upon its leader. It always retained complete control over the selection and promotion of elites to posts of leadership. Moreover, it was in a position to monitor the channels of its leader's communication with the outside, 'beyond the apparatus' and to control the upward flow of information and the downward flow of directives and their translation into reality.

While the General Secretary was under the thumb of the apparatus, the apparatus itself was not really controlled by anyone, at least after Stalin's death and especially after Khrushchev's period in office. As became absolutely clear in the early 1990s, it could simulate obedience as long as this would not endanger or in any way jeopardise its ruling status. Mikhail Gorbachev's attempts to change its role from society's boss to a more limited one failed.

The control of ideology was another feature of the developed Soviet regime. A complete monopoly of the 'only correct line' had been in place since the late 1920s. Any innovations could come only from higher party sources. But the main purpose of such a monopoly was not to preserve the purity of Marxist-Leninist dogma, but to cement and maintain ideological discipline. It amounted to a principle of 'non-freedom of information'. There were two radically different layers in the actual ideology of the party. The first one was external: it was declarative and largely camouflaging in nature. This external layer of ideology was propaganda for mass consumption. The second, internal, layer was designed for a narrow audience of the 'initiated', and in fact reflected the true ideology of regime. Understanding the difference between these two layers is crucial to interpreting the central core of Soviet rule. For example, the external layer preached the doctrine of equality, while the internal layer condoned rampant privilege, nepotism, protectionism and caste discrimination. The external layer championed internationalism while the internal layer promoted jingoism, antisemitism and hatred. Demagoguery about 'high-level democracy' thus masked cruel suppression of any opposition or independent thinking. Calls for efficiency sided with bureaucratic pseudo-activity on a monstrous scale.[2] What was said officially from high rostrums was usually contrary to what was said behind closed doors, and it was the latter that served as a practical guide for action.

The total dependence of the individual upon the state was a further crucial feature of the system. All channels for meeting essential human needs such as finding a job, educating one's children, seeking medical aid, or procuring housing came under the control of party and state. This naturally gave those in authority an enormous and inevitably corrupt influence. They could reward or punish an individual at will: he could be promoted or laid off; he could be given a decent place to live in or denied any shelter; he could be permitted to go abroad or forbidden even to read a foreign newspaper; he could be allowed to publish a book or his book could be banned. Dependence on the state also created a new class of elites with a vested interest in keeping the regime alive. They conspired to build highly stratified systems of distributing privileges and benefits. The system was like a multi-storeyed building: individuals were compelled to climb from floor to floor in the hope of receiving more benefits, often literally climbing over the bodies of others. The effect on public morale and personal morality was devastating.

Coercion and suppression were widely deployed. All Soviet rulers, and hence the apparatus, had an exaggerated interest in self-defence. For this reason, one of their central tasks from the earliest years was to set up a network of special agencies with wide powers. The brutal secret police machine that was created soon turned into a permanent tool of state policy. It not only continued to exist long after its original purpose was served, but it was continuously streamlined, refined and expanded. On rare occasions it was mildly rebuked in public for its zealotry. Nonetheless, throughout the time of the regime's existence it remained frighteningly powerful. Its permanent aim was to suppress all opposition and to make preventive assaults on any potential hotbeds of opposition. In this respect, the Soviets invented nothing new: they merely assimilated and modernised the ancient absolutist tradition of police reaction to any social unrest. Under the pretext of the dogma of 'moral and political unity', the party encouraged suspicion, conformism and intolerance. Only towards the end of the 1980s could people begin to break with the party, retreating from the 'gendarme's syndrome', which for decades inhibited every aspect of their lives.

Another principle of operation was the extensive use of various forms of forced labour. Today the whole world knows about the 'extermination labour camps' of the GULAG, in which millions of 'convicts' erected with their bare hands the 'great projects of Communism' on the bones of fellow inmates. 'Convict' labour was still used under Gorbachev, although on a smaller scale. But there were other forms of forced labour: army conscripts who built civilian facilities, citizens who were mobilised for harvesting, and millions who 'voluntarily' participated in *subbotniki* (unpaid work on holidays). Forced labour was always an essential part of Soviet economics. In a choice between an 'efficient society' and an 'obedient society', the regime invariably chose the latter.

It also acted whenever possible to discourage non-sanctioned initiative. In all spheres, the system relied upon pedantic, obedient performers instead of active, inquiring individuals. Even the best talents were tolerated only if under control, or, still better, if completely subservient to the state. On the other hand, the system moved to manipulate negative human attributes. One of the most widely manipulated human attributes was envy. It can be caused by another's talent, success, good fortune, even a beautiful wife or more capable children. One can envy anything under the sun. Envy is based on a form of natural inequality, but such inequality is subjectively perceived by the envious as injustice. It often provokes a perverted desire for revenge, for hurting the 'lucky bastard', for playing a 'dirty trick' on him, for bringing him failure or misfortune. In a Christian society, there is a system of moral standards that inhibits at least the cruellest forms of envy, but the relativism of 'revolutionary morals' permeating the entire ideological complex of Soviet socialism removed practically all ethical limitations. There were always more than enough artful 'soul catchers' among each regime's functionaries. There were people competent, willing and able to make use of human baseness—to advise the scoundrels how and what to do and how to suppress the pangs of conscience. The 'prize' for an informer could be double-edged: the material gains 'inherited' from the victim (office, status, housing, property) and the malicious satisfaction of 'revenge'. Other human vices shored up the rotting edifice of Soviet socialism: vanity, vainglory, love of power. The last two, when combined, were the cause of many shameful deeds, and allowed unscrupulous rulers to play on the weaknesses of morally sick men. And an even more universal tool of power is fear and the related wish to be among the hunters rather than the hunted. The party knew all too well how to intimidate its subjects and fill them with lasting fear. The mechanisms of exploiting every base human instinct operated at all levels of the power pyramid—from the Politburo to the Academy of Sciences, from the streets to the GULAG. Only the prizes were different, from high titles, broad powers and material abundance to miserable handouts and a chance to even a score with a prison mate. The negative incentives—persecution, deprivation, civil and physical death—varied little no matter what the level.

An important operating principle of all Soviet regimes was the exploitation of negative nationalism. It goes without saying that patriotism has positive and often lofty expressions, but this kind of 'politicised patriotism' was pure ideological manipulation. The party attempted to keep the numerous ethnic groups within the USSR hostile to one another, drawing on unsettled scores between non-Russian nationalities, especially in such tense and potentially explosive multinational regions as the Caucasus and Central Asia. As to the external world, the party made good use of the myth of the 'military threat' posed by the imperialist West. The USSR was characterised, by contrast, as a fortress under siege. This was very effective, as it was a long-established Russian tradition to regard the outside world as a host of enemies. The threat was widely accepted as a sufficient explanation for moral and physical deprivation, an active secret police, ideological suppression, and, of course, a militarised command economy. There was also routine manipulation of public consciousness. In the first decades after the Bolshevik revolution, the party particularly preyed on ignorant minds, but as time went by it became clear that orchestrated shouts of approval could be extracted not only from workers, but also from academicians and intellectuals who—unlike men in the street who may have sincerely felt lost or confused— were governed by a mixture of loyalty, fear, ambition, greed and conformism. Gradually, however, these techniques grew less effective. By the 1980s, fewer people were willing to participate in such puppet sideshows and more were inclined to make their own assessments, refusing to chew mechanically the ideological mash.

Soviet regimes also recklessly squandered their potential on various forms of 'pseudo-activity'. This troubling feature of Russian life was noticed by the Marquis de Custine during the reign of Tsar Nikolai I. The Marquis called Russia 'a country of facades'. One new aspect under the Soviets was 'pseudo democracy'. Every regime spent much effort in trying to create an image of a highly democratic society. No money was spared on this facade, but it was of very little use to society. One manifestation was a system of economic management dedicated to achieving favourable formal indicators instead of genuinely socially useful results. The pseudo-substitution of market mechanisms cost Russian society very dear. Everyone clearly realised it, but to renounce this system meant to renounce the omnipotence of the apparatus. Awareness of this fact for decades blocked and even now continues to interfere with overdue reforms. The struggle goes on and its prospects are not yet completely clear.

The logical outcome of many of these principles of operation was the rejection of the best people in every area of endeavour. Guided by sincere and patriotic motives, clever and earnest people more that once made selfless attempts to make the system more civilised, effective and human. Such attempts were made in economics, science, government, industry, and the arts—but as a rule, to little avail. At best, some inessential refinements were accepted. Radical reforms and ideas either drowned in red tape, were mutilated or were politically emasculated.

The law was reduced to an instrument of power. Such treatment of the law is usually described as Asiatic or Byzantine. It is a disdainful, pragmatic attitude that regards the law solely as an instrument of power instead of as a tool to realise the common contract and to protect individual rights. It is always the preferred option of tyrants and despotic governments. In the former USSR, the bulk of laws can be referred to by one of the two categories: declarative propaganda laws and laws of real action. All Soviet constitutions were prime examples of the first category. The laws of real action were drafted and approved without much ado or public discussions. They were first confirmed in the highest party bodies and then rubber-stamped with little or no discussion in the 'supreme legislative organ'. They were often expressly repressive and prohibitive. Yet bad as many Soviet laws were in principle, their application was still worse. Their authors and executors in the apparatus did not even try to make-believe that they were concerned about human rights, for example. This is a problem the new Russia has inherited and must strive to overcome—lack of respect for and faith in the law.

Why did it happen? For some types of power, political modernisation is very dangerous because in the long run it almost always seems to stem from the carriers of new ideas, usually people of non-standard modes of thinking, with obviously expressed individuality and independence. They are often more intelligent than those vested with power and for this reason alone they pose a threat to the bureaucrats. The risks posed by political modernisation exceed any possible gain. In the Soviet system, everything above the mediocre, if not under complete control, was dangerous and harmful to the socialist regime. Much safer was promotion of the worst. The key moral attribute of the Soviet power pyramid's climbers was unprincipled, naked careerism. Every Soviet regime's ruling elite became, in effect, an anti-elite composed largely of the worst representatives of every stratum.

The conservative syndrome in Russian mass consciousness

Alexis de Tocqueville in his analyses stressed the important, sometimes crucial, role of habits of heart and mind of people in the political order. For better or worse this concept finds one more confirmation in the current dramatic events in Russia. The theme of this part of my chapter is the deep structure of Russian conservatism—the psychological constants of mass consciousness.[3] I define these constants as a conservative syndrome. This syndrome is the crucial obstacle to the social, political and economic modernisation of Russia. The psychological opposition to reforms is not fatal and can be overcome. But to underestimate or misunderstand this phenomenon could cripple or distort even the most progressive plans of the reformers. Moreover, the neglect of this syndrome may provoke actions by forces hostile to reforms, and encourage reactionary political forces. Unfortunately, we encountered this aggressive counter-reformism during the tragic Moscow days and nights at the beginning of October 1993.

Recent public opinion polls demonstrate a certain shift of public mood to the conservative side of the scale. Popular support for the 'new deal' of government still prevails in different degrees. But we also see that the anti-reformist mood remains strong. A readiness to conform is an important component of Russian political life. On my reading of polls conducted in late 1993, the aggressive forms of the conservative syndrome are shared by 15-20% of the adult population in central Russia. This certainly does not mean that all these people would struggle actively against the reformist course. But 15-20% offers a serious social base for passive long-term resistance to reforms by any appropriate means. Moreover, passive conservative feelings are found among even a larger proportion of population.

In the following paragraphs, I shall outline briefly the seven main constants of the conservative syndrome and also illustrate several points with empirical data. A representative all-Russian sample on the questions of interest here still does not exist: therefore I examine responses to questions about the political orientations of citizens which were included in two questionnaires used in an empirical project which the Politological Centre of the Russian Academy of Administration conducted in Vladimir *oblast'* in 1992 and 1993.

The first constant of the conservative syndrome is an anti-personal social attitude, expressed in the notorious Soviet slogan, 'everybody can be replaced'. The extremely brutal forms of this orientation manifested themselves under Stalinism and are usually associated with the GULAG archipelago and forced collectivisation. But actually this phenomenon has a much broader historical and cultural background. This inhuman anti-personalism runs directly counter to the personocentric spirit of Western civilisation. The essence of this attitude is to reject even a relative independence of the person. This aggressive anti-individualism has at least two basic features: a levelling psychology (pseudo-egalitarianism) and a compulsive pseudo-collectivism. Pseudo-egalitarianism masked as 'social justice', and pseudo-collectivism, are based on a dramatically anti-personal stereotype of 'all as one', implying situations where, irrespective of the will of the individual, he is involved in a sectarian joint activity where his personal opinion means practically nothing. The person is sacrificed, victimised in a vulgarised idea of unity and conformism. The social price of this sacrifice is to push out of normal social life (or physical life in Stalin's period) extraordinary and dissident-minded people who are capable of changing the society. The result of this 'anti-natural selection' over several generations was the deficit of people skilled in practical fields of activity which our country faced during *perestroika*.

The second constant is the complex of social inferiority and fear of changes. This is found at various levels of consciousness and social strata and derives from the intersection of two controversial components: on the one hand, a feeling of dissatisfaction and lack of prospects concerning the dominant social system; and, on the other, an awareness of one's own organic kinship with this system by virtue of which even a change for the better seems to threaten the routine 'harmony' and order of things. What is curious is that the complex persists even among the poor or underprivileged. Changes are feared even by many of those who could seem only to gain. Practically all sections of society (except elites) contain thick amorphous layers who are happy with the status quo. According to the polls just mentioned, 57.8% preferred 'stable and guaranteed modest wages' to 'the chance to earn very much but with the risk of bankruptcy'; the latter option was preferred only by 21.5%. Further, 62.9% in 1992 and 55.9% in 1993 presumed state support during the transitional period to be necessary. 58.9% considered that 'overly large differences in people's income are inadmissible'; only 25.4% accepted great differences. Here, we are obviously faced with a stereotype mentioned by the historian N.M. Karamzin when he said: 'We are less sensitive to the evil we know than to a new good we don't know at all'.

The third constant is the lack of moral regulators of social behaviour. The traditional system of moral values earlier predominant in Russia had been considerably weakened and then failed within the period from the middle of the 19th century to the middle of the 20th century. The process was unavoidable and historically grounded. The traditional system of morals had outlived itself and its decay was legitimate. However, against the Communist aspirations, another equally universal and inherently legitimate system of regulators has never replaced the former. All the attempts to cultivate a new 'communist' morality proved to be utopian. As a result, we came to a situation of moral anaemia, marked by a lack of internal moral standards. The notable growth of crime in the country is one symptom of this problem.

The fourth constant is inadequate development of a normal work ethic. For centuries, labour in Russia was mostly forced, with a considerable share of non-economic pressure and governmental control even in industry and trade, not to mention serfdom in agriculture. Many categories of labourers were alienated from the results of their own work and had no positive incentives to increase their efficiency. As a consequence, work—with some exceptions, such as work within the home or for the family—was psychologically disregarded as a kind of unprofitable conscription enforced from above. At the beginning of the 20th century many things started to change for the better in this respect. This process continued until 1917 and even during the early post-revolutionary years. But the totalitarian étatisation of work in practically all fields, particularly forced collectivisation, and extensive exploitation of prisoners' labour, nearly brought an end to this positive process of formation of a new—liberated—work ethic. Moreover, the unwritten law reigning in public opinion which was expressed in such informal rules as 'averaging', 'punished initiative', encouragement of passive obedience and servile loyalty, had made a considerable contribution to our further retreat from the logic of free labour relations. The regime relied not on social efficiency but on total control over the population. The way of thinking that was stimulated during the past, including the 'Communist' era, was totally opposed to the liberal Protestant ethical tradition. That is perhaps why I have had problems explaining to American students the core of popular Russian proverbs like 'honest labour brings no stone chamber', 'hard work is for a fool to jerk'. In my questionnaires these proverbs got the approval of 37.4% of respondents against 6.4% who disapproved. This phenomenon is one of the deeper roots of the high proportion of delinquency in our business.

The fifth constant is quasi-étatism or fetishisation of state power. In a political culture this should be understood as the conviction that the 'strong hand' of authoritarian state power is the main—if not the sole—foundation on which the whole social superstructure can be maintained. Its main attributes are a lack of confidence in law as an effective instrument for the protection of human rights, a fatal obedience to any instructions coming down from above, an identification of the state and society, and a 'formalised patriotism' the moral inadequacy of which was disclosed in the first half of the 19th century by Lunin and Chaadaev, and then by Herzen who mocked it as 'Petersburg patriotism'.[4] A further stereotype which is a base for quasi-étatism is a fear of 'chaos' and 'anarchy', as if it inevitably accompanies any liberalisation. The idea of freedom is displaced in popular consciousness by the idea of disorder. For people who spent all their lives as subjects of the omnipotent state, the condition of freedom seems unusual and dangerous. In reality, they fear not anarchy but the necessity to make personal, independent decisions about their own lives. Empirically this correlates with nostalgia for the 'command-and-control' system: 33% of the respondents in 1992 and 16.6% in 1993 wished to return to the pre-*perestroika* time, and also favoured restoration of strict statist control over the economy and trade and the enforcement of 'discipline and order'. The reformist course can be conducted and grasped only by persons who are freed from the false idea that a powerful central agency is the only guarantee of a country's welfare. In this context the degree of continuity in personnel, attitudes and modes of actions among the public employees inside the machinery of government inherited from the past seems dangerous for the reform process. It can be admitted only as a provisional measure, in limited spheres and under effective control. But the essence, role and capacities of Russian bureaucracy to conduct the politics of modernisation should be discussed specially and thoroughly.

The sixth constant is nationalism. That is too large a problem to be discussed in this brief outline of the conservative syndrome. I draw attention only to one aspect of it. Modern nationalism, including even great power chauvinism, as a rule has in its psychological roots an inferiority complex, heavily camouflaged and often not realised by the people themselves. And the ideology built up on that complex is always smeared with the tar-and-feather witch-hunting prejudice that 'the witch is somewhere else' and is imbued with a passion to put the blame for all one's troubles and bad luck onto certain foreigners instead of looking for it in one's own mirror.

The seventh constant is a system of moral justification of one's own passivity as a citizen. An active citizen's position, a developed sense of social responsibility, an initiative-minded disposition, are the most important factors that could make a success of reforms in the uncertain transitional period. On the other hand, the wish to shirk one's civic responsibility, the philosophy of a hen-pecked dupe, a conformist's mind and behaviour, are moral and psychological handicaps that obstruct this process. However, this syndrome very often appears not in its common guise but disguised by the life-saving instincts of the mind which can be more or less willingly adopted and approved by the social environment—or at least by a reference group of individuals—and which therefore may serve as a commonly acceptable moral excuse. Such mental tricks of double morality work not only for the by-standers or 'cheering crowds' but also for the self-deception of the individual so that he or she sincerely believes in them as true motives of his or her own behaviour. Let us recall some of its varieties: an ethic of the 'work horse' when a person is confident of the virtue of not interfering in things which are 'none of his business'; an ethic of one's inferiority and one's boss's superiority: 'Whatever I do nothing happens', 'They can twist me to a ram horn'. These are augmented by a marked loyalty to whatever happens according to the orders from 'above', which camouflages a pragmatic, selfish calculation, a practical desire to insure oneself against all sorts of risk; or a cynical disposition to make moral relativism a life-time principle.

Now, these features are not unique to Russia. They are also inherent, in some degree, in all human beings in different patterns of social and political order. But the problem is that in Russia (and the USSR) these modes of mind and behaviour were encouraged for centuries by a system of practical morality and the political regime. Any opposing system of norms was treated as a sort of dissident counterculture with the expected consequences. And now, when our society is at a crucial crossroad in its history, the conservative syndrome constitutes shackles on the legs. Moreover, we have seen that our society contains a rather serious fascist potential which can be transformed, in favourable circumstances, into terrible destructive energy.

Fortunately, the conservative syndrome is an important but not the only form of our public consciousness. The alternative system of social morality and psychology survived, in spite of all repression, and now, in the more favourable situation, its sprouts are developing rapidly. I consider this phenomenon as a 'syndrome of modernisation', of innovation. It is neither a mythical 'consensus' between these incompatible modes of mind and behaviour, nor political games on the top, but rather a balance of forces and dynamics of progress in the syndrome of modernisation that are the critical factors for the future development of Russia.

Russian political institutions in the Time of Troubles

During transitional times the role of political institutions seems rather controversial. They are to provide more or less quiet and gradual social development, yet they can serve as shackles of modernisation. This ambivalence has been a crucial characteristic of Russian political institutions in recent and, to some degree, present times. The basic antinomy is a controversy between new political purposes and inherited patterns of order and machinery of government. As I outlined earlier, the Soviet system was oriented to maximise the control function and guarantee the obedience of society. President Yeltsin and his team tried to use this strictly centralised, antidemocratic system as a tool for providing the course to decentralisation, democracy and market development. It sounds a paradox. However, it was all they had at their disposal then and one cannot blame them for that. But as a matter of fact the system began to resist innovations and to distort the very spirit of reform. On the political surface we could see a struggle between different branches of government. But on a deeper level it was a struggle between different models of order and patterns of order.

At present the Russian political system is in the process of moving from mono-organisational socialism—according to the definition of T.H. Rigby[5]—towards a pluralistic, open and market society. It is useful to examine Russia's political institutions in the light of this new course of our development.

Turning to the political crisis of September-October 1993, there is no shortage of comment about the presumably 'antidemocratic character' of presidential actions against the parliament. But the problem is that the Russian Supreme Soviet had never been a 'parliament' in the proper meaning of word. It had nothing to do with a key principle of parliamentarism—the separation of powers. On the contrary, an intertwining of politics, administration, the judiciary and even management was one of the core principles of the 'socialist political system'. The soviets originally were an instrument for seizure of power by mobilising a lumpenised, demoralised part of the population. Later the 'parliament' supplied democratic camouflage for an antidemocratic regime. It was never considered a true decisionmaking body. After 1991 the Russian parliament adopted a new role—to provide quasi-legal leverage for resistance to reforms. This was hardly surprising: the majority of deputies had been members of local Communist party elites. They were elected under one-party rule and reflected the same mentality, corporate purposes and mode of actions. The parliament, despite all rhetoric, became a system of fortifications which blockaded all the efforts of reformers.

For example, the inherited Russian Constitution had legalised in Article 104 the right of the Congress of People's Deputies to intervene in the jurisdiction of any organ. This unlimited jurisdiction provided a legal smokescreen for legislative intrusions beyond any reasonable limits. The so-called 'Mordovian case' is a good example in this context. (I am familiar with the details as I appeared as an independent expert during the hearing of this case in the Constitutional Court.) In autumn of 1992 the Supreme Soviet of the Mordovian Republic established the post of President and made the necessary amendment to the Republican Constitution. A president was elected in general elections to a five-year term, but seven months after the elections the president—a member of the Yeltsin team—obviously disappointed the leadership of the Republican Supreme Soviet. It abolished the very post of president, crossed out its own constitutional amendment and moved to dismiss the elected president as an ordinary employee. The selfish concern of members of the old communist *nomenklatura* to secure their dominant power positions clearly overrode legality and the will of the people, not to mention the principles of the rule of law. From episodes such as this we have reason to conclude that the system of soviets was a pseudo-parliamentary institutional remnant of communist rule. This false imitation of democracy is incompatible with true democratic development.

Equally sad is the short and dramatic story of our Constitutional Court. This institution was intended to be a guardian of the constitution but rapidly managed to discredit itself. Certainly, its position was rather difficult from the moment it was established. It had the mission of guarding a controversial, obsolete and regularly-amended Constitution. In the early stages of its activity it tried to keep a sort of balance and political neutrality. But starting with the 'Communist Party trial' the anti-reformist orientations step-by-step gathered force. The pro-communist majority of the Court became involved in the political games on the anti-presidential side.[6] This led to a practical halt to its work and in public eyes discredited the very idea of an independent institution of judicial control. Some members of the Court promoted the idea of collective resignation. In my opinion, this would have been the best possible solution, because such sacrifice could have saved the face of the institution—potentially one of the crucial institutions in a democratic society.

The general political orientation of the executive branch has been quite different. President Yeltsin is definitely devoted to the idea of broad social modernisation and made real progress in this direction. But, as I mentioned earlier, the push to destatisation, decentralisation and marketisation was conducted by centralistic methods and on the basis of a new command system. Considered abstractly, this is a nonsense. But in terms of the political situation of the recent past it was almost the sole realistic way, or, at least, the least evil way possible. Moreover, in the time of troubles, in conditions of unconsolidated democracy, lack of parliamentary traditions and an undeveloped multiparty system, the temporary dominance of the executive branch of government and even some authoritarian tendencies seemed inevitable. There were no other realistic alternatives to overcome the rigid resistance of the ultra-conservative Supreme Soviet and bureaucratic sabotage in administration. Yet in the process, new antinomies and new dangers have evolved. The stupid and irresponsible actions of demagogues in the soviets have discredited the very idea of constructive opposition. Russia has no serious tradition of the peaceful coexistence of authority and opposition—parliamentary or any other. On the contrary, we have a long tradition of unlimited, bureaucratic government, and an almost religious belief in the model of omnipotent state power—and recent events have worked in favour of that historical tradition. I fear that our communo-fascistic, 'intransigent' opposition has undermined faith in the positive capacities of a multiparty parliamentary system.

The October 1993 victory of democratic forces was a very important positive factor because the danger of losing everything had been extremely real. But it gave an impetus to the ideology of the one party system in some new form. In terms of short-term practical politics such a system has some advantages. Some elements of autocratic actions may be necessary for the effective conduct of reforms. But in terms of the 'next day of Creation' we could lay a foundation for new troubles in the future. Without the need to conduct a serious dialogue with opponents in a genuine parliament, even the most progressive politicians could degrade. We know that 'power tends to corrupt and absolute power corrupts absolutely'. And this danger, unfortunately, is rather probable in our historical context. Despite the impressive number of parties and blocs which took part in the 1993 election campaign, at the moment we hardly have more than a quasi-multi-party system. Most of our parties are ad hoc groups which have been organised to support more or less popular leaders. Our current political chess-board, and political debates within both reformist and anti-reformist camps, reflect more personal political ambitions than differences in political positions. Russia is not unique in this respect but in the Russian case it seems more alarming. The reason is the potential of forces which oppose the very idea of democratic development of the country.

Russia now moves through a critical crossroads. The old system is capable of regeneration and we have not yet arranged an appropriate system of institutions to guarantee the irreversibility of the process of political change. As a matter of fact, until now we have had only a substitution of ruling elites and ideology, but not a substitution of institutional foundations of order. The current situation may prove to be either an introduction to a new story or only a change of scenery for a new version of an old play with another cast of performers. It would be unforgivable naivete to suppose that a new system can be organised within a couple of years. But it also would be unforgivable lightmindedness to underestimate three main threats to the future of free Russia: the danger of a new communist or chauvinistic coup d'etat, the danger of a new oligarchy, and the danger of endless quarrels between different groups of reformers. The first is the most horrible but, in my opinion, the least probable. The second danger, involving a new uncontrollable oligarchy, looks the least evil but the most probable.

Most people in power now have no experience of positive dialogue with opponents. Moreover, an autocratic statist ideology, the idea of the 'strong ruling hand', still exists in the minds of both the governors and the governed. This essential part of Russian mass political consciousness has a profound influence on our political realities. Many people in our so-called democratic establishment actually adhere not to democracy in some pure sense of word but to effective central government with maximal guarantees for their own political careers. In this context the temptation develops to arrange not democratic but quasi-democratic political institutions. As we know, 'temporary' institutions have a tendency to self-perpetuate. The new Constitution adopted in December 1993 should be considered in this context. Very broad authority for the president can be justified positively in terms of urgent political needs. I would approve this Constitution without any doubts but with one addition: an article providing for reassessment of it after several years by a special Constitutional Assembly or in some other appropriate way. In the absence of such an article there is a danger that some provisional measures of this Constitution will serve not democracy but some new oligarchy. I am also worried by the danger of endless conflicts and struggle inside the democratic wing of our political spectrum. Quarrels among different groups of democrats are a familiar mode of existence for politicians in democratic societies. Under conditions of stable, long-term democracy this is not a danger. But the current Russian situation is different. The anti-democratic forces retain influential positions in our society. In favourable circumstances they could renew their counterattacks on the very foundations of democratic institutions. They are capable of rapid mobilisation, as they showed by regrouping after August 1991. In this situation a disintegration of democratic forces weakens the whole democratic movement and can bring new troubles both inside and outside parliament. As a rule, disorganised democrats lose in the struggle with well-organised and integrated anti-democratic forces.

At the moment we are experiencing the cloudy morning of a new political era in Russia. The results of the December 1993 elections have confirmed that Russian conservatism is still robust in both its 'classical' and renovative forms, and the balance of conservative and innovative forces in the State Duma is very unstable, as in the country as a whole. How the situation will develop depends on many factors. We have overcome a range of different obstacles on our way to a more open society, and the new Constitution can assist us along that path. However, a constitution is only capable of assisting people to save freedom to the extent that they wish to save it. While I hope the majority of our people have a will for freedom, taking into account our historical experience and current political situation it appears that an effective hierarchy of executive power in combination with the development of a multidimensional network of self-governing networks under law is necessary to create a system of reliable guarantees for the irreversibility of our reforms.

Notes

1 For more details, see A.V. Obolonskii, 'Kakuiu politicheskuiu sistemu my unasledovali (Anatomiia "doaprel'skogo" politicheskogo rezhima)', *Sovetskoe gosudarstvo i pravo*, no.10, 1990, pp.59-72.

2 A.V. Obolonskii, 'Biurokraticheskaia deformatsiia soznaniia i bor'ba s biurokratizmom', *Sovetskoe gosudarstvo i pravo*, no.1, 1987, pp.52-61. For more general discussion of bureaucracy, see A.V. Obolonskii, 'Biurokratiia i biurokratizm (K teorii voprosa)', *Gosudarstvo i pravo*, no.12, 1993, pp.88-99.

3 For a more detailed discussion of this syndrome, see A.V. Obolonskii, 'Mekhanizm tormozheniia: chelovecheskoe izmerenie', *Sovetskoe gosudarstvo i pravo*, no.1, 1990, pp.80-87.

4 A.I. Herzen, 'O razvitii revoliutsionnykh idei v Rossii', *Sochineniia* (Moscow: Nauka, 1956) Vol.III, p.449.

5 See T.H. Rigby, *The Changing Soviet System: Mono-organisational Socialism from its Origins to Gorbachev's Restructuring* (Aldershot: Edward Elgar, 1990).

6 See A.V. Obolonskii, 'V. Zor'kinu khorosho by vernut'sia v pravovoe prostranstvo', *Izvestiia*, 27 March 1993.

3   POLITICAL LEADERSHIP IN POST-COMMUNIST RUSSIA

ARCHIE BROWN

The task of leadership in the conditions of collapse of the Soviet Union has been a conspicuously difficult one. The legacy from the Communist period of a decaying economy, vast ecological disaster areas, uncertainty about the legitimacy of political institutions and the character of Russia's statehood meant that the problems facing the leadership in both the executive and legislative branches of government were grave indeed. They were compounded by a sense of loss of superpower status, together with concern for the fate of twenty-five million Russians, formerly Soviet citizens, who now found themselves in the Near Abroad—the former union republics of the USSR.

Yet, as President of Russia, Boris Yeltsin had a number of advantages both over his *de facto* predecessor, Mikhail Gorbachev, and as compared with the leaders of almost all the other Soviet successor states. Yeltsin's victory in elections in three successive years—in the Moscow constituency of the Congress of People's Deputies of the USSR in 1989, from his native Sverdlovsk (now restored to its old name, Ekaterinburg) in the election to the Congress of People's Deputies of Russia in 1990, and in the Presidential election of June 1991—gave him a greater democratic legitimacy than any other politician in the country. The fact that a mere two months before the attempted coup of August 1991 he had defeated five rivals for the Russian presidency, including ones whose views mirrored the beliefs and attitudes of the putschists, was of especial importance. It meant that the attempt to overthrow Gorbachev—and Yeltsin himself—between 18 and 21 August was undermined by the evident absurdity at that time of the plotters' claim to be reflecting popular opinion.

Yeltsin had a number of other advantages not available to Gorbachev. As a result of the failure of the August coup, the institutions which had placed major constraints upon Gorbachev's freedom of action, and whose leaders eventually adopted concerted measures to overthrow him, had been placed on the defensive. That was true of the KGB (whose chairman, Vladimir Kriuchkov, was but one of several leading figures from the security forces imprisoned for intimate involvement in the attempted coup), the army (since the Minister of Defence, Marshal Dmitrii Iazov, was also a member of the self-appointed State Committee for the State of Emergency), the Ministry of Interior (whose head, Boris Pugo, committed suicide the day after the coup collapsed), the military-industrial complex (whose chief, Oleg Baklanov, was a key putschist) and also of the economic bureaucracy (with no less a person than the Soviet Prime Minister, Valentin Pavlov, a participant in the coup attempt). The fact that all of these leaders were in prison (apart from the unfortunate Pugo who was dead) and that, more important, the powerful institutions they had headed were discredited in the eyes of Russia and the world gave Yeltsin a greater freedom of action than Gorbachev had ever possessed, at least in the short term. That ceased to be the case when in due course the policies Yeltsin espoused provoked their own backlash and a reassertion of the sectional interests of some at least of those institutions which were under a shadow in late 1991 and early 1992.

An even more important case than the major institutions mentioned above is that of the Communist Party. Initially suspended by Yeltsin because of the involvement of a number of its senior officials in the attempted coup, it reemerged under new leadership, but minus its property and special privileges. Most crucially, it did not return as part of the executive power structure, although a revived Communist Party gradually began to win a significant level of popular support in the course of the first two post-Soviet years. (Of the eight political parties or blocs which passed the 5 per cent threshold and won seats in the December 1993 elections to the State Duma, the Communist Party of the Russian Federation emerged as the third largest.)

It was not for nothing that the Soviet Union was frequently described as a 'party-state' in the Western political science literature. The Communist Party apparatus had indeed for most of the Soviet period played the 'leading role' in the political system which the Soviet Constitution (between 1977 and 1990) accorded it. It was also part of the cement which held the Soviet Union and, to a lesser extent, Russia together. Thus, its disappearance from the power structures had some negative consequences for the post-Soviet leadership, just as it latterly did for Gorbachev. The departure of a powerful, country-wide institution with an apparatus capable of implementing policy decisions emanating from the highest authorities in Moscow left something of a power vacuum. The benefits of its absence, however, greatly exceeded any advantages it had to offer for leaders bent on radical reform. The apparatus could be relied upon to act as an instrument of power of the top leader only so long as that top leader did not undermine its own interests. Its reaction to a leader who was interfering with, or even removing, the powers of the apparatus could be dangerously hostile. Senior party officials, with the tacit support of those at lower levels, had removed Nikita Khrushchev from power in 1964 and they turned against Gorbachev from 1989.[1]

The party bureaucracy had its own ethos and rules of the game which even a General Secretary could challenge only with caution. Gorbachev had, with great skill, bent those rules to his own reformist purposes throughout the greater part of his period in the highest office, but that same apparatus imposed limits on his scope of action and, even when purporting to implement policy, could distort or delay measures which were not to their liking. The more radical Gorbachev's reform programme had become, the more determined—and by 1989-1990 overt—had become the opposition to it from the greater part of the provincial party bureaucracy.

Thus, it was very much to Yeltsin's advantage that—thanks, partly, to his own efforts—he did not have a power-wielding Communist Party to contend with. He would scarcely have been in a position to support such a radical break with more than sixty years of economic policy as was epitomised by Egor Gaidar's liberalisation of prices in January 1992 had not the institutions of the party-state either been destroyed or in disarray. In addition to the weaknesses of institutions which, in other times and circumstances, would have been countervailing powers against a reforming presidency, Yeltsin benefited also from the additional prestige he had earned as the symbol of defiance against the August coup and the main beneficiary of the defeat of the plotters.

Yeltsin's advantages over the leaders of the other successor states were even clearer. Although the dislocation of industry caused by the breakup of the Soviet economy affected Russia adversely, given the preponderance of industry within the Russian Federation and the dependence, in particular, of most of the other former union republics on Russian oil and gas, Russia emerged in a stronger position to weather the new economic storms than the rest of the former Soviet Union. The three Baltic states are a partial exception to this generalisation, since they started with a more sophisticated service sector and the modest size of their economies meant that help from outside, particularly from Scandinavia, could make a positive impact relatively quickly. Russia's overwhelming military and economic strength was, nevertheless, seen as a threat even there, especially by Latvia and Estonia with their large Russian minorities which, in Moscow's view, were being treated unfairly. If the Soviet leadership, at such times when Gorbachev held the initiative within it, had latterly tried to hold the USSR together by persuasion and accommodation rather more than by coercion, Yeltsin's Russia had a freer hand to pursue its own self-interest in relation to states which had gained independence. Indeed, as an increasing number of the other successor states were by early 1994 beginning to see advantages in forming a loose confederation with Russia, the main issue for Russian decisionmakers became the economic price which Russia would find worth paying for such a political outcome. While a more institutionally viable Commonwealth of Independent States or some other confederal successor to the Soviet Union (excluding, almost certainly, the Baltic states) was agreeable in principle to most Russian decision-makers, there were limits to the extent to which Russia was prepared to subsidise its neighbours. The Russian leadership was therefore likely to pursue such a goal only if the economic price were not too high.

Russia has surmounted more than one crisis since the collapse of the Soviet Union, but none deeper than that which occurred in September-October 1993 following Yeltsin's forcible dissolution of the Congress of People's Deputies and the Supreme Soviet. The struggle reached the point at which a change of regime could have taken place and Russia might have reverted to a far more oppressively authoritarian political order than it had known since before the reforms of the second half of the 1980s. It would not have been a return to a classical Communist system. Marxism-Leninism was far too discredited for that, and many of those who were part of the anti-Yeltsin coalition, including the Chairman of the Russian Supreme Soviet, Ruslan Khasbulatov, were aware that there was no viable alternative to movement towards some kind of market economy. Yet if the army had made a different choice on the night of 3-4 October, there was a real possibility of an unholy alliance of unreconstructed Communists and ultra-nationalists taking power in a new coalition which would have swept Yeltsin from power and turned back the clock with a vengeance. By the time the mob led by General Al'bert Makashov stormed the Ostankino television station on the night of Sunday 3 October, it appeared that Yeltsin had little alternative but to reply to force with force.[2]

That is not to say, however, that such a failure of the political process was inevitable.[3] Yeltsin, it could be said, once again demonstrated his strength in a crisis. He had been less effective, though, in preventing matters reaching danger point. The Russian parliamentary leadership was more culpable than the executive in the breakdown of political relations which preceded the dissolution of the Supreme Soviet, but the issues were a good deal less simple and clear-cut than most Western politicians and many newspaper commentators seemed to think. In contrast with the editorial columns of the Western press and the unambiguous welcome given by presidents and prime ministers to the dissolution of the Supreme Soviet and Congress of People's

Deputies by Yeltsin in his Decree number 1400 of 21 September 1993, independent papers of liberal or centrist disposition in Russia itself adopted a more critical or nuanced stance.[4] While a majority of Russian intellectuals supported the dissolution of parliament, a minority argued that this action would make violent confrontation more rather than less likely, with the editor-in-chief of *Nezavisimaia gazeta* comparing Yeltsin's action to Nikolai II's disbanding of the Duma and the Bolsheviks' dispersal of the Constituent Assembly.[5]

The Russian parliament which, after a political struggle, elected Yeltsin as Chairman of the Supreme Soviet in 1990 and which, with Yeltsin's strong backing, chose Khasbulatov to succeed him in that office in 1991 was not a body in which there was a permanent majority of unreformed Communists and ultra-nationalists, even though—taken together—these groups formed a substantial minority. It was, therefore, a notable failure of coalition-building on Yeltsin's part to turn the parliamentary majority he could command, however precariously, in 1990-1991 into a determined opposition. There were members of Yeltsin's advisory Presidential Council who realised that it was just as important for the Russian President as for the President of the United States to spend much time courting members of the legislature whose votes were needed and to listen not only to his committed supporters among the deputies. But this view did not prevail in Yeltsin's innermost circle.

Conflicting jurisdictions

The breakdown of political relations between the executive and legislature in September 1993 must, however, be seen in a broader context. Russia throughout 1993 was facing a crisis of authority, although it was in the autumn that it took a more critical turn. Yeltsin finally dissolved the old parliament—an action he had already contemplated in March 1993 when he spoke of taking special powers[6]—because ambiguity concerning the locus of power was making Russia close to ungovernable.[7] This was commonly described in Russia in three different (but only superficially contradictory) ways as *mnogovlastie* (multiplicity of powers), *dvoevlastie* (dual power) and *bezvlastie* (absence of power).

Mnogovlastie referred to the fact that numerous political bodies were taking decisions not only independently of but also in contradiction to each other, with each claiming a superior authority over all rival jurisdictions. This was partly a centre-periphery problem with the decisions reached in Moscow unheeded in many Russian regions and in a number of the republics where non-Russians are the dominant nationality. Even within any one region there was frequently conflict between rival authorities, with the regional administrators appointed by Yeltsin pulling in one direction and the elected local soviets (often, however, chaired by the former Communist Party First Secretary of the region or district) pulling in another. Under the same rubric of *mnogovlastie* came the confusion within the Russian executive itself. The complete breakdown in relations between Yeltsin and his Vice-President, Aleksandr Rutskoi, was merely the most spectacular example of that. This last aspect of multiple power has been eradicated by the simple device of doing away with the vice-presidency,[8] but the struggle for control over resources between Moscow and a number of the regions and republics will be much less easy to resolve.[9]

It was to put an end, above all, to *dvoevlastie* that Yeltsin issued his decree dissolving the Russian Supreme Soviet and Congress of People's Deputies. There is no question but that dual power had done serious harm to Russia, both politically and economically. While for thoughtful Russian democrats, it was at least as important to avoid the opposite danger—that is, of a return to a legislative assembly which, as in pre-*perestroika* times, would be a mere rubber-stamp for executive actions—the intensity of the conflict in the first nine months of 1993 between the Supreme Soviet and the presidency was immensely damaging. Especially serious was the contradiction between parliament's laws and Yeltsin's presidential decrees and the lack of clarity as to which had supremacy. This dual power was, of course, personified by the increasingly bitter animosity between those former allies, Yeltsin and Khasbulatov.

As Yeltsin himself has acknowledged, he should have made a serious effort to have a new Constitution adopted and a date for fresh elections agreed in late 1991 or early 1992 when his public standing was still sufficiently high for him to have persuaded the Congress of People's Deputies to vote for its own dissolution and replacement by a new bicameral parliament. To have done this by political persuasion would have been greatly preferable to dissolving the legislature by decree. That latter action was not only to leave Russia without a legislative assembly or elected local authorities for several months but to lead, directly or indirectly, to the suspension of the Constitutional Court, the temporary banning of some twenty newspapers,[10] and the tightening of governmental control over, and censorship of, television (which, in the light of the dramatic drop in newspaper circulation, has become overwhelmingly the most important means of mass communication).

That *something* had to be done to break the deadlock is, however, beyond question, for *mnogovlastie* and *dvoevlastie* led to what many Russians preferred to term *bezvlastie*, an absence of effective and legitimised power whereby the confusion within the Russian government, the contradictions between laws and decrees, and the lack of agreement on the jurisdiction of different political authorities promoted disrespect for decrees and laws alike. Thus, Yeltsin—like Gorbachev before him—was issuing *ukazy*, some of which had no effect beyond the grounds of the Kremlin, not being obeyed even in Moscow, not to speak of Chechnia, Tomsk or Tatarstan.

The lack of agreement on the locus of legitimate power and authority was a matter of concern not only for constitutional lawyers and political analysts; it had a direct and harmful effect on the economy. It helped discourage the large-scale foreign investment which Russia needs and which might make its own contribution to promoting political stability and to reversing the decline in production that continues to take place. The legal and political risks for foreign investors were sufficiently high that, while most multinationals wanted (and want) a foothold in Russia in the hope of better times to come, they did not wish to put many eggs in the Russian basket. The confusion concerning ownership rights, for example, meant that Western investors had to try to reach agreement with republican, regional or city authorities *and* with the central government in Moscow. Although time-consuming and burdensome, any alternative left foreign companies open to the risk of rejection by whatever authority was not party to the agreement.

Public opinion

The context of Yeltsin's dissolution of parliament was, therefore, one in which the status quo was barely tolerable. But that is not to say that something could not have been done earlier and differently, by political rather than administrative means, legally rather than unconstitutionally. This could most easily have been achieved not later than early 1992, although even as late as 1993 it might have been possible to end the deadlock by a compromise based upon simultaneous presidential and parliamentary elections. This was rejected at different times throughout the year both by the presidential side and by the legislature. But while Khasbulatov and the Supreme Soviet leadership were at least as much to blame for the failure to agree on such a compromise as the President and his advisers, Yeltsin made his task harder by offering jobs in government to those in the legislature whom he wished to reward or win over rather than keep uncommitted centrists and potential supporters in the Supreme Soviet, listen to their concerns and engage in a genuinely two-way dialogue. Yeltsin had the advantage that he remained the most popular—or, more precisely, the *least unpopular*—politician in the country, although he had seen his standing drop drastically from its peak in the summer of 1991. He was far more popular than Khasbulatov, in particular, and, as the referendum conducted in April 1993 confirmed, the presidency as an institution was more popular than the legislature elected in 1990. Yeltsin had a 'power to persuade' that he failed to exercise to the full.

There has been a general decline in trust in politicians in Russia as compared with the more optimistic days of 1989. The Director of the major Russian opinion polling institution, Iurii Levada—who succeeded Tat'iana Zaslavskaia as Director of this All-Russian Centre for the Study of Public Opinion in early 1992—published survey data just two months before Yeltsin's dissolution of the Congress of People's Deputies and the Supreme Soviet which showed that in each year since 1989 people had reported a lower level of participation in political life than the year before and a declining interest in politics.[11] Part of the context both of Yeltsin's turn to coercion on 21 September in his struggle with the Russian legislature and of the disappointing outcome for Yeltsin and his supporters of the December 1993 elections is to be found in the results of a survey conducted throughout the country by Levada's Centre between September 9 and 21. On the eve of the dissolution of parliament only 6 per cent of respondents 'fully shared the views and positions' of Yeltsin with the figure rising to 32 per cent when those who supported him with various reservations are added. 56 per cent of respondents indicated their lack of support for the Russian President. In a more direct question, in which respondents were asked whether they approved or disapproved of how Yeltsin coped with his responsibilities, 25% approved and 72% disapproved.[12] As part of the same survey conducted just before the dissolution of the legislature, respondents were asked the following question: 'If presidential elections in Russia were held in the next week and you had to choose between Boris Yeltsin and Aleksandr Rutskoi, how would you vote? Or, perhaps, you would not participate in the elections?'

The results were:

Would vote for Yeltsin	25%
Would vote for Rutskoi	22%
Would not participate in the elections	53%

In other words, Yeltsin's lead over Rutskoi was an uncomfortably narrow one on the eve of the sequence of events which began with the dissolution of parliament on 21 September and ended with the imprisonment of Rutskoi on 4 October. There was evidence also—which the December 1993 parliamentary elections, on the whole, confirmed—of widespread apathy.

The decline in Yeltsin's popularity over time is detailed in the following Table and Figure, both based upon data compiled by the All-Russian Centre for the Study of Public Opinion:

Table 3.1: Levels of Support for Boris Yeltsin, July 1991– September 1993

Which statement would you choose to describe your attitude toward the Russian President?	VII 1991	X 1991	III 1992	IX 1992	I 1993	V 1993	IX 1993
Fully share the views and positions of Yeltsin	29	15	11	5	5	9	6
Am ready to support Yeltsin while he is the leader of democratic forces	11	17	9	8	11	10	9
Did not like Yeltsin much before but hope that in future he will be of use to Russia	16	10	4	7	6	6	4
Support Yeltsin because of lack of other worthy political leaders	15	20	15	15	16	18	13
Liked Yeltsin before, but recently became disenchanted	7	11	18	30	29	18	26
Have no adherence to Yeltsin	8	10	13	21	16	20	22
Support anybody but Yeltsin	3	2	5	6	6	5	8
Hard to answer	12	15	26	10	12	14	12

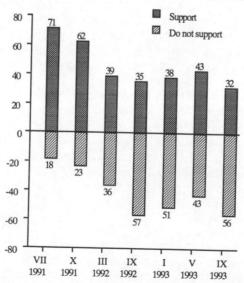

Figure 3.1: Support for Boris Yeltsin 1991-1993

In many ways this decline in Yeltsin's standing mirrors that of Gorbachev. The important difference, however, is that—contrary to widespread Russian and Western mythology—Gorbachev was still the most popular politician in his country five years after he became Soviet leader and the precipitous decline in his domestic standing occurred within his *last* two years as chief executive. In contrast, Yeltsin's decline in popularity, though by 1993 it had still not reached Gorbachev's lowest point in 1991, took place during his *first* two years.[13]

Even though Yeltsin's popularity had suffered a sharp decline, his personal standing ran ahead of support for the policies of his government. A survey conducted for a British team of researchers by the Institute of Sociology in Moscow of 2,030 randomly chosen respondents in fifty regions of Russia between 25 June and 26 August 1993 found that only 9 per cent thought that government action 'reflected the wishes of ordinary people' as compared with 69 per cent who thought it did not.[14] In terms of political priorities the same survey showed an overwhelming concern with economic issues—an emphasis on the need for economic growth combined with a perhaps incompatible desire for economic stability. These top two preferences were named by 54% of respondents. The next highest category of priorities were 'law and order' issues mentioned by 19% of citizens (with 12% saying that their principal desire was to 'improve order in the country' and 7% mentioning the fully congruent issue of 'the fight against crime'). Democratic and libertarian values came much lower on the popular scale of preferences, the defence of 'freedom of speech' being the top priority for only 0.2% of respondents.[15]

Implications of the dissolution

Given the frequency and irresponsibility of the Russian legislature's amendments to the Constitution—which, in its origins, moreover, was still the 1978 Constitution of the RSFSR—Yeltsin and his advisers could command the support of a majority of professed democrats in Russia while dispensing with legal niceties. There were, however, a number of notable exceptions. One such person was Egor Iakovlev, the man who turned *Moscow News* (*Moskovskie novosti*) into a flagship of *glasnost'* after he became its editor in 1986 and who was later head of Ostankino television until he was unceremoniously removed by Yeltsin. In an interview for the newspaper *Novaia ezhednevnaia gazeta*, Iakovlev accused the intelligentsia of not being prepared to stand independently on their own feet and of snuggling up close to the power-holders once again.[16] Another dissentient voice was that of the writer, Andrei Siniavskii, who spent seven years in a labour camp in the Brezhnev era for the 'crime' of 'anti-Soviet propaganda'. Siniavskii, who, like Iakovlev, observed how difficult it was to be on a different side from that of his close friends, noted: 'almost the entire Russian intelligentsia is for Yeltsin, but I am against'.[17] The most terrible thing for him, wrote Siniavskii, was that his old enemies were beginning 'sometimes to speak the truth' while the intelligentsia were 'welcoming everything emanating from the *vozhd'* and again calling for harsh measures'. But, he concluded: 'All this has been seen before. That is how Soviet power began'.[18]

In a nuanced critique of the dissolution of parliament, the political scientist, Igor' Kliamkin, argued that it would be crucially important to hold the forthcoming parliamentary and presidential elections simultaneously. That would not only help to counteract apathy but it would be less of a break with legality than electing a new legislature alone in the first instance. Such a parliament, he argued, would be all too easy to disband because it would have no real legal basis.[19]

Kliamkin's article was published before the announcement that there would be not only elections for a State Duma and a Federation Council—the lower and upper chambers of the new Federal Assembly—on 12 December but also a plebiscite that day on a new Constitution. Whether, however, that vote—in which almost 60 per cent of those who voted endorsed the Constitution and approximately 40 per cent opposed it—satisfies objections to Yeltsin's action on legal grounds is a moot point. An October 1990 Law on the Referendum of the RSFSR, which had not been annulled, stipulated that a majority of all registered voters was required to make constitutional changes by referendum; only 31 per cent of eligible voters supported the draft Constitution presented to them on 12 December 1993, but the vote was described as a plebiscite rather than a referendum.

Yeltsin appeared in September-October to commit himself very firmly to parliamentary elections in December 1993 and presidential elections exactly six months later—on 12 June 1994.[20] On a visit to Japan in mid-October 1993 he became angry when told that one of his advisers had reported that he was considering simultaneous elections for presidency and parliament 'sometime between December and March'. He told his questioner that such an adviser would no longer have a job, adding: 'The elections will be on 12th December to the Federal Assembly ... The presidential election will be on 12th June 1994. This has been determined and this is how it will be!'[21] Yet, speaking just one day after Yeltsin had objected to people in his entourage questioning his commitment to a 12 June presidential election date, the Russian Minister of Defence, Pavel Grachev, said that Yeltsin 'must continue as Russian president until 1996 when his term of office expires', adding that Yeltsin should 'be allowed to work in peace before a new presidential campaign begins in two years' time'.[22] Yeltsin himself appeared to come round to this view soon afterwards and abandoned his earlier promise to face the electorate in a June 1994 presidential election, even though Western leaders, in welcoming Yeltsin's dissolution of the old Russian legislature, had made much of the fact that Yeltsin had demonstrated his democratic credentials by being willing to face the electorate himself soon after the parliamentary election.

The showdown between executive and legislature, its violent dénouement in early October 1993 and Yeltsin's subsequent backtracking on the promise of an early presidential election did nothing to enhance popular interest in politics. On the contrary, disillusionment deepened and in November 1993 lack of interest in politics was greater than at any other time since the All-Russian Centre for the Study of Public Opinion began systematically investigating the issue. As few as 11 per cent of the population were either 'much interested' or 'very much interested' in politics in November 1993, as compared with 15 per cent in September of the same year, 21 per cent in September 1991 and 24 per cent in December 1990.[23] A highest-ever 60 per cent in November 1993, in the run-up to the parliamentary elections and the plebiscite on the new Constitution, expressed themselves to be 'little interested' or 'completely uninterested' in politics.[24]

The drastic measures of September-October 1993 were hailed by their supporters in Russia and the West as a victory for democracy and as preparing the way for a radicalisation of economic reform. Some scepticism about that seemed justified at the time and all the more so by March 1994, three months after the elections for a new legislature. While it was important to put an end to a destructive dual power—as distinct from political accountability and checks on the abuse of power—the manner in which the issue of *dvoevlastie* was eventually tackled by Yeltsin had a number of implications likely to do more harm than good to the causes of freedom, democracy and the rule of law in Russia. Moreover, the consequences for radicalisation of economic reform were far removed from those intended. Apart from the two months preceding the elections, when there was no legislature to exercise countervailing power and the government had a free hand, the dissolution of the old legislature and elections for a successor parliament resulted in a setback for proponents of economic 'shock therapy'. Gaidar's party, Russia's Choice, although it finished with the largest number of seats in the State Duma of any one party or bloc, received a substantially smaller percentage of the vote than Zhirinovskii's 'Liberal Democrats', and supporters of radical economic reform, of the kind favoured by Gaidar and the Minister of Finance, Boris Fedorov, found themselves in a minority in the new legislature. That body had, under the terms of the new Constitution, far fewer powers than its predecessor, but against that, it had the advantage of enjoying a fresher mandate not only than its predecessor but also than the President himself. In those circumstances Yeltsin had no choice but to offer Chernomyrdin as free a hand to make economic policy as he had offered Gaidar in 1992. No nomination as Prime Minister other than that of Chernomyrdin—a more cautious and politically pragmatic economic reformer than either Gaidar or Fedorov—would have been acceptable to the State Duma.

Both Yeltsin and the most radically reformist wing of his government underestimated the extent to which the grievances which had been voiced, often in harsh and outmoded rhetoric, by the legislature they had dispersed nevertheless reflected real interests in the society and real hardships being suffered by its members. Little comfort could be taken from the belief that their favoured candidates suffered in December 1993 from a failure to secure a larger turnout or from the notion that the demagogic Zhirinovskii had deprived the democrats and radical economic reformers of votes. A significant study by Whitefield and Evans has shown that supporters of anti-market, anti-privatisation economic policies and of nationalist and anti-democratic politics were the least likely to vote. Far from low turnout undermining the radical reformists' cause, the opposite appears to have been the case. It saved them from a still more serious defeat.[25] As for the Zhirinovskii phenomenon, the member of the Presidential Council of the Russian Federation who advises Yeltsin on regional policy, Leonid Smirniagin, who had access to a mass of data on the elections country-wide, reached the conclusion that Zhirinovskii's success had not been at the expense of the democrats but of the Communists. In Smirniagin's words, 'Zhirinovskii prevented a Communist landslide'.[26]

Conclusions

It is possible that if Yeltsin had created his own political party at an earlier stage in his presidency, this would have led to a somewhat less severe setback for radical reformers in the December 1993 elections than actually occurred, but given what we now know both about trends in public opinion during 1993 and about actual electoral behaviour in December of that year, it seems unlikely that the existence of a presidential party would have altered the result fundamentally. Perhaps, though, the failure to create such a party was harmful in a more general way.

Yeltsin's notion that he was 'above party' and that being President of all the people was incompatible with affiliation to a political party (when the experience of Western democracies suggests the reverse) did nothing to assist the formation of a viable party system in post-Soviet Russia. Political parties (with the partial exceptions of the revived Communists and, to a lesser extent, Zhirinovskii's Liberal Democrats) remain organisationally weak and inchoate.

The way in which Yeltsin chose to end the deadlock between the executive and the former legislature was to put it mildly far from optimal; some of its unfortunate implications are already being felt and they are likely to continue to be felt for some time to come. Five aspects in particular give cause for concern.

First, the precedent of forcible dissolution of an elected legislature was an unfortunate one. Much was made of the fact that the Congress of People's Deputies of the Russian Federation had been elected in Soviet times, but so had Yeltsin himself, albeit a year later. Most of the deputies had had to fight competitive elections and, in spite of the legislature's gross imperfections, the Congress and the Supreme Soviet were very different bodies from the old pre-reform Supreme Soviets. Once an elected legislature has been unilaterally dissolved by the executive, it becomes easier for a future President to do likewise. It would be fair to say, however, that Yeltsin himself could ill afford to dissolve a legislature for a second time, particularly one elected according to rules designed by the President himself and his political allies. Moreover, in any repeat of the 1993 showdown between presidency and parliament, it seemed quite probable that the senior ranks of the army and of the security forces would side with the legislature. The present parliament has, after all, a fresher mandate than Yeltsin; it is no longer led by an unpopular non-Russian, Khasbulatov (a Chechen); and its general disposition is more congenial to the military-industrial complex and the security forces than the policies with which Yeltsin has been associated since 1990.

Second, the events of 3-4 October—themselves a consequence of the unilateral dissolution of the legislature on 21 September— broke a taboo on political violence in post-Soviet Russia. While there was no doubt a greater willingness to resort to violence on the part of some of the hard-line military men opposed to Yeltsin than on Yeltsin's side—notably Generals Vladislav Achalov and Al'bert Makashov who joined Khasbulatov and Rutskoi in the Moscow White House—and while Rutskoi recklessly lent his support to acts of violence on the night of 3 October, there remain grounds for concern that the military response of Yeltsin on 4 October was disproportionate to what was required to end the standoff. Most of the deaths of those two days were on the 'parliamentary' side. Until that bloody showdown, Russia could with some justice congratulate itself on the fact that, in spite of the strains and hardships of the transition process, political violence had been avoided. Ordinary criminal violence had greatly increased, but—unlike the situation in several of the other post-Soviet successor states—there had not been a resort to arms in the pursuit of political goals.

Third, by taking the action he did on 21 September and on 3-4 October 1993, Yeltsin put himself and the presidency more in the debt of the 'power ministries'—the army, the Ministry of Interior and the security forces. The important role of the army on 4 October raises questions both about future politics and the economic reform. The army has been an important *instrument* of power in Russia for many decades, but throughout the Soviet period it was kept under strict political control. It was not allowed to become the *arbiter* of the fate of one group of politicians as against another. The nearest thing to an exception to this would probably be the support Marshal Zhukov accorded Nikita Khrushchev during the 'anti-party-group' crisis of 1957. Khrushchev, however, was soon able to use the levers of power which control over the party apparatus gave him to marginalise Zhukov. When Khrushchev was finally overthrown in October 1964, the army—unlike leading figures in the party apparat and the leadership of the KGB—played no part on one side or the other.[27]

Although showing an understandable reluctance to get involved in killing fellow-countrymen in the course of taking the side of one branch of power against another, the military—and Minister of Defence Pavel Grachev specifically—in the end played a highly visible part in the resolution of the extreme crisis of 3-4 October. As a result, the military influence in domestic and foreign policy was likely to be enhanced, since the military had become increasingly aware of the extent to which the President and the civilian government depended on them. By March 1994 there had already been signs of changes in Russian foreign policy which took the views of the military more fully into account. The presidential team was aware that if the army had made a different choice on those crucial days in early October, all the vocal support of President Clinton and a dozen or more Western Prime Ministers would not have kept President Yeltsin in office. Given that the Ministry of Defence had hitherto been espousing a somewhat different foreign policy towards the Near Abroad than the Ministry of Foreign Affairs, that could not but be of some political consequence.

Fourth, by abandoning much of the work of the Constitutional Commission of the previous legislature, which Yeltsin himself had once chaired, and having a new Constitutional draft prepared at short notice which greatly strengthened the presidential branch of government at the expense of the legislature, Yeltsin may have been guilty of putting short-term tactical advantage ahead of the strategy required for consolidation of democracy and the rule of law in Russia. The tactical advantage turned out, perhaps, to be even shorter-term than Yeltsin had in mind, inasmuch as the results of the December election meant that even though the new parliament had significantly fewer powers than its predecessor, its composition was such that it could not but at times be a thorn in the flesh of the President. As early as in late February 1994 it demonstrated that this could be so when it passed a resolution of amnesty which led to the release from prison of Rutskoi, Khasbulatov and those who had been arrested after the events of 3-4 October 1993 as well as declaring an amnesty for the coup plotters of August 1991. The latter had already in 1993 been released from prison and were awaiting resumption of their trial which had been interrupted several times. The outcome of the part of the resolution affecting the 1991 plotters (two of whom had actually been elected to the State Duma) remained unclear, for Russia's Supreme Court subsequently held that parliament had no right to grant an amnesty in the case of a trial which had already begun but not ended.

Notwithstanding the amnesty setback for Yeltsin, the fact remained that the Constitution adopted in December 1993 made the Russian political system more 'presidential' than it had been hitherto. The strength of the powers vested in the presidency was welcomed, almost alone among opposition political leaders, by Zhirinovskii who clearly hoped to inherit those powers in due course. The implications of that have been brought out in more general terms by Carla Thorson when she observed that 'a strong presidential republic, while it might work with Yeltsin at the helm, could be very dangerous in the hands of others'.[28]

A broader issue still, however, is the appropriateness of a presidential system for the consolidation of democracy in countries emerging from authoritarian rule. There is a growing comparative politics literature on 'the perils of presidentialism'.[29] While the new Russian Constitution owes something to that of the Fifth French Republic and comes into the category of 'semi-presidential government'[30] rather than that of pure presidentialism, it would appear, at least, to represent movement away from parliamentarism (especially as compared with the discarded drafts of the Constitutional Commission). Summing up the case for the advantages of parliamentarism as 'a more supportive constitutional framework' than presidentialism for consolidating democracy, Stepan and Skach note: 'its greater propensity for governments to have majorities to implement their programs; its greater ability to rule in a multiparty setting; its lower propensity for executives to rule at the edge of the constitution and its greater facility at removing a chief executive who does so; its lower susceptibility to military coup; and its greater tendency to provide long party-government careers, which add loyalty and experience to political society'.[31]

Fifth, and finally, the way in which the executive-legislature deadlock was ended in September-October 1993 adds to the difficulty of establishing a rule of law and due process within Russian society. It was neither the first nor the last example of an attitude in Russia within the ranks of professed democrats (as well, of course, as that of overt authoritarians) that 'the end justifies the means'. It would appear that those who in contemporary Russia see themselves as radical democrats include many who in psychology, as distinct from ideology, are neo-Bolsheviks whose fundamental outlook is akin to Lenin's *kto kogo* (who will crush whom).[32] Aleksei Kazannik, who had been Procurator-General for only a few months and whose attachment to democracy and the rule of law could scarcely be questioned, resigned after implementing the decision of the State Duma to amnesty those imprisoned as a result of their part in the August 1991 and autumn 1993 conflicts. Although Kazannik disagreed on political grounds with the State Duma's decision, he believed it to be in accordance with the Constitution and that, accordingly, in law he had no choice but to implement it. In a subsequent interview he related how, in a telephone conversation with the Russian President, he refused to accept Yeltsin's instruction to find a way of avoiding releasing the prisoners. Kazannik was not prepared to go along with the 'telephone law', whereby—as in Soviet times—politicians told the legal authorities how to interpret, bend or ignore the law.[33]

Compared with by far the greater part of the Soviet period and, for that matter, of Russian history, the top political leadership in post-Soviet Russia has been tolerant and benign. That, however, is not to apply the most stringent comparative yardstick. The task of legal and political institution-building has already been interrupted more than once. Only when it begins again in a serious way, and when the Russian political leadership finally breaks with revolutionary psychology and accepts the advantages of a rule of law and of evolutionary political change, will the chances of differences being settled on the streets once more have been significantly diminished.

Notes

This chapter is an expanded and updated version of my paper at the Canberra conference which draws also on my article, 'The October Crisis of 1993: Context and Implications', *Post-Soviet Affairs*, vol.9, no.3, July-September 1993. I am grateful to George Breslauer, the editor of *Post-Soviet Affairs*, for permission to republish some parts of that article.

1 See William J. Tompson, 'The Fall of Nikita Khrushchev', *Soviet Studies*, vol.43, no.6, 1991, pp.1101-1121; and William J. Tompson, 'Khrushchev and Gorbachev as Reformers: A Comparison', *British Journal of Political Science*, vol.23, part 1, January 1993, pp.77-105.

2 That view has been seriously questioned however by none other than Aleksei Kazannik, the Procurator-General appointed by Yeltsin after the violent showdown at the Moscow White House. Kazannik, a Yeltsin supporter, first came into the public eye in 1989 when he ceded his seat in the Supreme Soviet of the USSR to Yeltsin after a majority of deputies in the Congress of People's Deputies had tried to prevent Yeltsin's election to the inner body of the Soviet legislature. Kazannik, before his resignation as Procurator-General at the end of February 1994, had ordered an investigation into whether any talks on the surrender of the people in the White House were ever held, adding that, if there were none, 'then the actions of the authorities could be interpreted only as a different type of crime' and one motivated by the desire for revenge: *Komsomol'skaia pravda*, 18 March 1994, p.7.

3 Nor is to accept that, having dissolved parliament, Yeltsin and his colleagues were necessarily wise to besiege the White House they had defended two years earlier and cut off the lights, water, electricity and telephone (not to mention the telephone of the Chairman of the Constitutional Court, Valerii Zor'kin, in the Constitutional Court building when he was attempting to speak to leaders in the regions). Yeltsin and Zor'kin have produced their own fundamentally contrasting accounts of the September-October 1993 crisis. See Boris Yeltsin, *The View from the Kremlin* (London: HarperCollins, 1994); Valerii Zor'kin, 'Uroki oktiabria-93', *Konstitutsionnyi vestnik*, no.1 (17), March-April 1994, pp.7-19.

4 See, for example, *Nezavisimaia gazeta*, 23 September 1993 and subsequent issues; *Moscow News*, 1 and 8 October 1993; and *Novaia ezhednevnaia gazeta*, 1 October 1993. Most other newspapers of pro-democratic orientation, however, supported the dissolution of parliament, among them *Izvestiia*, which is generally pro-Yeltsin.

5 Vitalii Tret'iakov, 'Ikh vsekh nuzhno ostanovit'', *Nezavisimaia gazeta*, 23 September 1993, p.1.

6 Yeltsin, in a television broadcast on 20 March 1993, indicated that he had signed a decree in which he was taking special powers, but this may have been a testing of the waters. Following condemnation by Valerii Zor'kin, the Chairman of the Constitutional Court as well as by Khasbulatov, on the basis of what they had been led to believe would be in the presidential *ukaz*, Yeltsin eventually issued a decree more anodyne than that which he had hinted at (not to mention that which he eventually issued on the evening of 21 September).

7 Russia, indeed, was already in the throes of a triple crisis—(i) a crisis of power and authority; (ii) a crisis of national identity and of nationality relations; and (iii) an economic crisis. Only the first can be discussed within this chapter, although in a number of respects these crises were, and are, interrelated.

8   Rutskoi had shown himself to be an emotional politician with no
    coherent intellectual position. He was increasingly drawn into an
    alliance with the ultra-nationalists and unreconstructed Communists
    from whom he had earlier differentiated himself. The turning of
    Rutskoi from a useful ally into an implacable enemy owed a good deal,
    however, to the tactless way in which the Russian President and his
    aides treated him almost from the outset of the Yeltsin presidency. To
    note that the alienation of Rutskoi was an unnecessary error on the part
    of the President's team does not mean that Yeltsin had made a wise
    choice of running-mate in the summer of 1991; on the contrary, it was
    an error of comparable magnitude to Mikhail Gorbachev's selection of
    Gennadii Ianaev as Soviet Vice-President. Still less does it excuse
    Rutskoi's criminal folly on the night of 3 October when he called for the
    violent storming of the Mayor's office and the Ostankino television
    centre in Moscow.

9   The regional and local soviets were also disbanded and elections for new
    local councils scheduled for 1994. This will not necessarily end the
    struggle for power, however, given the evidence that 'the struggle is
    not so much over reform per se as over the control of resources'. See
    Jeffrey Hahn, 'Attitudes Toward Reform Among Provincial Russian
    Politicians', *Post-Soviet Affairs*, vol.9, no.1, 1993, pp.66-85 at p.84.

10 Banned altogether on 13 October 1993 were *Den'*, *Narodnaia pravda*,
    Russkoe delo, *Russkoe voskresenie*, *Russkie vedomosti*, *Russkii puls*,
    Russkii poriadok, *Za Rus*, *Nash marsh*, *Natsionalist*, *Russkoe slovo*,
    Moskovskii traktir, *Russkii soiuz* and *K toporu*. The more important
    newspapers, *Pravda* and *Sovetskaia Rossiia* were treated differently in
    form but not in essence. In contravention of the Russian press law,
    their editors-in-chief were dismissed by the Russian Ministry for Press
    and Information and they were informed that if they were to be allowed
    to re-register as publications, they would have to change their names.
    In fact, they succeeded in resuming publication under their familiar
    names. *Rossiiskaia gazeta*, the main mouthpiece of the Russian
    parliament, was initially banned, but resumed publication on 5 October,
    by which time it had been transformed into the newspaper of the
    Russian Council of Ministers. In addition, the newspaper *Glasnost'*—the
    reactionary position of which belied its title—was closed down because it
    had 'failed to undergo registration', *Russkii Vestnik* was instructed to
    mend its ways and then apply for re-registration and *Eshche* was
    suspended. (See BBC *Summary of World Broadcasts*, SU/1821 B/4, 16
    October 1993.) Most of these newspapers were able, one way or another,
    to resume publication, sometimes after changing their name. Thus, the
    nationalist *Den'* (The Day) became *Zavtra* (Tomorrow), while retaining
    the same editor-in-chief, Aleksandr Prokhanov.

11 Yuri Levada, 'Tired of Politics: the electorate in 1993', *Moscow News*,
    no.30, 23 July 1993, p.3.

12 I am most grateful to Professor Levada for supplying me with the survey
    data cited above and below.

13 It was as late as May 1990 that Yeltsin overtook Gorbachev as the most
    popular politician in Russia and the Soviet Union. (See 'Reitingi Borisa
    El'tsina i Mikhaila Gorbacheva po 10-bal'noi shkale', All-Russian Centre
    for the Study of Public Opinion, 1993).

14 These and other interesting data are to be found in an article by
    Stephen Whitefield and Geoffrey Evans, 'The Russian Election of 1993:
    Public Opinion and the Transition Experience', *Post-Soviet Affairs*,
    vol.10, no.1, January-March 1994, pp.38-60.

15 Whitefield and Evans, 'The Russian Election of 1993: Public Opinion and the Transition Experience'.

16 Egor Iakovlev, 'Ia teriaiu liudei, v kotorykh byl vliublen ...', *Novaia ezhednevnaia gazeta*, 1 October 1993, p.2.

17 Andrei Siniavskii, 'Vse eto uzhe bylo', *Nezavisimaia gazeta*, 13 October 1993, p.5.

18 Siniavskii, 'Vse eto uzhe bylo'.

19 Igor' Kliamkin, 'Vopros o kharaktere vyborov iavliaetsia strategicheskim', *Novaia ezhednevnaia gazeta*, 1 October 1993, p.2.

20 Yeltsin issued a decree on 23 September 1993, stating that the presidential election would take place on 12 June 1994 and that the Federal Assembly must adopt an appropriate law to facilitate this not later than 1 February 1994.

21 Press Conference in Tokyo on 13 October, NHK TV. See BBC *Summary of World Broadcasts*, SU/1819 C/2, 14 October 1993.

22 Interfax news agency report of a speech by Grachev delivered on October 14. See BBC *Summary of World Broadcasts*, SU/1821 B/1, 16 October 1993.

23 Leonid Sedov, 'Mezhdu putchem i vyborami', *Ekonomicheskie i sotsial'nye peremeny: monitoring obshchestvennogo mneniia* (VTsIOM), no.1, January 1994, pp.14-15 at p.14.

24 Sedov, 'Mezhdu putchem i vyborami'.

25 Whitefield and Evans, 'The Russian Election of 1993: Public Opinion and the Transition Experience'.

26 Leonid Smirniagin, Seminar on 'The regional dimension of Russian politics' at St Antony's College, Oxford, 31 January 1994.

27 For a good account which makes use of much of the recent evidence, see Tompson, 'The Fall of Nikita Khrushchev'.

28 Carla Thorson, 'Russia's Draft Constitution', *RFE/RL Research Report*, vol.2, no.48, 3 December 1993, pp.9-15 at p.15.

29 See, especially notably, Juan J. Linz, 'The Perils of Presidentialism', *Journal of Democracy*, vol.1, no.1, Winter 1990, pp.52-69; and Alfred Stepan and Cindy Skach, 'Constitutional Frameworks and Democratic Consolidation: Parliamentarism versus Presidentialism', *World Politics*, vol.46, no.1, October 1993, pp.1-22.

30 See Maurice Duverger, 'A New Political System Model: Semi-Presidential Government', *European Journal of Political Research*, vol.8, no.2, June 1980, pp.165-187.

31 Stepan and Skach, 'Constitutional Frameworks and Democratic Consolidation: Parliamentarism versus Presidentialism', p.22.

32 Traces of such an outlook could be observed in an article by Vasilii Seliunin in which the view, 'he who is not for us is against us', came through strongly. Liberal critics of Yeltsin's action on 21 September, such as the economist and politician, Grigorii Iavlinskii, and the editor-in-chief of *Nezavisimaia gazeta*, Vitalii Tret'iakov, who were oddly described as 'opportunists' (although they had not backed what to most people looked at that time like the winning side) and unprincipled, were drenched in a flood of accusations entirely Soviet in spirit, notwithstanding the differences of ideological orientation. See Seliunin, 'Krakh opportunizma', *Izvestiia*, 8 October 1993, p.4.

33 In his interview Kazannik said: 'I tried to put an end to the policy of telephone law in relation to the Procurator-General': *Komsomol'skaia pravda*, 18 March 1994, p.7.

4 The Shape of the Russian Macroeconomy

WILLIAM MALEY

Our century has been a harsh one for the people of Russia. Their nascent experiment with responsible government came to a screeching halt when detachments of Red Guards dissolved the Constituent Assembly in early 1918, and within three decades they were exposed to the whirlwind effects of crash industrialisation, agricultural collectivisation, the Great Terror, and the German invasion, all of which cost countless lives.[1] With the death of Stalin in March 1953, things took a turn for the better. However, the command economy which his successors inherited, while it generated some increases in average living standards, could not match the performance of the liberated capitalist systems of Western Europe, the United States, and East Asia.[2] This failure lay at the heart of the push for economic reform that Mikhail Gorbachev embraced during his period as General Secretary of the Communist Party of the Soviet Union from 1985 to 1991.

The larger story of Gorbachev's tenure, and of the unravelling of the Soviet Union itself, has been well told on a number of occasions, and there is no need to repeat it here.[3] It is a dramatic and in some ways tragic tale, of a transitional leader of enormous energy whose policies acquired a momentum of their own which caused him to lose not only control of the political agenda, but even a clear sense of its shape. In no area was this more marked than that of the economy. In Gorbachev's last year of office, marked by an unusual degree of confusion and incoherence in economic policymaking, Russian real gross domestic product fell sharply—by 9% according to the International Monetary Fund (IMF) and by 17% according to the USSR State Committee for Statistics[4]—and consumer prices reportedly rose by 89.1%.[5] Over four million working days were lost in strikes,[6] and one hundred million Soviets allegedly lived in poverty.[7] It is difficult to imagine a more perturbing inheritance for Gorbachev's successors. This point cannot be made too strongly, given the disposition of some commentators, with singularly shaky records where analysis of the Soviet economy was concerned,[8] to heap opprobrium on reformers such as Egor Gaidar and Boris Fedorov who were charged with the thankless task of cleaning out the Augean stables.

The economic system of the Soviet Union was in its conception one of the most centralised that the world has ever known, and in its functioning one of the most bureaucratised.[9] Both the Soviet Government and the Communist Party of the Soviet Union were intimately involved in the making of economic policy. The governmental hierarchy, at the apex of which stood the Council of Ministers, consisted of what became over time an increasingly complex array of branch ministries and state committees to which were linked 'enterprises' (*predpriiatiia*), charged with performing specific tasks within the constraints set by superordinate authorities. The party hierarchy was responsible at all levels for ensuring that non-party organisations followed policy and met plan targets. The basic planning organisation was the State Planning Commission (*Gosplan*), set up originally in 1921. Five Year Plans set out broad forecasts—and more importantly, targets—for important economic aggregates such as investment, output of consumer and capital goods, agricultural production, and consumption. They also shaped the general structure of Annual Plans, which provided operational details for the attainment of the objectives which they embodied.[10] Agriculture was based on state farms and collective farms, although the output of private plots contributed significantly to welfare.

Given the importance of economic factors in democratic transitions,[11] it is little wonder that the shape of the Russian macroeconomy is now a topic of intense concern for Russians and non-Russians alike. This in itself is testimony to how fast events have moved in recent years. In command economies, the very concept of the 'macroeconomy' is an elusive one. While fat books of aggregate statistics relating to economic performance at national, republican, and sectoral levels of the Soviet Union were issued by the State Committee for Statistics,[12] the use of planning agencies rather than market mechanisms to determine the values of key economic variables such as product price and quantity, and more generally the proportions of real national income to be devoted to consumption and to capital investment, obviated the need for macroeconomic policies to control inflation or eliminate unemployment. The planned economy, indeed, was widely defended as a 'rational' solution to the miseries of the downside of the capitalist trade cycle which had surfaced so dramatically during the Great Depression.[13] Unfortunately, like most magic solutions to complex problems, the 'rational' planned economy depended upon heroic assumptions about the ability of bureaucracies to accomplish the centralised coordination of a vast array of information which markets accomplish in a decentralised fashion,[14] and these assumptions were never realised beyond the pages of socialist theory. Furthermore, 'coloured' markets flourished, adding to the problems of planners.[15] For all these reasons, economic reconstruction in Russia came to involve a dramatic push to replace bureaucratic modes of coordination with market modes, and this in turn focussed attention on macroeconomic issues which the very nature of the command economy had long suppressed.

The remainder of the chapter is divided into four sections. The first section briefly discusses the focus of macroeconomics, and highlights some of the major schools of macroeconomic thought and their relevance to the transition from 'really-existing' socialism. The second discusses the macroeconomic inheritance of Gorbachev's successors, and the macroeconomic policy alternatives which were available to address the dilemmas which his successors faced. The third examines the substance and politics of macroeconomic policy in post-communist Russia. The fourth and final section discusses macroeconomic policy in the light of the December 1993 elections, and the subsequent purge of reformers from the government of Prime Minister Viktor Chernomyrdin.

The nature of macroeconomics

In the Western world, 'macroeconomics' is no longer quite as fashionable as once was the case. From the late 1960s, Keynesian policies of demand management by the state which had been credited with creating two decades of prosperity began to lose their lustre. With the collapse of the Bretton Woods system of fixed currency exchange rates, the rocketing of crude oil prices, and the development of interest group structures which gradually corrupted the framework of rules with which private entrepreneurial activity was conducted,[16] there emerged problems of unemployment and inflation with which standard macroeconomic policies proved unable to cope. To some economists, this simply proved the pseudoscientific character of macroeconomics, especially when allied with the use of complex mathematical models to intimidate rather than illuminate.[17] To others it suggested rather the limitations of macroeconomic policy, especially when confronted with long time-lags, and unstable consumer and producer behaviour in an uncertain world. Yet while the hubris associated with the Keynesian revolution has dissipated, some of the key problems which countercyclical policy was designed to address remain troubling.

One important response to the apparent failures of Keynesian demand management came in the form of monetarist policies.[18] Inflation—a key political problem in pluralist systems, since increases in the general level of prices erode the living standards of those on fixed nominal incomes—could be viewed at its crudest as a monetary phenomenon, with too much money chasing too few goods. While inflation theoretically could result from an increase in the velocity of circulation of a fixed quantity of money, the lesson of monetarism was that the quantity of money should be tightly controlled. In particular, governments were enjoined to make sure that their receipts from taxation and responsible borrowing covered their expenditures, so that there was no need for deficit financing through the Central Bank of a kind which would directly increase the money supply and risk the creation of inflationary pressures.

A second key response to the perceived breakdown of Keynesian management strategies was a growing scepticism about the virtues of governmental provision of services. Public investment, so long seen as an effective antidote to the 'bust' phase of the capitalist trade cycle, was increasingly—although not uncontroversially—viewed as 'squeezing out' private investment which could employ the same numbers of workers, but at lower cost. This led to pressure to 'privatise' those parts of the public sector providing services which in principle could be provided by the private sector. While some voices pointed out that privatisation was not the same as the replacement of monopoly with competition,[19] the privatisation of state-controlled industries in Western countries proceeded apace. This marked a turn not simply to a new approach to macroeconomic policy, but away from macroeconomics as a whole. The role of government was not to 'manage' the economy, but to ensure a stable framework of institutions—including the institution of money—within which the fruits of 'microeconomic reform' could be exploited. This was not, however, to suggest that one could draw a sharp distinction between 'real' and 'monetary' economies. On the contrary, despite abundant endowments of the factors of production—land, labour, capital—an economy could stagnate if inappropriate frameworks of rules were used to structure the conduct of economic activity.

These post-Keynesian perspectives are by no means irrelevant to economies in transition from the command system to the market. This is transparently the case where the call to privatise is concerned, but is also true of the demand for monetary discipline. Fundamental imbalances between supply and demand are not absent from command systems: they simply manifest themselves in the form of shortages, queues, or excessive money holdings rather than price rises. These imbalances give rise to complex macroeconomic problems once the transition to the market gathers speed. Management of these problems is especially complicated when economic change is associated with political democratisation. In a democratic polity where economic considerations may significantly shape the attitudes of voters and thus the fortunes of political actors, it may be unrealistic to expect that the state will eschew a significant economic role if voters are risk-averse. It is quite reasonable to hope that the state in such circumstances will pursue macroeconomic stability by establishing a framework of rules within which private activity will be conducted, by pursuing fiscal and monetary policies which ensure a stable currency, and by providing a social security floor which will protect the fragile democratic transition from destruction by the alienated victims of radical microeconomic reform. The danger is that the state will feel constrained to do much more, undercutting the transition process as a whole.

The macroeconomic inheritance

The fiscal and monetary problems of transition in Russia came in a number of forms, but four were particularly striking.[20] Together they constituted a formidable challenge to economic reformers, who had fewer instruments of macroeconomic management at their disposal than do finance ministers and central bankers in developed capitalist economies; and who also faced opponents not noted for their scruples.[21]

First, the newly-independent Russia was confronted by a massive abundance of savings in private hands, representing repressed inflation on a large scale. This 'savings overhang' reflected the largely illusory character of 'real wage increases' during the 'era of stagnation'. It was indeed the case that increases in nominal wages had exceeded increases in official prices, but since consumers were unable on a sufficient scale to exchange their additional roubles for locally-produced goods and services, were unable to purchase imports because the rouble was not a hard currency, and could not invest their rouble holdings through a private capital market, they had little choice but to hold their 'real wage increases' in the form of savings. This led to a widening gap between the prices which were administratively fixed for goods, and those which would have prevailed in a free market—so that price liberalisation, essential if prices were to serve as signals to allow efficient allocation of resources, became politically ever more difficult, as a significant increase in prices was sure to result. Measuring the scale of the savings overhang involves numerous assumptions, but econometric analysis suggests that the wealth overhang of households in 1990 fell somewhere between 159 billion and 183 billion roubles, and that the proportion of wealth held in monetary as opposed to real form had increased from 57.1% in 1965-69 to 87.2% in 1985-89.[22]

Second, physical output was falling as the erosion of the power of governmental and party hierarchies caused centralised control over local economic activity to break down. It became increasingly difficult for enterprises to obtain supplies of essential inputs, and as a result, problems in one sector of the economy tended to be replicated more widely. Supplies of consumer goods were also disrupted: in a 1990 survey of emigres, 'staples and vegetables were reported to be regularly available in the stores by less than a third of the respondents', indicating 'a marked decline compared with previous years in the availability of the most basic foods in the Soviet diet'.[23] The problem of supplies arose not simply from the emergence of local autarky, especially in the sphere of agriculture, but also from the inefficiency of the Soviet transport system, which was unable to protect consignments of capital or consumer goods from being pillaged before they reached their destination. In addition, the system was riddled with corruption, against which official anti-corruption campaigns proved largely ineffective.[24] Falls in output are not *ipso facto* undesirable: the collapse of a loss-making enterprise, leading to an immediate output fall, may be part of a process of structural adjustment which will lead to higher levels of productivity and real income per capita. However, output falls which result from bottlenecks created by dysfunctional organisational structures have nothing to commend them, and this was substantially what the Soviet economy experienced in the late 1980s and early 1990s.

Third, the state budget was plunging deeper and deeper into deficit. In 1991, according to the IMF, the overall budget deficit amounted to 482 billion roubles, or 26% of gross domestic product, compared to 8.5% of GDP in the previous year.[25] Furthermore, this deficit was largely financed through the printing of money which goes a long way towards explaining the surge in inflation mentioned at the beginning of this chapter. There were a number of reasons why this deficit emerged. Production falls diminished the real tax base in a system dominated by indirect taxation.[26] The anti-alcohol campaign of the early Gorbachev period cut especially deeply into state revenues. Furthermore, the collection of key indirect taxes became administratively unmanageable as firms slipped from central control. Finally, the recovery by the central authorities of taxes which republican authorities were charged with collecting became politically controversial.

Fourth, the collapse of the Soviet Union raised serious problems about the future role and status of the rouble. To encourage foreign investment in Russia, it was vital that the rouble become convertible, so that dividends could effectively be paid to investors in the currencies of their choice, and at a rate accurately reflecting the real rate of return on their investment.[27] However, this would require a difficult process of adjustment, as the officially-fixed exchange rate between the rouble and major

Western currencies such as the US Dollar, Sterling, and the Deutschemark diverged sharply from the rouble's real external value, and the USSR's external debt at the end of 1991 totalled US\$67 billion.[28] Furthermore, the replacement of the Soviet Union with the Commonwealth of Independent States (CIS) pursuant to the December 1991 Minsk Agreement meant that as long as a common 'rouble zone' persisted, the Russian Government would face the dilemma of whether to finance credits in roubles granted by other instrumentalities within the CIS.

These problems were of course recognised by serious Russian economists well before the collapse of the USSR,[29] but the political process in the USSR's final years was not geared to generate appropriate solutions. Gorbachev's concept of *perestroika*—which for him was compatible with the assertion that socialism and public ownership 'hold out virtually unlimited possibilities for progressive economic processes'[30]—initially amounted to little more than an item of rhetoric, and embraced significant oscillations in policy, although innovations such as the 1988 Law on Cooperatives had a symbolic significance outweighing their direct economic effects. By 1990, the fundamental flaws of the Soviet economy were well publicised in the popular press, but the erosion of Gorbachev's popularity left him increasingly vulnerable to conservative forces resistant to reform. To provide only one example, the Shatalin plan for economic reform, entailing price liberalisation and stringent monetary controls, was sacrificed by Gorbachev in the face of pressure from the industrial establishment, prompting Academician Shatalin to comment in a devastating open letter to Gorbachev that 'a politician should not stay on beyond the point where people feel pity for him'.[31] It took the failed coup attempt of August 1991 to break the stalemate and provide an opportunity for radical economic reformers to come to the fore.[32] The most significant of these figures was Egor Gaidar, Deputy Prime Minister for Economic Affairs in the Russian Government from November 1991, and Acting Prime Minister of the Russian Federation from June-December 1992.

When one compares the different proposals for economic transition that surfaced at this time, one is immediately struck by the lack of fundamental divergence among the more serious contributors over the nature of the *ultimate objective* of change. Most economists of any standing took a market economy, with the bulk of productive assets in private hands, as the ultimate objective of reform. However, there were significant differences between these economists as to the appropriate priority and timing of different elements of the transition process—and when one moved beyond the ranks of professional economists, one found very significant divergences of opinion as to the appropriate objectives of economic reform. This lack of consensus, when reflected in different patterns of control in different policymaking agencies, in large measure accounted for the problems of macroeconomic management in the post-Soviet era.

The most intellectually troubling of these disputes related to timing and pace of reform. On the one hand, Sir Karl Popper, long a proponent of 'piecemeal' as opposed to 'holistic' social engineering, argued in 1991 that those seeking to manage the transition from command to market economies should 'start from the assumption that any ostensibly fool-proof scheme can be fooled, and that it is their job to test it for potential weaknesses by trial and error. A slow, empirical type of approach is what is required'.[33] Such an approach could also be supported by reference to the familiar defence of incrementalism in public policy, or even to the conservatism of conventional welfare economics which endorses change only when no one is made worse off.[34] Markets are not simply the product of self-interest: they are complex social institutions which result from the development of systems of rules which ensure that agents compete by striving to sell cheaper or higher quality goods.[35] Elements of this approach found favour with the liberal economist Grigorii Iavlinskii, who argued that 'economic policy must be formulated for the achievement of long-term goals'.[36] On the other hand, one could question whether the incrementalist approach, conceived as a normative model of policy change, was either desirable,[37] or directly relevant to the unique problem of dismantling an entire command-administrative order. A drawn-out process of change could simply facilitate countermobilisation by conservative opponents of change—and this argument carried force in Russia, where the managers of 'rustbelt' enterprises with no future in an efficient, productive economy were nevertheless strongly represented in the Russian Congress of People's Deputies elected in March 1990 and inherited by post-Soviet Russia. This was among the factors which prompted Gaidar to attempt to implement what came to be known as *shokoterapiia*, or 'shock therapy', comprising price liberalisation and monetary constraint.[38]

The substance and politics of macroeconomic policy

On 2 January 1992, the new Russian government liberalised prices on a wide range of goods. The rationale of price liberalisation—which had been a component of a number of the reform packages of the Gorbachev era—was to eliminate the savings overhang, and to allow market forces to determine appropriate relative prices, so that resources would increasingly be directed to the production of goods in high demand. The effects of price liberalisation were felt immediately. According to official statistics, producer prices in industry rose by 382% in January, and by 3,275% in 1992 as a whole; food prices rose by 306% in January, and by 2,033% in 1992 as a whole; and the Laspeyres Consumer Price Index rose by 296% in January, and by 2,318% in 1992 as a whole.[39] At the same time, for many consumers there was a fall in the amount of time spent queuing, an indication that prices were beginning to play a rationing role.[40]

The label 'shock therapy' for the policy of price liberalisation was nonetheless an unfortunate one, for it created expectations of short-run improvements as a result of price liberalisation which were not met, and probably could not have been. A number of institutional features of the Russian economy frustrated hopes of rapid improvements in the structure of production; and within a short space of time these were greatly complicated by political factors.

The high degree of monopolisation in the Russian economy meant that newly-liberalised prices rose more sharply than was necessary to eliminate the savings overhang, largely because price setters were spared the discipline of competition.[41] While the possibility of selling goods at higher prices had been designed to lure new producers into markets, and thus to boost output, monopolies found that they could reduce production and increase prices, but because of inelastic demand still increase their revenue in the process. Furthermore, supply-side limitations prevented market entry within Russia, and since the rouble was not convertible, there was no prospect of competition from imports to dampen price effects. One of the obstacles to the opening of the Russian economy was undoubtedly the caution of Western governments and financial institutions, notably the G7 states and the IMF, in extending financial assistance to the Russian Government during the period of reform, and for this they were later savaged by reformers. The caution was to a degree understandable, since few economies could have so closely resembled a 'black hole' as did the Russian, but it created both political and economic problems for reformers. In 1992 and 1993, the G7 announced official financial assistance to Russia through the IMF of US$14 billion: of this total, US$2.5 billion was actually delivered, US$1.5 billion being a first tranche of the so-called 'Systemic Transformation Facility'.[42] Only in May 1992 was an initial agreement reached on transition to current account convertibility of the rouble, and even then, uncertainties remained as to the nature and source of a stabilisation fund. Yet such a fund, permitting the government to defend the established rate, is vital if convertibility is to be credible.[43]

However, the most acute problem which the reformers faced was that they were unable to ensure that monetary and fiscal discipline was maintained. For this reason, the label 'shock therapy' was doubly unfortunate, since monetary discipline is essential to any strategy worthy of that name. Russia in 1992 witnessed an expansion of credit which was virtually guaranteed to produce high levels of inflation. In mid-July 1992, Viktor Gerashchenko replaced Georgii Matiukhin as Chairman of the Russian Central Bank, and instituted a 'loose credit' policy: according to one analyst, Central Bank credits in 1992 amounted to 40% of gross domestic product.[44] Credits were seen as one solution to the problems created by a vast growth in 'inter-enterprise debt'. This was partly a result of the primitive state of the Russian financial system, but more fundamentally a result of negative real interest rates and the effective absence of hard budget constraints for enterprises, given the absence of a credible bankruptcy system.[45] Real arrears peaked in June 1992 at 299 billion roubles, more than double the real bank credit level of 140 billion roubles,[46] and roughly 50% of gross domestic product.[47] Gerashchenko also justified the loose credit policy by pointing to a rise in the transactions demand for cash—reflected in a cash shortage which emerged shortly after price liberalisation[48]—while ignoring the fall in the assets demand for money. Finally, the continuation of the 'rouble zone', which held Moscow hostage to the central banks of other CIS states, was a recipe for uncontrollable monetary expansion. With a lag of 3-4 months, an increase in the money supply tended to be reflected in an increase in the general level of prices.[49] By December 1992, the monthly rate of increase of the Laspeyres Consumer Price Index had reached 25.3%, compared with 7.1% in July.[50]

If monetary indiscipline in 1992 undercut the claim that the government's economic policy amounted to 'shock reform', so did events in 1993. The year began on a strange note, when Prime Minister Chernomyrdin attempted to introduce legal controls on retail prices—a recipe for emptying the shops, which he was rapidly obliged to abandon.[51] This did nothing to establish his credentials as an economist, and may have contributed to an even more bizarre episode in July, when Gerashchenko—apparently without wide consultation—announced a confiscation of currency under which banknotes 'in amounts exceeding 35,000 roubles' would be consigned to six-month time deposits.[52] This was described by Finance Minister Fedorov as 'stupid, outrageous, and senseless'.[53] During 1993, a continuing source of monetary stress arose from the need for Central Bank credits to fund a budget deficit which the Parliament seemed intent upon elevating to an irresponsible and unsustainable level, and this was undoubtedly one of the factors which led to the return of Gaidar to the government as First Deputy Prime Minister from 18 September 1993, and President Yeltsin's final confrontation with the Parliament. At the end of the year, the Finance Ministry reported that the budget deficit had been reduced to 9.2% of gross domestic product—although some reports suggested that this was achieved either through creative accounting which deferred certain expenditures until 1994, or through the simple expedient of not paying wages and salaries, while other reports suggested that the figure was simply understated, and may have been as high as 15.5%.[54] On the other hand, 1993 did witness some positive developments, notably the establishment of new currencies by all CIS states except Tajikistan, in effect putting an end to the rouble zone.[55] Furthermore, figures suggested a moderation of retail price inflation to 940% in 1993, and an increase in real incomes.[56]

The catastrophic failure of monetary discipline during these years was firmly rooted in the politics of the period. As inefficient enterprises faced the prospects of ruin, there was strong political pressure for the supply of credit to postpone the evil day. The institutional structures for the making of macroeconomic policy were unable to resist these pressures and the inflationary effects proved enormous. Gerashchenko claimed the independence of a *Bundesbank* chairman without displaying the hostility to inflation which characterises the *Bundesbank*'s operations.[57] Only in November 1992 was he formally brought within the ranks of the government,[58] and the broader political turmoil which followed almost immediately meant that the constraints which this imposed upon him were minimal. Gerashchenko's position was bolstered by opposition to the government's policies from the Congress of People's Deputies, and especially from its ambitious Speaker, Ruslan Khasbulatov, who had an interest in promoting the Congress at the expense of the presidency since, as an ethnic Chechen, his prospects of ever being elected president were slight. However, while personality clashes certainly contaminated the struggle over economic policy, there were two deeper bases for the clash. The first was a conflict of interest between those who wished to protect their managerial positions in existing enterprises, and those who wished to see industrial restructuring. The second was a conflict of vision between those who favoured markets, and those who—whatever the content of their rhetoric—still yearned for a command-administrative system. And while it would be naive to think that the opponents of reform were motivated by motives much higher than the protection of the privileged positions which they had enjoyed under the Soviet system,[59] there is no doubt that the spectre of unemployment they conjured up inspired great fear amongst Russian voters.

Prospects for reform

The December 1993 elections put paid to Gaidar's Second Spring, and he resigned as First Deputy Prime Minister on 16 January 1994. In the absence of evidence to the contrary, the failure of his Russia's Choice bloc to win anything like an absolute majority in the State Duma was read as a censure of radical economic reform, even though Russia's Choice emerged as the largest single named bloc in the Duma. The removal of all significant reformers except Privatisation Minister Anatolii Chubais from the Chernomyrdin government was a fairly predictable response to the apparent discontent of the electorate. Nonetheless, for a number of reasons it would be premature to conclude that radical economic reform in Russia is no longer possible.

First, the pain of the transition process may have been overestimated. Statistics which suggest a dramatic decline in output may reflect more the inadequacy of the Russian system of data-gathering during a transitional phase than a recessed economy.[60] There are strong reasons for doubting whether macroeconomic aggregates adequately capture the output of newly-emerging firms, or the impact on citizen welfare of the increased availability of services. Furthermore, aggregate figures can mask significant regional variations in economic performance, of a kind which might show in a more favourable light the economic achievements in regions where local authorities supported the reform process.[61] Finally, there is strong evidence that the Russians, while not necessarily entrepreneurial, are extremely enterprising in undertaking a range of monetised and non-monetised economic activities which protect their standards of living even in the face of unemployment.[62]

Second, survey evidence raises at least some doubts as to whether the December 1993 elections should be read as a repudiation of economic reform, rather than some other developments blamed on the government, such as rising crime[63] or declining Russian self-esteem—both of them concerns into which Zhirinovskii was able to tap.[64] Separate surveys have also shown continuing high support for a market economy: even after the elections, and in a climate of economic pessimism, 63% of voters held the view that a market system was 'right for Russia'.[65]

Third, while macroeconomic policy is in a state of turmoil, other reforms are progressively changing the fundamental bases of economic interests in Russia. Microeconomic change in the form of privatisation, discussed in more detail in this book by Robert F. Miller and Stephen Fortescue, may ultimately have radical effects on the structure and operation of the Russian economy.

The fear of unemployment may, however, hamper economic reform in the future. At some point, an increase in unemployment in Russia will almost certainly occur if significant industrial restructuring is to be carried out. Too many workers remain employees of subsidised enterprises which are value-subtracting in the sense that they take valuable assets in the form of raw materials and convert them into less valuable manufactured goods. The obliteration or massive reorganisation of these rustbelt enterprises is essential if Russians are eventually to enjoy the standards of living which their Western counterparts have long taken for granted, and labour shedding is unavoidable. Nonetheless, the fear of unemployment at the level of the mass population is widespread, and undoubtedly genuine given Russia's rudimentary social security system. In the same sample which saw 63% of respondents endorsing a market economy, 58% pronounced unemployment 'unacceptable'.[66] There is already a high level of disguised unemployment in Russia—in the form of workers forced to work short hours or take unpaid holidays—which belies the official claim that unemployment remains low,[67] and a January 1994 study by the International Labor Organization reportedly put the real level of unemployment in Russia at more than 10%.[68]

It is a delusion of meliorist intellectuals that if one searches for long enough, one is sure to find costless or low-cost solutions to complex political and economic problems. In politics there are always choices, but none may be especially attractive. Fear of the sociopolitical consequences of unemployment is perfectly legitimate, and one should not idly recommend policies if suffering is a predictable consequence: the workers in the rustbelt are after all the victims rather than the architects of the command-administrative system. However, one must equally recognise that there may be costs associated with *not* attempting the replacement of the rustbelt. Those who sabotage reform may simply be maintaining their position at the expense of the welfare of future generations. There is no shortage of commentators recommending a 'middle way' for Russia,[69] but Chernomyrdin's 'market without the bazaar',[70] his 'non-monetarist methods',[71] still remain little more than facile slogans—notwithstanding the decision of the IMF to transfer the second US$1.5 billion tranche to Russia.[72] The subsidisation of rustbelt enterprises entails either inflation, or a transfer of real resources from potential successes to established failures. Chernomyrdin and the conservatives can no more escape this poisoned chalice than could Gaidar. With the defeat of reform, Russia stands on the brink of painful economic choices. However, if hyperinflation comes about through further financial indiscipline, the reformers may yet enjoy a Third Spring.

Notes

1 See R.W. Davies, Mark Harrison and S.G. Wheatcroft (eds), *The Economic Transformation of the Soviet Union, 1913-1945* (Cambridge: Cambridge University Press, 1994).

2 See Mervyn Matthews, *Poverty in the Soviet Union* (Cambridge: Cambridge University Press, 1986); Igor Birman, *Personal Consumption in the USSR and the USA* (London: Macmillan, 1989); Mervyn Matthews, *Patterns of Deprivation in the Soviet Union Under Brezhnev and Gorbachev* (Stanford: Hoover Institution Press, 1989).

3 See especially John Miller, *Mikhail Gorbachev and the End of Soviet Power* (London: Macmillan, 1993); Stephen White, *After Gorbachev* (Cambridge: Cambridge University Press, 1993).

4 *IMF Economic Reviews: Russian Federation* (Washington DC: International Monetary Fund, 1993) p.86; and Keith Bush, 'The Disastrous Last Year of the USSR', *RFE/RL Research Report*, vol.1, no.12, 20 March 1992, pp.39-41 at p.39.

5 See Philip Hanson, 'The Russian Economy in the Spring of 1992', *RFE/RL Research Report*, vol.1, no.21, 22 May 1992, pp.24-29 at p.25. As this figure shows, it is misleading to claim, as does Jonathan Steele, 'Gaidar's poor guidance', *The Guardian*, 19 January 1994, p.18, that as a result of the price liberalisation of January 1992, 'Gaidar was the man who started the inflationary spiral'.

6 *The Economy of the Former USSR in 1991* (Washington DC: International Monetary Fund, 1992) p.9.

7 BBC *Summary of World Broadcasts*, SU/0961/i, 4 January 1991.

8 See, for example, John Kenneth Galbraith, *The New Industrial State* (Harmondsworth: Penguin, 1974) p.120.

9 For the best overview of the structure and functioning of the Soviet economy, see Ed A. Hewett, *Reforming the Soviet Economy: Equality versus Efficiency* (Washington DC: The Brookings Institution, 1988).

10 For a detailed examination of the evolution of these organs, see R.A. Belousov, *Istoricheskii opyt planovogo upravleniia ekonomikoi SSSR* (Moscow: Mysl', 1987), 26-49, 107-126.

11 See Seymour Martin Lipset, 'The Social Requisites of Democracy Revisited', *American Sociological Review*, vol.59, no.1, February 1994, pp.1-22.

12 See, for example, *Narodnoe khoziaistvo SSSR za 70 let: Iubileinyi statisticheskii ezhegodnik* (Moscow: Finansy i statistika, 1987).

13 For a sample of this kind of argument, see Maurice Dobb, *Soviet Russia and the World* (London: Sidgwick & Jackson, 1932).

14 See F.A. Hayek, *Individualism and Economic Order* (Chicago: University of Chicago Press, 1948); Don Lavoie, *Rivalry and Central Planning: The Socialist Calculation Debate Revisited* (Cambridge: Cambridge University Press, 1985).

15 Aron Katsenelinboigen, 'Coloured Markets in the Soviet Union', *Soviet Studies*, vol.29, no.1, January 1977, pp.62-85.

16 Mancur Olson, *The Rise and Decline of Nations: Economic Growth, Stagflation, and Social Rigidities* (New Haven: Yale University Press, 1982).

17 See F.A. Hayek, *The Fatal Conceit: The Intellectual Errors of Socialism* (London: Routledge, 1988) p.98.

18 While the Quantity Theory of Money is one of the most venerable of economic identities, its classic modern defence can be found in Milton Friedman, 'The Quantity Theory of Money—A Restatement' in Milton Friedman (ed.), *Studies in the Quantity Theory of Money* (Chicago: University of Chicago Press, 1956) pp.3-21.

19 Samuel Brittan, 'Privatisation: A Comment on Kay and Thompson', *The Economic Journal*, vol.96, no.1, March 1986, pp.33-38.

20 For more detailed discussion, see János Kornai, *The Socialist System: The Political Economy of Communism* (Princeton: Princeton University Press, 1992) pp.529-564.

21 One of the most notable was Vice-President Aleksandr Rutskoi, who by February 1992 was already deriding the reform process: for an uncritical presentation of his views, see Jonathan Steele, *Eternal Russia: Yeltsin, Gorbachev and the Mirage of Democracy* (London: Faber & Faber, 1994) p.292. As his irresponsible conduct in October 1993 demonstrated, Rutskoi, a former air force officer with a record of activities during the Afghan war which cries out for detailed examination, had far more in common with Hermann Goering, another air-ace-turned-politician, than with J.M. Keynes. See R.J. Overy, *Goering: The 'Iron Man'* (London: Routledge & Kegan Paul, 1984).

22 *A Study of the Soviet Economy* (Paris: IMF, World Bank, OECD & EBRD, 1991) Vol.I, pp.388-390, 412.

23 Mark Rhodes, 'Food Supply in the USSR', *Report on the USSR*, vol.3, no.41, 11 October 1991, pp.11-16 at p.13.

24 Leslie Holmes, *The End of Communist Power: Anti-Corruption Campaigns and Legitimation Crisis* (New York: Oxford University Press, 1993).

25 *The Economy of the Former USSR in 1991*, pp.12-13. For further discussion, see Keith Bush, 'The Russian Budget Deficit', *RFE/RL Research Report*, vol.1, no.40, 9 October 1992, pp.30-32.

26 On the structure of the taxation system, see Michael A. Newcity, *Taxation in the Soviet Union* (New York; Praeger, 1986).

27 On convertibility, see Timothy N. Ash, 'Problems of Ruble Convertibility', *RFE/RL Research Report*, vol.1, no.29, 17 July 1992, pp.26-32.

28 *IMF Economic Reviews: Russian Federation*, p.116.

29 For a discussion of the genesis of economic reform proposals in the USSR, see Pekka Sutela, *Economic Thought and Economic Reform in the Soviet Union* (Cambridge: Cambridge University Press, 1991).

30 Mikhail Gorbachev, *Perestroika: New Thinking for Our Country and the World* (London: Collins, 1987) p.83.

31 *Komsomol'skaia pravda*, 22 January 1991.

32 For a detailed discussion of the vicissitudes of Gorbachev's economic strategy, see Marshall I. Goldman, *What Went Wrong with Perestroika* (New York: W.W. Norton, 1992).

33 '"The Best World We Have Yet Had": George Urban Interviews Sir Karl Popper', *Report on the USSR*, vol.3, no.22, 31 May 1991, pp.20-22 at p.20. For the distinction between piecemeal and holistic social engineering, see Karl Popper, *The Poverty of Historicism* (London: Routledge & Kegan Paul, 1961) pp.64-70.

34 See David Braybrooke and Charles E. Lindblom, *A Strategy of Decision: Policy Evaluation as a Social Process* (New York: The Free Press, 1963) pp.81-110; Iain McLean, *Public Choice: An Introduction* (Oxford: Basil Blackwell, 1987) p.182.

35 See Chandran Kukathas, David W. Lovell, and William Maley, *The Theory of Politics: An Australian Perspective* (Melbourne: Longman Cheshire, 1990) pp.64-68. The (perhaps apocryphal) story of Kiev minibus operators who 'competed' by paying *mafiosi* to hurl bricks through the windscreens of each others' vehicles clearly illustrates that not all competition is *market* competition.

36 See Grigorii Iavlinskii, 'O novoi politike pravitel'stva', *Voprosy ekonomiki*, no.2, February 1993, pp.112-123 at pp.118-119.

37 See Robert E. Goodin, *Political Theory and Public Policy* (Chicago: University of Chicago Press, 1982) pp.19-38.

38 Egor Gaidar, 'Logika reform', *Voprosy ekonomiki*, no.2, February 1993, pp.12-16. Th

39 *IMF Economic Reviews: Russian Federation*, p.88.

40 Richard Rose, Irina Boeva, and Viacheslav Shironin, *How Russians are Coping with Transition: New Russia Barometer II* (Glasgow: Studies in Public Policy no.216, Centre for the Study of Public Policy, University of Strathclyde, 1993) p.23.

41 For a discussion of the problems of monopoly from an anti-reformist point of view, see Iurii Sukhotin, 'Reforma v Rossii: nauka protiv populizma', *Svobodnaia mysl'*, no.5, March 1993, pp.3-13 at pp.6-7.

42 *IMF Survey*, 7 February 1994, p.45.

43 For a discussion of this problem, see Alan Smith, *Russia and the World Economy: Problems of Integration* (London: Routledge, 1993) pp.193-194.

44 Jeffrey D. Sachs, 'Prospects for Monetary Stabilization in Russia', in Anders Åslund (ed.), *Economic Transformation in Russia* (London: Pinter, 1994) pp.34-58 at p.39. The 40% was made up of 22% to enterprises, 10% to other CIS republics, and 8% in budget financing facilities.

45 See Erik Whitlock, 'A Borrower and a Lender Be: Interenterprise Debt in Russia', *RFE/RL Research Report*, vol.1, no.40, 9 October 1992, pp.33-38; Jacek Rostowski, 'The Inter-enterprise Debt Explosion in the Former Soviet Union: Causes, Consequences, Cures', *Communist Economies & Economic Transformation*, vol.5, no.2, 1993, pp.131-159.

46 Rostowski, 'The Inter-enterprise Debt Explosion in the Former Soviet Union: Causes, Consequences, Cures', p.151.

47 See Jacek Rostowski, 'Dilemmas of Monetary and Financial Policy in Post-Stabilization Russia', in Anders Åslund (ed.), *Economic Transformation in Russia* (London: Pinter, 1994) pp.59-79 at p.73.

48 *IMF Economic Reviews: Russian Federation*, p.29.

49 See 'Rossiiskie finansy v 1993 g. (Obzor Ministerstva finansov Rossiiskoi Federatsii, podgotovlennyi pod rukovodstvom B.G. Fedorova)', *Voprosy ekonomiki*, no.1, 1994, pp.4-85 at p.16.

50 *IMF Economic Reviews: Russian Federation*, p.88.

51 Keith Bush, 'Chernomyrdin's Price Control Decree Is Revoked', *RFE/RL Research Report*, vol.2, no.5, 29 January 1993, pp.35-37.

52 *Rossiiskaia gazeta*, 27 July 1993, p.1.

53 *Nezavisimaia gazeta*, 30 July 1993, p.1.

54 See 'Rossiiskie finansy v 1993 g. (Obzor Ministerstva finansov Rossiiskoi Federatsii, podgotovlennyi pod rukovodstvom B.G. Fedorova)', p.41; *The Financial Times*, 24 December 1993; Elizabeth Teague, 'Crisis Over Unpaid Wages', *RFE/RL News Briefs*, vol.3, no.5, 24-28 January 1994, p.5; Keith Bush, 'Budget Outturn in 1993', *RFE/RL News Briefs*, vol.3, no.10, 28 February-4 March 1994, p.5.

[55] See Erik Whitlock, 'The Return of the Ruble', *RFE/RL Research Report*, vol.2, no.35, 3 September 1993, pp.34-37; Erik Whitlock, 'The CIS Economies: Divergent and Troubled Paths', *RFE/RL Research Report*, vol.3, no.1, 7 January 1994, pp.13-17. The negotiation of a monetary union between Russia and Belarus in April 1994 appears to fall well short of reviving a significant rouble zone: see Ustina Markus, 'The Russia-Belarusian Monetary Union', *RFE/RL Research Report*, vol.3, no.20, 20 May 1994, pp.28-32.

[56] Keith Bush, 'Real Incomes Rose in 1993', *RFE/RL News Briefs*, vol.3, no.6, 31 January-4 February 1994, p.6.

[57] For a comparative analysis of central bank independence, see Kanishka Jayasuriya, 'Political Economy of Central Banks', *Australian Journal of Political Science*, vol.29, no.1, March 1994, pp.115-134.

[58] *Izvestiia*, 17 November 1992, p.1.

[59] See Mervyn Matthews, *Privilege in the Soviet Union: A Study of Elite Life-Styles under Communism* (London: George Allen & Unwin, 1978).

[60] On some of the problems of statistics gathering, see P. Guzhvin, 'Rossiiskaia statistika segodnia i zavtra', *Voprosy ekonomiki*, no.5, 1993, pp.4-13.

[61] See Philip Hanson, 'Local Power and Market Reform in Russia', *Communist Economies & Economic Transformation*, vol.5, no.1, 1993, pp.45-60.

[62] See Richard Rose, 'Toward a Civil Economy', *Journal of Democracy*, vol.3, no.2, April 1992, pp.13-26; Richard Rose and Yevgeniy Tikhomirov, 'Who Grows Food in Russia and Eastern Europe?', *Post-Soviet Geography*, vol.34, no.2, 1993, pp.111-126; Richard Rose, 'Contradictions between Micro- and Macro-Economic Goals in Post-Communist Societies', *Europe-Asia Studies*, vol.45, no.3, 1993, pp.419-444; Richard Rose and Ian McAllister, *Is Money the Measure of Welfare in Russia?* (Glasgow: Studies in Public Policy no.215, Centre for the Study of Public Policy, University of Strathclyde, 1993); and Rose, Boeva, and Shironin, *How Russians are Coping with Transition: New Russia Barometer II*, pp.18-37. This is true also of Ukraine, which has avoided starvation even though its general economic performance has been far worse than Russia's: see *The Economist*, 7 May 1994.

[63] On crime rates, see Sheila Marnie and Albert Motivans, 'Rising Crime Rates: Perceptions and Reality', *RFE/RL Research Report*, vol.2, no.20, 14 May 1993, pp.80-85.

[64] See Elizabeth Teague, 'Who Voted for Zhirinovsky?', *RFE/RL Research Report*, vol.3, no.2, 14 January 1994, pp.4-5.

[65] William L. Miller, 'Zhirinovsky's Voters: Two-wave Opinion Poll from Glasgow University Team', 21 February 1994, p.3.

[66] Miller, 'Zhirinovsky's Voters: Two-wave Opinion Poll from Glasgow University Team', p.3.

[67] See Sheila Marnie, 'Who and Where Are the Russian Unemployed?', *RFE/RL Research Report*, vol.2, no.33, 20 August 1993, pp.36-42; Rose, Boeva, and Shironin, *How Russians are Coping with Transition: New Russia Barometer II*, p.13.

[68] Robert Lyle and Keith Bush, 'ILO Study on Unemployment in Russia', *RFE/RL News Briefs*, vol.3, no.6, 31 January-4 February 1994, p.2.

[69] See, for example, Robert V. Daniels, *The End of the Communist Revolution* (London: Routledge, 1993) pp.179-190.

[70] Mikhail Berger, 'Glava Rossiiskogo pravitel'stva obeshchaet strane rynok bez bazara', *Izvestiia*, 15 December 1992, p.1.

71 Erik Whitlock, 'Chernomyrdin on Wage and Price Controls', *RFE/RL News Briefs*, vol.3, no.5, 24-28 January 1994, pp.2-3 at p.3.
72 *The Financial Times*, 28 March 1994

5 REFORMING RUSSIAN AGRICULTURE: PRIVATISATION IN COMPARATIVE PERSPECTIVE

ROBERT F. MILLER

You have to look the truth in the face: without the modernisation of the machinery and tractor pool in Russian agriculture there's no future at all. However paradoxical it may sound, without such technology there is not even the hope of survival.[1]

For all the talk of the importance of changing property relations—that is, privatisation—as the solution to the accumulated disasters of Russian agriculture, in the short term at least, the simple home truths conveyed by the above quotation from a recent survey of problems with the 1993 harvest are worth keeping in mind. While the theoretical and practical-legal issues connected with the destruction of the old, centralised collective and state farm system and its replacement with various forms of private agriculture are certainly deserving of major attention and will occupy the major part of this chapter, it is necessary to address as well some of the more mundane questions currently facing the Russian Government as it strives to become self-sufficient in food production. Agricultural subsidies and the import of foodstuffs continue to account for a huge share of Russia's budget deficit, and it is becoming increasingly recognised that food self-sufficiency is an essential component of any program of general economic reform. It is perhaps the one area where import substitution makes good economic sense—however much such an argument may distress Australian trade officials.

There can be no doubt that a change in the system of property relations in agriculture is a necessary element of reform. Even if some forms of collective or group farming are retained in the short run, the need for them to operate in a more or less free-market context, to show a profit—or at least avoid catastrophic losses—and to be subject to bankruptcy and liquidation procedures if they cannot do so is by now pretty well universally accepted. There can also be little doubt that an immediate shift to private, family farming is not a realistic possibility. Even in former socialist countries like Poland and Yugoslavia, where small family farms accounted for approximately eighty percent of total arable land, the summary liquidation of the former socialist *latifundia*-type farms is recognised as a costly proposition and has not been as vigorously pushed by the post-communist regimes as one might have expected. For various reasons, this problem—largely due to the relatively low levels of mechanisation of the socialist sector—has not really arisen in China and Vietnam; but elsewhere, for reasons to be considered in this paper, the rationale for the retention of some form of group or cooperative farming is becoming part of the new conventional wisdom of agricultural reform.

Political considerations have been a major element in the choice of solutions to these problems in Russia and other former communist countries. Economists, especially Western consultants, have often tended to ignore this dimension of the reform process. Local operators do not have this luxury, especially where, as in Poland, democratic procedures have become more than merely symbolic. The question of who gains from privatisation—genuine entrepreneurs or old *nomenklatura* apparatchiki—is the central issue here, and much has been written and said on this by both domestic and foreign critics of privatisation. But in the long run, as long as a genuine market in land and producer goods and a genuine market for agricultural commodities comes into being, the foreign economists may turn out to have been right: it may not really matter.

The list of topics that could be considered in an essay like this is almost endless. I shall necessarily have to concentrate on a few important ones, although for the sake of as comprehensive treatment of the real issues as possible, I shall be erring on the side of extensiveness, rather than intensiveness.

Privatisation and what it entails

In the majority of post-communist systems, especially where large numbers of former communist cadres—ostensibly turned 'democrats' and 'reformers'—continue to hold positions of influence, privatisation is not quite what it seems. As a general rule, all that is entailed in the 'privatisation' of formerly state-owned or state-controlled enterprises (among the latter, especially the kolkhoz) is the transfer of responsibility for financing, management and supply of production inputs from the state budget to the enterprise itself. In the words of one Russian specialist: 'Privatisation, in essence, presupposes the determination of a concrete owner of property, and its aim consists in the combination of producers with property and in the formation of a real boss.'[2] In short, financial and managerial independence.

In many cases under this formula—by far the majority in Russia—the structure and *modus operandi* of the enterprise, not to mention the management personnel, have hardly changed at all. Even where genuine privatisation has taken place—for example, the breakup of the former state agricultural enterprise into independent family farms—much of the former nexus of supply, sales and agro-technical services has been retained or recast in a cooperative form that is strongly reminiscent of the old patterns.[3] Unfortunately, many of the associated infrastructural elements of the old system no longer function, so that without active state support, the survival of such nominally privatised enterprises without heavy state subsidies will probably soon become problematical.

In light of the general dissatisfaction with the old Soviet agricultural system, its persistence in the post-Soviet period may seem surprising and highly dysfunctional for thoroughgoing economic reform. Whether it is a good or a bad thing is beside the point, however. Given the nature of the transformation process and the continuity of the *dramatis personae* involved, it was probably inevitable, at least in the short run. Even in Poland, where the socialist sector was far less pervasive and dominant in agriculture, it has taken four years of concentrated effort to achieve just the first stage of the privatisation of some 60% of that country's collective and state farms: namely, the transfer of their land and assets to the state treasury. By the end of March 1993, only 1% of this land had undergone the second stage of being sold to private persons; another 7% had been leased.[4]

In Bulgaria, where the commitment of post-communist governments to the restoration of private farming has been at least verbally more insistent, the restitution of private farms appears likely to reach 70% by the end of 1993. However, the majority of such farms are tiny (averaging only 1.2 hectares), and 45% of them do not intend to farm their plots themselves. The result has been a resurgence of producer-type cooperatives of various types, which may not prove to be viable in competing on the world market; indeed, they may not even be able to compete against imports on the domestic market.[5]

Clearly, serious impediments to agricultural reform exist in these countries. They are similar, but not identical, to problems of privatising the state industrial sector. In some respects the problems are worse in agriculture. That sector still tends to be neglected by the new state authorities, just as it was by their communist predecessors. Peasant interests remain the least likely to be effectively articulated through normal policymaking channels, although in Poland, in September 1993, they ultimately succeeded in organising themselves to win a substantial share of the popular vote and, in October, to have one of their own elected as Prime Minister. Russian peasants did almost as well in the parliamentary elections of 12 December 1993 and managed to have a leader of the Agrarian Party, Ivan Rybkin—a veteran Communist Party functionary—elected to the potentially very important post of Speaker of the lower house, the State Duma.[6]

While in Russia and some of the other countries of the Commonwealth of Independent States (CIS), the number of private family farms is growing rapidly, they still account for only a small share of the land and commodity production. Results of farm privatisation through the first quarter of 1993 are shown in the following table:[7]

Table 5.1: Private (family) farms in the Russian Federation and other states of the CIS at the end of First Quarter 1993

	Number of farms	Average size (hectares)
Russia	240,000	43
Ukraine	20,700	20
Kazakhstan	11,100	531
Kyrgyzstan	16,700	23
Belarus	9,400	20
Uzbekistan	5,800	9
Armenia	246,000	1-2
Tajikistan	8	45
Turkmenistan	100	11
Moldova	500	3

The same source indicates that the total amount of land in private farms by May 1993 had reached 17 million hectares. However, the 10.3 million hectares of these in the Russian Federation accounted for only about 2% of the land in kolkhozy and sovkhozy subject to ownership reorganisation—some 440 million hectares—in that republic.[8] According to Nefedov, these private farms in 1992 accounted for less than one percent of the total gross output of agricultural commodities, although in some commodities, such as vegetables, their contribution is somewhat more significant.[9] By the end of 1993 private farms had already increased their land holdings to about 5% of agricultural land and were producing more than that proportion of agricultural commodities, although their economic situation remained far from rosy. Indeed, for the moment, growth seemed to be stagnating at this level.[10]

Readers will recall the conventional wisdom of the Soviet period that the private plots of the farmers, occupying only 3 % of the total arable land in the USSR, accounted for 25-30% of gross output. What was not often mentioned, except by a few Western observers, such as K.-E. Wädekin, was that these private plots depended for many of their agro-technical and other inputs on the kolkhozy and sovkhozy in which they were located. The change in the relationship between these collectives and the new class of private farmers in the past couple of years has evidently substantially reduced the latter's productive and marketing potential. It is clear that if the regime wishes to complete the restructuring of the agricultural system and promote the economic viability of the private peasant farms, it will have to be more determined and more consistent in the formulation and application of agricultural policy. In the run up to the December 1993 elections, Yeltsin seemed committed to doing something like that.[11] Now that the results are in—highly unfavourable to the continuation of reforms—a hiatus on 'affirmative action' for the private farming sector seems to have set in.

Government policies on agricultural reform

There has hardly been a dearth of legislative enactments on agricultural policy in recent years; indeed it is the only area of agriculture which seems to be in surplus. According to Wegren, from the Second Congress of Deputies of the RSFSR in late 1990 through March 1993, more than 40 legislative acts and prescriptions had been adopted on agriculture.[12] In November 1990 an important 'Law on Peasant Farms' (amended on 27 December of that year) was passed, making it possible for peasant farms to obtain land, mainly on an long-term, inheritable leasehold basis.[13] But the ownership rights to such land were strictly limited. Indeed, until President Yeltsin's Decree of 27 October 1993 'On Regulation of Land Relations and the Development of Agrarian Reform in Russia', the political obstacles to consistent land reform and privatisation remained almost insuperable.[14] This was true at the local level, as well in the Supreme Soviet and the Congress, where agricultural policy became an important rallying point for conservative forces.

The main concession of the 1990-1992 legislation was to make private farming one of a number of forms of farming that were considered legitimate, but local practice made it perhaps the least favoured form. Peasants seeking to take advantage of the new possibilities often suffered discrimination in the supply of production and technical services, as well as funds and credits for operating expenses. Furthermore, the jealousy of less enterprising neighbours, with or without the connivance of the local authorities, often led to unhappy consequences for the new farmers, and many of them gave up the effort after a brief trial period. During 1992, more than 5000 peasant farms went under.[15]

By late 1993 it was being claimed that 'under existing financial conditions' more than 30% of private farms faced collapse 'in the very near future' (*v blizhaishee vremia*).[16] More optimistic assessments noted, however, that even where the failure rate of private farms was highest, reaching 3-4%, the result had been a shaking out of the less viable farms, accompanied by an increase in average farm size and in the total area under private ownership.[17]

Party conservatives at the local and intermediate levels made sure that discrimination against peasant 'separatists' went unpunished. They knew that they had considerable support in high places for their opposition to the breakup of the socialist sector farm system. Indeed, Vasilii Starodubtsev, the chairman of the Agrarian Union, the main organisation nominally representative of agricultural interests (but actually the defender of the interests of kolkhoz and sovkhoz management and the associated bureaucracy), had been a member of the 'State Committee on the Emergency Situation' which staged the 19-21 August 1991 putsch to overthrow Gorbachev. His Union and the closely associated Agrarian Party continued to fight the introduction of genuine privatisation and agricultural reform right up until the promulgation of Yeltsin's decree on 27 October 1993.[18] Many of their critical observations on the weaknesses of the reforms to date were far from absurd, but the main aim of their activities was obviously to limit genuine change as far as possible. A good example of the rearguard opposition to reform can be seen in an account of the damage done by government policy in Tver' Province by one of the main newspapers of the anti-Yeltsin conservatives, *Sovetskaia Rossiia*, in July 1993. After describing difficulties experienced by collective and state farms struggling to maintain production in the face of what he calls the chaos and malevolence of government policy, the author concludes: 'The truth is that the countryside is being methodically and consistently ruined, it is doomed to a slow death. Mercilessly being undercut by the economic axe, the sovkhozy and kolkhozy are falling one after another. This is in total conformity with the anti-peasant policy of the president and the government. Even previously flourishing farms are on the verge of perishing'.[19]

However serious their accusations of economic ruination in agriculture—and this could hardly have been the aim of conscious governmental policy—the conservatives clearly regard the maintenance of the old farming structures as vital to the preservation of their power base throughout the country. Yeltsin's victory over the old parliament and his subsequent decrees suggested that the conservatives had lost this first skirmish; the old structures seemed vulnerable precisely because of their association with his enemies. The election results soon proved, however, that this was more of an advantage than a disadvantage for the agrarian conservatives. In any case, even if the reformers had won on 12 December 1993, some variant of large-scale, group farming would have had to be fashioned to replace the old ones until genuine private farming could develop sufficient strength to take up the burden of commodity production.

Regarding the general politics of agricultural transformation in Russia, it is interesting to contrast Yeltsin's (and Gorbachev's) approach to reform—and agricultural reform in particular—to that of the Chinese communists under Deng Xiaoping. Instead of confronting the opponents of reform head-on by seeking to smash their political base, the Chinese, by what Susan Shirk has called 'particularistic contracting', managed to enlist selected local cadres in the cause of economic reforms by interesting them in the material payoffs that could accrue to the structures they controlled and to them personally. This approach avoided direct challenges to existing power relationships (at least in the short run) and created a vested interest in reform.[20]

Whether such a strategy could have worked in the USSR and Russia is a moot question. The personal authority of a leader like Deng in the Chinese system was probably much greater for legitimising a major change in the direction of policy against entrenched bureaucratic interests than a Gorbachev or a Yeltsin could ever aspire to. Moreover, the pseudo-ideological rigidity and hierarchical organisational integrity of the Soviet bureaucracy, which enabled, not to say impelled, it to marshal its forces against transparently subversive change, probably would have made the Chinese approach ineffective in the Soviet case. It would have taken more authority than Gorbachev ever possessed to legitimise 'particularistic contracting' in the USSR. Nevertheless, the Chinese alternative of economic reform with delayed, non-confrontational political reform will obviously supply grist to the mill of those, both within and outside the CIS, who argue that there was another path to reform, which could have avoided the wholesale destruction of Soviet socialism and the USSR.

Yeltsin's ruthless but successful disposal of the parliamentary and regional opposition to agrarian reform in September-October 1993 seemed suddenly to have improved at least the possibility of change. The Decree of 27 October 'On Regulation of Land Relations and the Development of Agrarian Reform in Russia' removed all restrictions on land ownership and classified it as 'real estate' (*nedvizhimost'*). This made possible for the first time the creation of a market in land, something that many have considered a *conditio sine qua non* for the fundamental reform of Russian agriculture.[21] It establishes procedures for the granting to individuals of the title to specific land holdings and shares related to specific quantities of collectively owned assets. It also guarantees the sanctity of these property rights, while establishing procedures for resumption of land by the state for its purposes.

At the same time, the Decree allows citizens and juridical persons to opt voluntarily for collective or joint utilisation of their land.[22] Existing collective and state agricultural enterprises are required to issue land titles and property share certificates to their members. Individual recipients have the right to choose either to receive and/or purchase the land allotments accruing to them or to pool their land certificates and property shares to create more economically viable farms—without the need to gain assent from other members of the collective. However, by allowing, if not exactly encouraging, the pooling of land and other private resources and giving other members of collectives the first right of refusal on the sale of the land by individual members, the Decree implicitly leaves a loophole for existing kolkhozy and sovkhozy to preserve themselves through the 'back door', so to speak.[23] Only time will tell whether this possibility will be used by local managers and politicians to continue to sabotage consistent reform. Indeed, a subsequent decree by Yeltsin reduced the power of the local authorities to act as land holders with pre-emptive rights over land sales. It is worth reiterating that there could be valid economic reasons for not allowing the privatisation of land and the creation of small family farms to proceed at a rapid pace. In the words of an *Izvestiia* columnist, under the new Decree: 'The peasants will be going over from collective property to private property, not by decree of the president or the government, not by coercion, but only voluntarily. Moreover, if you look at the matter realistically, you have to admit that in many farms people simply do not have the possibility of earning their bread without working together'.[24]

The 27 October Decree removes many of the previous limitations and ambiguities of previous legislation on the privatisation of Russian agriculture. How rapidly the peasants take up the new opportunities will be a matter of current economic realities, but also of local politics.

Problems of the Transition Period

As we have seen, under the previous 'reform' legislation there was little change in the basic structure of agricultural production. As of 1 January 1993, some 8,592 (66%) of the 13,022 kolkhozy in Russia that were subject to ownership transformation had carried out some form of reorganisation. However, only 551 of them had transformed themselves into 'associations of peasant farms', while 2,495 had become 'joint-stock companies', 976 had been transformed into cooperatives, and 4,671 had chosen to adopt 'other forms'—that is, had decided to remain as is.[25] Of the 19,061 sovkhozy, 8,378 (44%) had undergone transformation, of which 393 had become associations of peasant farms, 3,149 joint-stock companies, 749 agricultural cooperatives, and 4,087 had chosen 'other forms'—that is, stayed the same.[26] It remains to be seen just how fast and how far the new Decree will change these patterns. By mid-1993, virtually all (90+%) of collective and state farms had undergone some form of restructuring, and the proportion of those electing to stay the same had declined to about one-third.[27] Even under the previous reforms, managers of collective and state agricultural enterprises were subject to fines for delaying the restructuring process, but such penalties as were levied on violators did not seem to have a decisive effect on accelerating the process, and the changes actually made were often merely nominal. As has been noted, the reasons for obstructionism were largely political, but not exclusively so.

Even where transformation of ownership was only nominal, the system as a whole could not help but change. The old system of centralised planning, finance and supply had largely broken down. Although 'state orders' for agricultural output continued to be issued by the government (indeed, the old term 'compulsory deliveries' continued to be used), the payment for procured output and the supply of funds for investment and operating expenses to the farms could no longer be guaranteed. The introduction of a tax on land in October 1991, had undercut much of the old rationale for compulsory deliveries (that is, as an obligation to the state for the free use of state land).[28] The farms were presumably happy to have the security of state orders and compulsory deliveries in the absence of a functioning market for their products.[29] But they were far from happy with the failure of the state to pay for the commodities delivered, nor were they enchanted with the level of state purchase prices.

The state budget had allocated some 2.2 trillion roubles in credits and loans for the 1993 agricultural year; yet when it came time to pay the farms for their delivered produce, there was often no money in the till.[30] During critical stages of the crop year in 1993 the press was rife with complaints of lack of funds for the farms to purchase fuel and lubricants, agricultural chemicals, farm machinery or spare parts. A Decree of 22 September 1993, 'On Settling Accounts for Agricultural Products and Food Commodities' rushed through by Yeltsin after dissolving parliament, sought to compel procurement agencies and processing industries to pay off their debts to farmers by imposing severe cash penalties (one percent for each day of delay).[31] But these measures did not seem to be any more effective than previous legislation. There just wasn't enough money available to pay for the commodities regardless of the penalties for late payment.[32]

These financial difficulties, together with prolonged inclement weather during the harvest season, kept the outturn for the year well below optimistic preliminary forecasts and threatened to jeopardise preparatory work on the next year's harvest. Kazakhstan, upon which Russia (along with Belarus and other former republics) had begun to rely to make up their own shortfall and avoid undue reliance on hard-currency grain imports, was experiencing not dissimilar difficulties of its own and was beginning to see the merits of exporting whatever surplus it had to hard-currency payers, who paid for shipments on time and often at higher prices per tonne.[33] Thus, the barter trade among former Soviet republics, upon which the various CIS governments have been relying to keep them running until their respective economic houses were in order, seems to have broken down as well.

One of the main problems of the agricultural reforms thus far—a direct result of the vain effort to keep control over some prices (mainly of food items) while freeing up prices in the rest of the economy—has been the revival of what Trotsky in the early 1920s had called the 'scissors crisis'. That is, there has been a growing disparity between what the farmers must pay for their manufactured inputs and what they receive for their commodities. An agricultural official reports that in the last two years the price of industrial goods had risen by more than 1000 times, while that for agricultural produce by only (!) 300-350 times.[34] Evidence from Poland immediately after the introduction of economic reforms suggests that this may be a generic problem of the transforming post-communist economies. The monopoly position of state industrial enterprises and the monopsonistic situation of the official procurement organs in these countries, which allows them to set prices without regard to market conditions, combine to keep the farm sector at a disadvantage vis-a-vis their customers and suppliers.

The author of a recent article in *Sel'skaia zhizn'* has even interpreted this situation as an implicit government strategy to keep the peasants and agriculture outside the workings of the market.[35] Whether that is true or not, the effect has been precisely that. The article reported on a conference in late October in Ufa, Bashkortostan, of officials of regional agro-industrial organs, which was addressed by Deputy Prime Minister A.Kh. Zaveriukha. The author describes deep splits among these officials on agricultural policy and their fears concerning Yeltsin's foreshadowed Decree 'On Regulation of Land Relations ... '. Zaveriukha had some encouraging words on the government's ability to keep agricultural production from falling as fast and as far as industrial output, but he admitted few grounds for real optimism in the immediate future, largely because of the straitened financial situation of the government.[36]

One important problem that is not mentioned as often as it should be by Russian commentators is the shrinking of consumer demand for food, which places serious constraints on the government's ability to free up agricultural procurement prices entirely to help close the 'scissors' with manufactured inputs, in response to the suggestions of some critics of government policy. The fact is that despite reduced output, farms, procurement agencies and processing plants have been encountering serious difficulties in disposing of their output, owing to the cutback in consumer demand in response to the sharp jump in retail prices during the past two years. Even such staples as potatoes and eggs had become difficult to sell, not to mention meat and vegetables.[37] Only bread grains seemed to continue to be fully saleable. Critics are claiming that the quality of the Russian diet is fast retrogressing to the level of the 1950s and 1960s.[38]

Against this background, the situation of the emerging independent private farms has been particularly desperate. They are among the last to be paid for the sales of their produce through official channels. The reduction in consumer demand has also limited the profitability of their sales on the private market, which had traditionally been the main source of income from private plots on kolkhozy and sovkhozy. The scarcity and high prices of machinery and other manufactured inputs have made it even more difficult for independent farmers to obtain the equipment required for commercial farming. Moreover, the high interest rates on credits and bank loans (now running at from 140 to over 200%) and the imposition of tight repayment schedules by the few commercial banks willing to lend or invest in agriculture make it impossible for them to operate like normal farmers. It was estimated by the Russian Ministry of Agriculture that as of 2 April 1991 the establishment costs of setting up a peasant farm averaged approximately 374,000 roubles, or US$15,000.00.[39] The cost has undoubtedly risen considerably in the intervening years, so the burden of the transition to private family farming is obviously immense, not to say impossible, for the foreseeable future.

In view of these material difficulties and the local political and psychological obstacles facing the would-be family farmer, it is not surprising that the private sector has yet to become a significant contributor to total agricultural production.[40] Nor is it surprising that farmers have been something less than ecstatic over Yeltsin's Decree of 27 October 1993 which was designed specifically to encourage private farmers. Former First Deputy Premier Egor Gaidar, the most consistently committed economic reformer in Yeltsin's entourage, sought to assure private farmers in a speech to the leaders of the Association of Private Farmers (AKKOR) in early November 1993 that the government indeed valued their efforts and counted on them for the future of Russian agriculture. He promised to give their needs a high priority but admitted that the government had often erred in the past by making promises that could not be kept. In future, he said, no one would be receiving preferred credit conditions: the government would no longer make up the difference between preferential and commercial interest rates. All obligatory deliveries were to be abolished by 1994, and the burden of tariffs and quotas on imports and exports was to be removed. The state would be purchasing only what it absolutely required for its food reserves and would pay attractive prices for its purchases.[41]

How much encouragement the peasants derived from Gaidar's assurances and what practical consequences will flow from them in terms of the expansion of the private farm sector were vividly illustrated by the results of the 12 December elections. Gaidar himself was one of the first casualties of the electoral debacle, so his thoughts on the future course of agricultural reform and development are no longer of any practical relevance. One of his arch rivals in the government, Deputy Prime Minister Zaveriukha, one of the main victors in the elections and the darling of the agrarian conservatives, has evidently been given his head by Yeltsin. Consequently, the prospects for genuine agricultural reform have suddenly become worse than at any other time in the post-August 1991 putsch era. Agriculture is evidently fated to resume its status as one of the blackest of the 'black holes' of the Russian economy.

Problems and prospects for Russian agriculture in the mid-1990s

Against the litany of the woes of Russian agriculture presented in the preceding sections, the comments by Gaidar that Russia intends to return to the world market as an exporter of grain may appear wildly fanciful.[42] As noted earlier, original forecasts of a record crop of 120-125 million tonnes of grain in 1993, were scaled back to the previous year's level of 107 million tonnes, and even that was not guaranteed because of problems with finance, storage, transport and the weather. Nevertheless, although supply problems remained 'sticky', important shifts were taking place in the structure of demand which no longer made the attainment of objectives like Gaidar's entirely improbable.

For one thing, the state has apparently gone out of the business of supplying feed grains for the livestock industry. According to Gaidar, the effect has been to cause livestock raisers to shift to green feed and to dispose of many of their animals to private farmers, who reputedly have a higher interest in maintaining higher quality, more productive herds. Lower quality animals— 'which produce nothing but manure'—have been sent off to abattoirs.[43] Consequently, an important component of the demand for grain has largely disappeared.

For another thing, the volume and structure of state grain reserves have been significantly altered. In place of the former system of a single, centralised state reserve which was drawn upon to distribute grain to the regions and capital cities, a two-tiered structure has been introduced: one, a central fund (scheduled to acquire 12 million tonnes in 1993) to cover the needs of large cities and of certain non-grain-growing regions, the other, a regional fund (of 20-23 million tonnes) to be distributed and paid for by the regions.[44] It remains to be seen just how effectively this new arrangement will work in practice. On the face of it, the reduced volume of state purchases and the transfer of major responsibility for grain reserves to the regions should leave a considerably greater share of procurements to market forces. The government evidently intends to avoid its previous heavy-handed involvement in price setting, which should allow greater stimulus for producers. Meanwhile, the existence of the reserve funds will provide the latter with at least a basic level of market security. Chinese experience with similar policies in the past two years has not shown entirely satisfactory results, however.[45] It is evident that a good deal more remains to be done in fashioning the instruments of an agricultural market in the transforming socialist and ex-socialist economies.

Furthermore, these countries' basic commitment to self-sufficiency in food places certain constraints on their willingness to rely entirely on market forces to determine supply, especially of grain products. From the standpoint of conserving scarce hard-currency reserves, this orientation makes a certain amount of sense. There is a school of development theory which argues that investment should be concentrated on the growth of high value-added manufacturing for export; the successful development strategies of the Asian NICs are often adduced as evidence for this proposition. In fact, there seems to be no reason why a country with Russia's (or China's) resource endowments and traditions of agricultural production should not be able to cover its food needs and even have something left over to export. But the transformation costs of doing so may be so high as to divert scarce resources from more productive purposes. In any case, as a result of the reduction of centralised demand (and the shortage of hard currency), Russia was able to reduce its imports of grain in 1993 to 10.4 million tonnes, the lowest quantity in many years.[46]

The political dimension of the reform syndrome will also have to be taken into consideration. Unlike in China (at least so far), the fledgling institutions of democratic politics in Russia and the other European states of the former socialist world have enhanced the political leverage of organised agrarian interests. In Poland they have managed to elect a government; in Russia, the Agrarian Union-Agrarian Party bloc delivered a surprisingly high vote in the December parliamentary elections, coming in fourth among the parties that made it into parliament, with 55 seats. (Gaidar's 'Russia's Choice' movement was in first place with 76 seats, followed by Zhirinovskii's Liberal-Democratic Party, with 63 seats. The Communist Party of Ziuganov came in a poor fifth, with only 45 seats.)[47]

Indeed, on the eve of the elections there were already signs that the Russian Government, sensing disaster, was gearing itself up to satisfy a number of the agrarians' demands.[48] The list of pre-election demands presented by the so-called 'agricultural lobby' included (1) the diversion to the agricultural sector of 15% of hard-currency earnings from Russian exports; (2) minimum purchase prices for farm products in order to close the 'scissors' between manufactured input prices and agricultural producer prices; and (3) tariff protection for domestic farm products and the elimination of subsidies on agricultural imports.[49] Analogous demands were being voiced by Polish farm interests, and the previous government of Hanna Suchocka argued insistently against them in the name of consistent economic reform ... with devastating consequences.

The same thing has evidently happened in Russia. As we have seen, Egor Gaidar also tried to argue the farm lobby out of its demands for special treatment, which ran counter to the reform program of macroeconomic stabilisation and constituted an unbearable burden on the state budget. Given the differences between the Russian and Polish constitutional structures, a substantial vote for the agricultural lobby in the parliamentary elections theoretically might not be quite so disastrous for the cause of reform. Everything depended on Yeltsin's personal preferences and how he chose to interpret the results of the election. There is evidence that soon after the election results were in, Yeltsin, turning away from the reformers, whose inadequate electoral performance had deeply disappointed him, had begun meeting with centrist and conservative representatives of major interest groups, including the agricultural lobby, to seek out their support in the future battle with a hostile Duma. He reportedly declared himself ready to abandon previous reform efforts in agriculture and promised a decided relaxation of financial and budgetary constraints on that sector.

One of the best indicators of Yeltsin's present intentions with respect to economic reform in general and agriculture in particular was his refusal to accept Gaidar's and Finance Minister Boris Fedorov's ultimatum and sacrifice Zaveriukha, and the other *bete noire* of the reformers, Russian Central Bank Governor Viktor Gerashchenko, on the altar of economic and fiscal reform. Both of the latter are committed to an alternative vision of transformation, based on maintaining production and relegating the fight against inflation to a secondary role. Zaveriukha has reportedly demanded a support package for agriculture worth up to 14 trillion roubles, which domestic and foreign critics warned would totally destroy the budget.[50] Other sources indicate that the ultimate bill for agricultural survival may amount to as much as 34 trillion roubles, which would represent a major part of the anticipated blowout of the state budget.[51] While Zaveriukha is far from being a total ignoramus in matters agrarian—indeed, he has some sensible ideas on the development of the wholesale trade system, which Yeltsin seems to have accepted—his priorities for addressing the nation's agricultural woes are hardly compatible with financial stability and the transformation to private agriculture. Whatever the final outcome in terms of state expenditure on agriculture, it is clear that despite his victory in the referendum on the new constitution, Yeltsin's political position has been substantially weakened vis-a-vis the conservative parliamentary opposition. His concessions on government personnel and his relative silence since the formation of the new government suggest that Prime Minister Chernomyrdin, whose wishes on these matters proved to be decisive, has become a much more equal partner of Yeltsin in executive-branch policy making and will be a much more important factor in shaping the overall atmosphere on economic transformation than had previously been the case. Whether Yeltsin will again find it necessary or, indeed, possible to reassert his authority in reform policy matters will depend very much on the economic results of the new 'third way' approach to reforming the Russian economy.

Consequently, as a result of the electoral victory of the conservative forces on 12 December 1993, it seems probable that the structure of Russian agriculture will remain much the same in its broad outlines as it has been since the onset of mass collectivisation in the 1930s. Namely, large, basically extensive types of farms will continue to predominate in grain and technical crop farming and probably in beef production as well. In spite of changes in ownership patterns (whether genuine or merely nominal) and the best intentions of the surviving reformers, the majority of these farming enterprises will undoubtedly continue to require considerable government support. Under Zaveriukha and his like-minded colleagues, that support will be more enthusiastically and more generously supplied than would have been the case had Gaidar and Fedorov remained in government. This will apply equally if not more so to the newly emerging collectives and cooperatives of individual farmers, not to mention the private family farms.

As the opening quotation in this essay suggests, furthermore, without a substantial renewal of the farm machinery manufacturing, sales and service system, no ownership sector of Russian agriculture can become efficient and competitive. The whole industry requires restructuring to become more demand-oriented and 'customer-friendly'. At present, the prices of the machinery produced by the industry, the range of products available, and the low level of quality and reliability are such that farms are simply not prepared to buy them. In future a good deal more attention will also have to be paid to the production of smaller tractors and accessory equipment that is more suitable to private farming. Finally, a good deal of investment will have to be made in rural infrastructure: roads, transportation, communications and agricultural services are all things that have been woefully neglected during the final decades of Soviet rule.

None of these requirements can be met cheaply. International experience suggests, further, that commercial sources of financing will be hard to come by; there are many more profitable sectors than agriculture in which foreign and domestic capital are likely to invest. That means the Russian government, despite its commitments to privatisation and the market, will have to remain much more heavily involved for the foreseeable future in financing and otherwise facilitating agricultural reconstruction and development than is suggested by the tenor of recent agrarian legislation. Paradoxically, the conservative team around Zaveriukha and the Agrarian Party will be more forthcoming on such problems than their reformist opponents would have been, but the opportunity costs in terms of damage to the rest of the economy—and ultimately, to agriculture itself—are likely to be high. Privatisation will conceivably succeed eventually in some form or another, but the ultimate structure of Russian agriculture may well look quite different from what is usually connoted by private farming. Sixty years of collective and state farming are bound to have left an imprint on the structure and psychology of Russian agriculture, which reformers, with the best will in the world, would have had a hard time erasing. The current agrarian leaders are unlikely to have many illusions on this score.

Notes

1 Boris Svishchev, 'Obratnyi schet', *Sel'skaia zhizn'*, 19 October 1993, p.2.
2 A.P.Sokolov, 'Nekotorye voprosy privatizatsii sobstvennosti v kolkhozakh i sovkhozakh', *Ekonomika sel'skokhoziaistvennykh i pererabatyvaiushchikh predpriiatii*, no.7, 1991, p.15.
3 For a good general summary of these developments see Stephen K. Wegren, 'Trends in Russian Agrarian Reform', *RFE/RL Research Report*, vol.2, no.13, 26 March 1993, pp.46-57.
4 Louisa Vinton, 'Privatization in Poland: A Statistical Picture', *RFE/RL Research Report*, vol.2, no.32, 13 August 1993, p.61.
5 Michel L. Wyzan, 'Bulgaria: The Painful Aftermath of Collectivized Agriculture', *RFE/RL Research Report*, vol.2, no.37, 17 September 1993, pp.34-41.
6 Aleksandr Bykovskii, 'Agrarnik—u rulia Dumy', *Sel'skaia zhizn'*, 15 January 1994, p.1.
7 Viktor Nefedov (Deputy Chairman of CIS Statistics Committee), 'Chislo fermerskikh khoziaistv v SNG vozroslo do 540 tysiach', *Izvestiia*, 22 May 1993, p.4.
8 Calculated from data in Wegren, 'Trends in Russian Agrarian Reform', p.53.
9 Nefedov, 'Chislo fermerskikh khoziaistv v SNG vozroslo do 540 tysiach', p.4.
10 Valerii Konovalov, 'Fermerstvo ostanovilos' v roste', *Izvestiia*, 12 January 1994, p.2.
11 See, for example, the Decree of the Council of Ministers of the Russian Federation of 18 November 1993 'O merakh gosudarstvennoi podderzhki agropromyshlennogo kompleksa v 1993-1994 godakh', *Sel'skaia zhizn'*, 7 December 1993, pp.1-2, which provided additional financial sweeteners for the agricultural sector as a whole, designed evidently to appeal to the votes of the majority of the farm population for the President's reform team.
12 Wegren, 'Trends in Russian Agrarian Reform', p.47.
13 See M.S. Pashkov, 'Zakonodatel'stvo RSFSR o krest'ianskikh (fermerskikh) khoziaistvakh', *Ekonomika sel'skokhoziaistvennykh i pererabatyvaiushchikh predpriiatii,*, no.7, 1991, p.53.
14 'Krest'iane poluchaiut zemliu, kotoruiu obeshchali im Bol'sheviki v 1917 godu', *Izvestiia*, 29 October 1993, pp.1-2.
15 Wegren, 'Trends in Russian Agrarian Reform', p.52.
16 Valerii Konovalov, 'Fermery usomnilis' v svoei nuzhnosti gosudarstvu, no vitse-prem'er Gaidar ikh somneniia razveial', *Izvestiia*, 6 November 1993, p.2.
17 Konovalov, 'Fermerstvo ostanovilos' v roste', p.2.
18 See the account of a letter from Starodubtsev and other agrarian conservatives to Yeltsin 'Uslyshat' trevogu derevni', *Izvestiia*, 28 October 1993, p.1.
19 Iurii Burov, 'Spasut le selo ... begemoty?', *Sovetskaia Rossiia*, 20 July 1993, p.1.

20 Susan L. Shirk, *The Political Logic of Economic Reform in China* (Berkeley: University of California Press, 1993). Shirk does not consider agricultural reform in her book, but the approach seems to apply to it as well. I am indebted to Mr Chris Buckley of the Contemporary China Centre, Australian National University, for calling this book to my attention.

21 For a view in favour of this proposition, but one which criticises the Decree as not going far enough, see Andrei Lazorevskii, 'Po proektu ukaza Prezidenta zemlia ostaetsia u kolkhoznykh "feodalov"', *Izvestiia*, 26 October 1993, p.2.

22 Decree of 27 October, *Izvestiia*, 29 October 1993, pp.1-2.

23 Precisely the outcome feared by Lazorevskii, 'Po proektu ukaza Prezidenta zemlia ostaetsia u kolkhoznykh "feodalov"'.

24 Elena Iakovleva, 'Nakonets-to utverzhdaetsia chastnaia sobstvennost' na zemliu', *Izvestiia*, 27 October 1993, p.2.

25 Wegren, 'Trends in Russian Agrarian Reform', p.54.

26 Wegren, 'Trends in Russian Agrarian Reform', p.55.

27 Stephen K. Wegren, 'Rural Reform in Russia', *RFE/RL Research Report*, vol.2, no.43, 29 October 1993, pp.44-45.

28 'O plate za zemliu', Law of the RSFSR of 11 October 1991. This and associated rules for land valuation and enabling legislation can be found in *ESPP*, no.2, 1992, pp.23-29.

29 For a good account of the balance of positive and negative attitudes on the continuation of compulsory sales to the state see Wegren, 'Rural Reform in Russia', pp.48-49, based on interviews in selected rural regions of Russia in July and August of 1993.

30 See the interview with Deputy Chairman of the Russian Federation Council of Ministers in charge of agriculture A.Kh. Zaveriukha, 'Legkoi zhizni zhdat' nel'zya', *Sel'skaia zhizn'*, 14 October 1993, pp.1-2. See, also, the sad tale of the sugar beet industry in Lipetsk Oblast', where one *sovkhoz* was owed 0.5 billion rubles by industry and the state despite large expenditure items of its own, for example 3 million rubles for spare parts. Sergei Brovashov, 'Kazhdyi sam po sebe', *Sel'skaia zhizn'*, 23 October 1993, pp.1-2.

31 'Ob uporiadochenii raschetov za sel'skokhoziaisvennuiu produktsiiu i prodovol'stvennye tovary', *Ekonomika i zhizn'*, no.44, 1993, p.6.

32 The chief of the Riazan Oblast Agricultural Administration, A.V. Kiriushkin, blamed the Russian Government for this situation. Interview by Anatolii Zholobov, 'Umel vziat', umei i otdat'', *Sel'skaia zhizn'*, 16 October 1993, p.2.

33 Elena Iakovleva, 'Kazakhstan vriad li vypolnit kokchetavskie soglasheniia po postavkam zerna v Rossiiu', *Izvestiia*, 18 September 1993, p.4. Belarus has returned this year to the old practice of sending farm machinery and operators to Kazakhstan to help with the harvest in return for a million tonnes from this year's grain harvest. Mikhail Shimanskii, 'Budet li Balarus' s khlebom—zavisit ot Kazakhstana', *Izvestiia*, 14 August 1993, p.4.

34 That is, of course, in current prices. Interview with G.G. Kol'tsov, First Deputy Head of Administration of Krasnodar Krai, 'Pora nozha ... i nozhnits', *Sel'skaia zhizn'*, 19 October 1993, p.1.

35 Petr Shcherbakov, 'Krest'iane poka vne rynka', *Sel'skaia zhizn'*, 4 November 1993, p.2.

36 Shcherbakov, 'Krest'iane poka vne rynka', p.2.

[37] See, for example, Galina Budeeva, '"Nevyezdnye" ... ovoshchi', *Sel'skaia zhizn'*, 23 October 1993, p.1; Valerii Tatarenkov, 'Gore s kartoshkoi', *Sel'skaia zhizn'*, 4 November 1993, p.1; Valerii Savel'ev, 'Ovoshchnoi vopros', *Sel'skaia zhizn'*, 26 October 1993, p.1.

[38] Ol'ga Akulova, 'Sosiska ... v zerkale statistiki', *Sel'skaia zhizn'*, 23 December 1993, p.1.

[39] N.I. Evseev, 'Organizatsiia i funktsionirovania krest'ianskikh (fermerskikh) khoziaistv v RSFSR', *Ekonomika sel'skokhoziaistvennykh i pererabatyvaiushchikh predpriiatii,,* no.10, 1991, p.10. Calculations of the US$ value are mine, using the exchange rate prevailing at that time, when I was in the then USSR.

[40] Conservatives point to the insignificance of private production with unconcealed derision. Iurii Burov, for example, notes that in Tver' Oblast', the private sector, with ten percent of the cropland, produces only 0.9% of the province's meat output, 1.3% of the milk and 1.1% of the grain: *Sovetskaia Rossiia*, 20 July 1993, p.1.

[41] Konovalov, 'Fermery usomnilis' v svoei nuzhnosti gosudarstvu, no vitse-prem'er Gaidar ikh somneniia razveial', p.2.

[42] Interview with Gaidar by the veteran economics commentator Otto Latsis, 'Rossiia namerena vernut' svoi status eksportera zerna', *Izvestiia*, 23 October 1993, pp.1-2.

[43] Latsis, 'Rossiia namerena vernut' svoi status eksportera zerna', pp.1-2.

[44] 'Agricultural Market: Administered Prices and Imbalances', *Business Observer*, English-language supplement to *Ekonomika i zhizn'*, October 1993, p.6.

[45] According to Professor Andrew Watson of Adelaide University in an unpublished seminar paper on the Chinese grain trade, Contemporary China Centre, Research School of Pacific Studies, Australian National University, 17 November 1993.

[46] Keith Bush, 'Grain Imports Down', *RFE/RL Daily Report*, 12 January 1994.

[47] 'Balans sil v Gosurdarstvennoi Dume', *Argumenty i fakty*, no.4, 1994, p.2.

[48] According to an agricultural official quoted in the 3 November 1993 issue of *The Journal of Commerce*, cited by Keith Bush, 'Agricultural Lobby Submits Its Wish List', *RFE/RL Daily Report*, 4 November 1993.

[49] Bush, 'Agricultural Lobby Submits Its Wish List',

[50] Keith Bush, 'Projected Deficit to Grow', *RFE/RL Daily Report*, 25 January 1994.

[51] Keith Bush, 'Farm Support', *RFE/RL Daily Report*, 4 February 1994.

6 PRIVATISATION OF LARGE-SCALE RUSSIAN INDUSTRY

STEPHEN FORTESCUE

In these grim times for economic reform in Russia, privatisation is often described as one of reform's few success stories, and with Anatolii Chubais the last reformer left in the government a success story which might yet be maintained. Even if Chubais is unable to continue to force the pace, it is considered by many that privatisation has gone too far to be reversed. This creates the hope that the new economic class which should arise from privatisation will provide a bulwark against anti-market forces in the future.

It is not the purpose of this chapter to examine the validity of such hopes in detail or conclusively. It will do no more than look at some particular aspects of privatisation, but in a way which should contribute to an understanding of the place of privatisation in the current state of the Russian transition.

We examine privatisation in the Russian industrial sector, and will be concerned with what in the literature is described as 'large' privatisation, that is, of enterprises large enough to require a sufficient complexity of management that the issue of the separation of ownership and management will be relevant.[1]

The aims of privatisation

We will focus on the benefits that privatisation should bring to the Russian economy under two broad headings. The first deals with the benefits of introducing a new form of ownership; the second with the opportunity privatisation provides for the restructuring of Russian industry.

Privatisation should bring to enterprises new, more responsible owners. These are owners who will have greater incentives to ensure that their enterprises operate efficiently and profitably than was provided by the diffuse and bureaucratic 'collective ownership' of the command-administrative model. They should be able to operate under a hard budget constraint, that is, they should not require state subsidies. And they should bring to their enterprises new investment, either from their own resources or from other private investors.

Particularly in large industrial enterprises privatisation should lead to an improved owner-manager relationship. Following the decades of *melochnaia opeka* (petty tutelage) by Soviet planning agencies and branch ministries, it is considered that managers need to be given greater independence and responsibility. However the experience of Gorbachev's Law on the Enterprise, in the mould of the communist reform doctrine of radical decentralisation without changes in property rights, is said to demonstrate the dangers of leaving management without any higher level of control. That control should be provided by shareholders, in a serious but 'hands off' way.[2]

The second benefit of privatisation is that it should provide the basis for industrial restructuring. Among the serious problems of Soviet industry were such structural distortions as a bias in favour of the large over the small enterprise, an extremely high degree of monopolisation, and the *vedomstvennost'* or 'departmentalism' derived from a rigid, sectorally based industrial structure. The shock therapy economists who introduced economic reform to Russia had an inherent distrust of the use of direct government intervention to correct these problems. It is particularly noticeable that shock therapy sequences exclude demonopolisation, partly because it is seen as too hard to achieve in the time scales required, but also because it requires a degree of state intervention, and therefore room for the pleading of special interests, that is seen as dangerous. The necessary changes are therefore brought about by allowing the privatisation as independent entities of enterprises down to the production unit level, meaning the breaking up of the large production cum administrative empires.

The ownership benefits of privatisation, in particular, would seem to point to a 'sell to the highest bidder' approach. Privatisation and corporate governance theory suggests that owners should be clearly identifiable, as distinct from diffuse, so that responsibility can be allocated and ownership can be readily transferred if required. Owners should have indicated their strong commitment to the success of their enterprises by investing their own money in them. Identities and commitment are most clearly indicated through 'highest bidder' auctions. This approach indeed dominated the initial privatisation programmes and legislation, both in the Soviet Union and Russia.[3] However as time went on the approach changed considerably. Probably partly because of a realisation that there would be few bidders at 'highest bidder' auctions, but also because of political and social pressures, two other approaches came to dominate. The strongest was workforce ownership; citizen ownership, through the 'voucher' system, also became an important and innovative aspect of Russian privatisation.

It appears that in Russia a residual commitment to socialist principles led to particularly strong support for worker ownership, on the grounds that it is only fair that those who produce an enterprise's output and profits should have full control over those profits, particularly given the strong fear that a 'highest bidder' approach would rapidly lead to very high levels of redundancies. Workforce ownership, it was claimed, would be economically efficient, since workers who own productive assets and the returns from them have a strong incentive to make the best use of them.

There were others who rejected the rigours of the 'sell to the highest bidder' approach, but who at the same time believed workforce ownership to be unjust to those who happened not to work in sectors of the economy that were susceptible to profitable privatisation. This recommended an approach which gave a share in the nation's industrial assets to all citizens. The usual method is to issue to all citizens, free or for a nominal sum, 'vouchers' which can be used to buy shares in enterprises, either directly or through investment funds. This form of privatisation is seen, in a Thatcherite way, as producing a large shareholding public which will be committed to social, political and economic stability. More basically, it should also overcome the practical problem of lack of demand for privatised assets in the 'sell to the highest bidder' approach.

Procedures and outcomes[4]

In July 1992 all large Russian enterprises, with the exception of those in some sensitive sectors of the economy, were subject to compulsory privatisation, meaning that by October 1992 they had to submit to the government's privatisation agency, *Goskomimushchestvo* (GKI), a proposal on which form of privatisation the workforce preferred. Two major forms of privatisation were available. In the first option the workforce received free of charge 25% of statutory (*ustavnyi*) capital in the form of special shares without voting rights. Workers could then buy, for either cash or vouchers, voting shares worth up to 10% of statutory capital at a 30% discount on face value with three years to pay. Senior management had the right to purchase up to 5% of shares at face value. In the second option the workforce received no special or discounted shares, but was entitled to purchase 51% of normal shares at a price 1.7 times face value, again in cash or vouchers.[5]

It can be seen that the second option guaranteed a workforce ownership outcome.[6] Initially 63.7% of workforces chose it, a percentage which increased with time.[7] Many of the 34.5% who chose the first option also intended to gain a controlling parcel of voting shares, through taking up their options on discounted shares and buying further shares at voucher auctions.

It is at these auctions that citizens are able to bid for shares using the 'vouchers' which were distributed to them in the last quarter of 1992. A surprising 96% of the population took up their vouchers, and by the beginning of December 1993, 115 of 160 million vouchers had been used in one way or another.[8] About half of the vouchers that have been disposed of by their owners were paid into investment funds, which in September 1993 had invested about 40% of their vouchers in shares. Shares not paid into investment funds were invested directly in shares by individuals, either by workers taking up shares in their own enterprises or people simply investing in enterprises that took their fancy.[9] The latter 'small investor' group is apparently not a large one.[10] Shares that are left after the workforce has taken up its allocation and the voucher auction has been held can be put out to tender, to be bought for cash or vouchers by professional investors, including from abroad. The tenders, which are usually for 10-15% of shares, generally have conditions attached. The one that receives the most current attention is the investment that is required of the successful tenderer, but obligations to maintain production profile and employment levels have also been common. Tender is seen by reformers as the closest thing to a 'highest bidder' system they can get to, although as a Western consultant's report points out, interested investors can buy up shares without taking on tender obligations and there are no sanctions that can be applied to investors who disregard their obligations anyway.[11] Finally, the state often retains a small but strategic shareholding of around 20%, although in a not insignificant number of enterprises in key sectors of the economy the state retains either a 51% holding or a single 'Golden Share' (a share which gives a veto over a range of corporate activities, primarily reprofiling).[12]

In summary, by November 1993 10,500 of 14,500 major enterprises slated for privatisation had been transformed into joint-stock companies, that is, had had their privatisation plans approved and had at least allocated shares to their workers.[13] The great majority had chosen the second form of privatisation, guaranteeing a 51% workforce shareholding. This means that despite significant holdings in other hands, for the moment workforce ownership is dominant.

Are the new owners good owners?

Most corporate governance specialists are highly suspicious of workforce ownership, on the basis of the tendency of worker owners to demand higher than desirable consumption payments at the expense of investment.[14] Workforces use their majority shareholdings to extract from management—who now depend for their jobs on getting majority support at shareholder meetings—promises of the maintenance of employment and social infrastructure spending. This was most evident at one of the earliest shareholder meetings at a newly privatised enterprise, the Vladimir Tractor Factory. There the workforce held 48% of shares (presumably they had chosen the first form of privatisation and had built up their shareholding since privatisation), the state represented by the regional property fund had 29%, an investment fund 'Alpha' 10%, and a Russian-US joint venture 'Renova' 12%. 'Renova' was the vehicle of a former finance director of the enterprise now working for the World Bank. He endeavoured to obtain a majority at the first shareholders' meeting, but eventually the workforce was swayed by the promises to maintain employment and social infrastructure of the incumbent director.[15]

Although clearly there are other major factors involved, workforce ownership is perhaps not irrelevant to the massive declines in industrial investment in recent times. Statistics indicate a staggering proportion of profits going to consumption funds rather than investment,[16] and enterprise-level evidence reveals the freezing of production investment spending while employment and social infrastructure spending are maintained. KamAZ, for example, froze investment in the production sphere but continued to build flats for its workers.[17] The maintenance of employment levels also means the maintenance of consumption spending at higher levels than are necessary to ensure adequate investment.[18]

Workforce ownership means not only that the workforce is able to put undue and inappropriate pressure on management. The workforce-management relationships just described also tend to mean that there is no proper 'ownership' control over management. As long as their employment and social welfare needs are met, the workforce is likely to leave management to its own devices. Worker owners do not have the interests that non-worker owners have. Dividends are likely to be seen as less important than wages and other forms of social consumption. Although they presumably would want to ensure the viability of their enterprise, its market value, that is, its share price, should be of no particular interest since they should not be interested in selling their shares. Recent survey evidence shows a big decline in the belief of managers that worker ownership will improve productivity (although managers still support the concept so as not to antagonise the workforce).[19]

It is in this context that many commentators positively evaluate any evidence of enterprises passing out of the control of workforces. Although privatisation procedures have made it very difficult for 'new entrepreneurs', that is, professional, non-management investors, to obtain controlling shareholdings in major privatising enterprises, they are able to buy significant shareholdings at voucher auctions, particularly if they operate together with a major voucher investment fund. Although the 'new entrepreneur' described above was not able to get control of the Vladimir Tractor Factory, he and his backers were able to get two seats on the board.

Such investors are also able to buy out workforce shareholdings after privatisation has been completed. Enterprises by law are not allowed to close their share registers, that is, individual workers cannot be prevented from selling their shares on the open market.[20] There is also evidence that even enterprises that were most determined to maintain closed registers have been forced to open them in order to attract new equity capital, in circumstances when reasonably priced debt capital is virtually impossible to obtain.[21] For a very clear example of the workforce selling out its shareholding, see the takeover by the major privately owned oil corporation 'Hermes' of the Tiumen' Shipbuilding Factory. 'Hermes' bought the factory in order to shift production over to oil industry equipment.[22]

There are those, usually on the radical reform side of things, who see these sorts of outcomes as ideal. New aggressive owners will either replace or put some ginger into existing management; if the new owners intend to take on the management role themselves, usually they will rely sufficiently on investor partners to have some sort of external control exercised over them. The intended outcome at the Vladimir Tractor Factory would have been seen as ideal. Someone from the industry, indeed from that very enterprise, would have taken on the main executive role, but with backing from professional investors who would presumably have kept an eye, but not too close a one, on how their investment was being managed. This might appear to require some brave assumptions as to the competence of investment fund managers. However it has been pointed out that, given that the funds' tasks should not include close operational involvement in the enterprises in which they have invested, one can easily exaggerate the degree of 'technical' competence required.[23]

Those who put their hope in this outcome presumably hope that 'new entrepreneurs' will help solve one of the major problems of the transition, that of new investment. It is hoped that they will bring new investment into enterprises, whether it be their own personal wealth or that of the institutions that are backing them. One suspects, however, that their own personal wealth might be overestimated—it is cheaper to buy a Mercedes than a new production line. It is also not easy to identify the institutions that will provide capital injections. Voucher investment funds have vouchers, not money. Commercial banks prefer to lend what money they have to commercial organisations, whose rapid turnover of funds protects them and their creditors to some extent from inflation. Foreign investors are a potential, if controversial and currently less than totally enthusiastic, source. One of the main sources of investment so far have been other enterprises, usually the so-called *smezhniki*, that is, those above or below the enterprise in the production process.

If none of these sources are adequate the spectre is raised of the state having to provide investment funding even to privatised enterprises. This is a spectre in the eyes of the shock therapists because it involves the dreaded 'picking winners' and the opening up of the government to the dangers of the pleading of 'special interests'. There is no reason why privatised enterprises are necessarily immune from the need for a soft budget constraint, that is, having the government bailing them out even to cover their operating costs. Certainly such cases are not rare in the West, and one notes Yeltsin's November 1992 decree guaranteeing privatised firms the same access to state credits as state-owned enterprises.[24]

The issue of sources of financial backing for privatised enterprises is important not just for its relevance to the government's budget deficit. If enterprises are unable to get finance from private sources they are far more likely to be sucked back into state-dominated, 'corporatist' industrial management structures. This becomes relevant to the restructuring of Russian industry.

Industrial restructuring

As already mentioned privatisation legislation gave the right of privatisation as an independent entity to all enterprises with existing status as a legal entity. In general terms this covered most physically self-contained production units.[25] Although large numbers of production units had lost their independent legal status during Brezhnev's amalgamation campaigns, the coming of *khozraschet* late in the Brezhnev period and the cooperative/small enterprise movement of the Gorbachev period again increased the numbers of enterprises with the status needed to privatise as independent entities.

The granting of the right to privatise to relatively low-level production entities appears to have been a conscious decision, designed not only to finish off the already mortally wounded branch ministries, but also to get Russian industry back to basic building blocks so that a new structure, away from the traditional Soviet sectors, could be built.[26] The greater flexibility that would thus be introduced into Russian industry would contribute to the breaking up of the monopolies that dominated the economy, at a time when a more formal demonopolisation policy was seen as too hard.

There is some, admittedly limited, evidence of these benefits already flowing from privatisation. Although much of the incentive for this particular development probably flows more from what hard budget constraint has now been imposed on Russian industry than from greater independence for production units through privatisation, there is evidence of enterprises reprofiling their production assortments, with this often involving moving into areas previously dominated by monopolies. Products for which there are no demand are being dropped, sometimes with great heartache as managers consider the production and technical skills that are being lost.[27] Some enterprises find themselves having to change their production profiles entirely. Many of the strongest examples come from defence industry enterprises, which have been forced to take conversion seriously, like it or not. In doing so, some make clear their willingness to take on established monopolists. For example, the Kirov Factory, facing a catastrophic decline in demand for its tractors, was prepared to take on monopolists in turning to the production of turbines, locomotives and forestry equipment (as well as set up a strategic alliance with KamAZ to produce minitractors).[28] We have no data to give us a sense of how widespread the shifts in product profile and mix are or the extent to which products are being dropped not because they are not needed or wanted but because there is no money for their purchase. But there is prima facie evidence of the sort to give some heart to neoclassical economists looking for signs of market-driven flexibility.

We also find evidence of enterprises that, following true Soviet autarkic principles, might previously have tried to produce everything themselves now looking to buy in components from outside suppliers. Although KamAZ has been forced by the fire in its engine shop to go faster in this direction than it might have otherwise chosen, the enterprise's general director claims that the successful search for components' suppliers from former defence industry producers had already been underway for some time.[29]

Sometimes these new supplier relationships seem to be purely contractual 'buy' relationships. However we also see efforts to create closer relationships, but falling short of old Soviet-style hierarchical relations. These are what in the Western literature are called 'hybrid' institutions. They include the provision of financing and know-how to suppliers by purchasing enterprises,[30] cross-shareholdings, strategic alliances and joint ventures.[31] Such joint ventures and strategic alliances have sprung up more or less spontaneously over the last year or so. Sometimes they consist of enterprises engaged in the same area of production activity, and often seem primarily intended as buying cartels, although the joint funding of research is also often a feature. A regional basis is also not uncommon.[32] Others are alliances of diverse enterprises for the manufacture of a new product. As already mentioned, these alliances often include enterprises, usually from the defence industry, which are reprofiling their production activities. They also often involve the introduction of competition into what previously had been a monopolistic or oligopolistic sector.[33]

These sorts of new structures appear to be more common among the more dynamic enterprises in Russian industry. Enterprises set them up because they see a positive gain to be won. They are attempting to find a compromise between the chaos of purely market relationships in an economy which does not really have a market and the rigidities of Soviet-style hierarchy. They are of considerable comparative interest, in that they show signs of being within the category of hybrid structures, between market and hierarchy, which has attracted considerable theoretical interest in the West in recent years,[34] and are becoming an increasingly important part of Western industrial practice, particularly in the form of strategic alliances in hi-tech industries.

While these sorts of structures might be taken as an indication that privatisation, along with other aspects of economic reform, is introducing to the Russian economy a welcome new element of flexibility and responsiveness to demand, there are many who see the destruction of old hierarchies as a catastrophe. While that destruction cannot be put down just to privatisation—the disintegration of the USSR and the increasing 'regionalisation' of Russia have certainly played their part—the right of low-level production units to privatise as independent units is seen as speeding the process along, and therefore contributing to the collapse of long-standing and intricate supply networks and 'technological complexes' (at the same time as doing nothing to remove monopolies, since all it does is create new, smaller ones).[35] This has led to persistent demands to reverse the rights of legal entities to privatise, through insisting that units which are an integral part of a larger organisation can break away only with the agreement of the workforce of the whole larger organisation. There has also been considerable stress on the need to maintain 'technological chains' during privatisation. The Higher Arbitration Court has indeed been prepared to place barriers in the way of the independent privatisation of technologically-linked units. The principle applied in litigation has been that enterprises with a different technological function have a greater right to independence from parent organisations than those with a like or linked technological function.[36]

In general it can be said that there seems still to be in the post-Soviet psyche little concept of the possibility of, to use Western terms, a 'buy' rather than 'make' decision within a single technologically defined sector.[37]

This 'make' orientation has also been a major component in the debate over the proper role of the 'commercialised' descendants of the branch ministries and new supra-enterprise management bodies. With the transition from the command-administrative system the branch ministries rushed to convert themselves into new 'commercial' organisations, bearing a whole range of Western-sounding corporate names—*kontserny, korporatsii, assotsiatsii, kholdingi*. The language of the top managers of the new organisations made it clear that they expected to maintain over their member-enterprises something like the control they had exercised over them under the old regime.[38]

However these expectations have to be seen in the context of the major breakdown in central planning and consequent disappearance of many of the powers of the old branch ministries, and the legal guarantees of enterprise independence under Gorbachev's Law of the Enterprise and subsequent Russian legislation. It might be this, rather than poor data, that explains the paucity of information on the concerns and associations. The indications are that *Gasprom*, the successor to the Ministry of Gas Industry, goes closest to maintaining Soviet-style control over its enterprises.[39] The others represent their industrial sectors in tripartite negotiations on wages and work conditions.[40] Many of their other publicised activities could be seen as part of a 'lobbyist' function.[41] More prosaically, they organise exhibitions and trade fairs.[42] Where the evidence is most strikingly lacking is on the functions which they themselves stress most strongly— integrated investment and technology policies, implying some scope to reallocate resources from one enterprise to another. The lack of evidence might be a result of a problem in our available sources of information. But it cannot be excluded that in the current climate the concerns and associations are simply unable to exercise that sort of control over enterprises or even provide a forum at which agreement can be reached among enterprises.

Certainly the 'industrialist' lobby seems to feel that the powers available to supra-enterprise organs are inadequate. With the increasing influence of the industrialists in policymaking through 1992 proposals for various forms of more tightly integrated corporate structures became insistent. These ranged from the proposals of then Minister of Industry Titkin for the great bulk of Russian industry to be allocated among a few hundred state holding companies, presumably under the control of his ministry,[43] to the defence-industry based 'locomotives' or 'financial-industrial groups' of the Shulunov-Kokoshin plan.[44]

For much of 1992-1993 the proponents of tighter corporate structures concentrated on the so-called 'holding companies', in which a central apparatus would hold major shareholdings in a range of related enterprises. Some of the former branch ministries had declared themselves to be holding companies at the time of the collapse of the Soviet Union, and reformers feared that the new campaign was an effort to recreate the ministries. However when Yeltsin's decree of 16 November 1992, 'On measures for the realisation of an industry policy in the privatisation of state enterprises', with its accompanying 'Temporary regulation (*polozhenie*) on holding companies created through the transformation of state enterprises into joint-stock companies', appeared,[45] it placed considerable controls on the new structures legislated for in the decree. They could not be the legal successors (*pravopreemniki*) of the old concerns and associations, although it was suggested that the older organisations would be allowed to remain in existence if they reregistered within two months. The most significant part of the regulation was that which established that an enterprise could be taken over by a holding company only with a 50% vote of its workforce, not forgetting that privatisation procedures also make it difficult for holding companies to obtain majority shareholdings in enterprises that are determined to maintain their independence. According to the decree, disputes over subsidiary status were to be resolved by joint commissions of GKI and GKAP (the anti-monopoly committee), hardly supporters of the old branch ministries and their successors. Holding companies, both at the time of their creation and through subsequent takeovers and mergers, were subjected to market share controls (35%). Somewhat improbably, they were not allowed to fix the prices of or be involved in the sale of the output of their subsidiaries, primarily it seems to prevent transfer pricing within the holding companies. The decree clearly was not a charter for the recreation of the branch ministries. To the extent that workforces were given the right to veto the buying up of their enterprises by holding companies, Russian enterprises continue to enjoy greater protection from takeover than their Western counterparts.

With their failure to guarantee control of enterprises by holding companies those wanting corporate integration have turned their attention to 'financial-industrial groups'. There are primarily distinguished by their combining a range of production and financial institutions, supposedly along the lines of South Korean *chaebols*. President Yeltsin issued a decree on such structures on 5 December 1993.[46] It shows all the signs of GKI distrust of integration in the Russian economy.[47] It bans the participation in the groups of enterprises with more than 25% state ownership, concerns and associations, and holding companies with less than 50% of their capital in the form of material assets. It also forbids any cross-shareholdings among the members of the grouping, a substantial limitation even in terms of established market economies, especially those with more 'interventionist' orientations. Groups whose members employ large numbers of workers or who have monopoly positions, including at the local level, can be formed only with the agreement of, among others, GKI and GKAP.

GKI has maintained its position as various government bodies have considered the registration of the first group. It is to be called *Ural'skie zavody* (Urals factories), and is a collection of eleven industrial enterprises, one research institute, and six financial and trading organisations from the Urdmurtia defence industry sector. GKI has rejected the initially proposed structure, on the grounds that it violated the ban on cross-shareholdings. At last report Oleg Soskovets, first deputy prime minister and a leading 'industrialist', was advising *Ural'skie zavody* not to wait for government approval and simply get to work. This would mean, however, that without registration the group would not get such privileges as reduced VAT on intragroup transfers and group-wide taxation (allowing the netting of tax liabilities between profitable and loss-making participants).[48] There is no mention in the legislation or commentary of state involvement in the funding of groups. However it is difficult to imagine that their financial components will not be used as a conduit for state investment credits.

It should be noted that there is no reason to believe that the enterprises involved in *Ural'skie zavody* or many holding companies are so involved against their will. It appears that GKI is unwilling to agree readily to even to such voluntary associations, and is certainly determined to avoid a situation in which integrated structures could be created and enforced through administrative fiat.

As already mentioned, the defenders of the old ministry-based concerns and associations and the proponents of the holding company and financial-industrial group approaches to integration give absolute priority to technology issues in decisions on integration and the boundary of the firm. It would be easy to conclude that such a position is nothing more than a cover for 'departmentalist' desires to protect old institutions and their powers, that these are people born and bred on hierarchy rather than contract, and decisions to make rather than buy. That could well be the case.[49] One cannot fail to note however that buy decisions can be made and contracts drawn up only when a market exists. For many Russian enterprises a market does not exist—either for finance or for inputs. In those circumstances one should not be surprised by the attractiveness of 'make' over 'buy' decisions and involvement in structures with access to state funds. It was a well-known feature of Soviet attempts at decentralising reform that enterprises did not necessarily want the independence that was supposedly being offered them. Although one suspects that many enterprises in integrated structures are probably trying to have their cake and eat it, to be independent but also have the security of association when needed, one should not necessarily be surprised at their willingness to accept hierarchy.

While I would not want to be seen as a supporter of the old branch ministries or their successors, the point needs to be made that there is nothing inherently wrong with hierarchy or integration. One feels that not only Russian reformers but also Western Sovietologists became overcommitted to the view that the answer to the problems of central planning was decentralisation. Western theory and practice would suggest that this is not necessarily the case—a huge range of considerations have to be taken into account in order to determine the ideal boundary of the firm.[50]

Despite that, one suspects that in conditions of a genuine market for finance and inputs the balance would shift far more decisively in favour of 'buy' decisions than it is at the moment. One's fear is that, despite the opportunity for a fresh start provided by the highly disaggregative privatisation programme, the institutional structures already in place and on the way to being relegitimised in recent discussions and legislation will make it difficult to move in that direction when the time comes. That is why one appreciates GKI's caution.

Conclusion

Two major problems, or potential problems, for the privatised Russian economy have been identified, firstly, that the dominance of workforce ownership will mean the loss of many of the corporate governance advantages of privatisation; and secondly, that pressure for greater integration of privatised enterprises will lead to a recreation of old excessively centralised and bureaucratised administrative structures with too ready access to state credits.

I will stick my neck out and predict that the dominance of worker ownership will not continue. Although workforces have fought hard to obtain and retain it, the pressures to dilute it through bringing in outside equity will be overwhelming. This is particularly the case if, as one suspects, much of the push for workshop ownership comes from managers fearful of losing their jobs and powers if new owners come in. These managers can be bought off by new investors (one hears of Russian managers being given seats on the boards of foreign companies in return for delivering a majority shareholding), or they can lose the backing of the workforce if they cannot maintain the flow of goodies.

If it is the case that workforce ownership will be gradually replaced, into whose hands will enterprises fall? Will they be taken over by new structures or old? Perhaps the words 'old' and 'new' are inadequate here. Better words might be, on the one side, 'hybrid', 'flexible', 'profit-oriented', as opposed to 'hierarchical', 'rigid', 'subsidy oriented'. We certainly should not fall into the trap of assuming that any form of integration is inevitably an old branch ministry reincarnated. Which type of structure will come out on top, beyond the very real possibility that they will each come out on top in different parts of the economy, depends on how financial structures will develop, how willing and welcome foreign investment will be, and, most importantly, what government policy will be. There is some justifiable fear that government policy is inexorably moving towards the latter type of structures, although Chubais's continued position in the government leaves some room for optimism.

Notes

This chapter draws on three earlier papers by the author: 'Privatisation of Russian industry', *Australian Journal of Political Science*, vol.29, no.1, March 1994, pp.135-153; 'Organization in Russian industry: beyond decentralization', *RFE/RL Research Report*, vol.2, no.50, 17 December 1993, pp.35-39; and 'Enterprise reform in Russia', paper presented to 'Workshop on enterprise reform', Centre for Chinese Political Economy, Macquarie University, 3 September 1993. They contain more detail on most of the issues covered here and some not covered here at all.

1   The current definition of a large enterprise, taken from the new Privatisation Programme referred to below, is one which on 1 January 1992 had fixed assets of more than 1 billion roubles.

2   This approach requires acceptance of the currently popular 'revisionist' view of the theory of the Western firm, which revises the long held view that shareholders were at a serious disadvantage in their

relations with management. See David Soskice, Robert H. Bates, and David Epstein, 'Ambition and Constraint: The Stabilizing Role of Institutions', *Journal of Law, Economics and Organization*, vol.8, no.3, 1992, pp.547-560 at p.556; *The Economist*, 24 April 1993, pp.77-78.

3   See Stephen Fortescue, 'The privatization of Soviet large-scale industry', in Hans Hendrischke (ed.), *Market Reform in the Changing Socialist World* (Sydney: Macquarie Studies in Chinese Political Economy no.4, Macquarie University, 1992).

4   The most recent 'State Programme for the Privatisation of State and Municipal Enterprises in the Russian Federation', signed into law by a presidential decree of 24 December 1993, sets out in detail the latest procedures. It does not differ essentially from the previous 1992 Programme, although it does formalise state majority and 'Golden' shareholdings and branch agency involvement in a way that was previously avoided. The new Programme can be found in *Sobranie aktov Prezidenta i Pravitel'stva Rossiiskoi Federatsii*, no.1, 1994, article 2. For commentary comparing it to its predecessor by a senior Russian privatisation official, see *Ekonomika i zhizn'*, no. 2, 1994, p.1 of supplement. For accounts of the earlier Programme, see Stephen Fortescue 'Privatisation of Russian industry', *Australian Journal of Political Science*, vol.29, no.1, March 1994, pp.135-153

5   A third option allowed a group of managers to take operational control of the enterprise for up to 12 months, during which time they could exercise an option to buy 20% of shares at face value. The workforce as a whole could buy a further 20% at a 30% discount. An insignificant number of enterprises chose this option.

6   Although it should be noted that many major corporate decisions, including changing an enterprise's Statute (Articles of Association), require a 75% majority, and that in Western practice holdings of considerably less than 50% are often sufficient to exert predominant influence.

7   *Ekonomika i zhizn'*, no.2, 1994, p.14 of supplement.

8   *Kommersant*, 18 December 1993, p.3. The deadline for their use was extended from 31 December 1993 to the middle of 1994.

9   *Ekonomika i zhizn'*, no.43, 1993, p.14.

10   *Kommersant*, 24 December 1993, p.8.

11   *A Study of the Russian Privatisation Process: Changing Enterprise Behaviour* (Moscow: KPMG Management Consulting in association with the Centre for Economic Reform and Transformation, Heriot-Watt University and SovEcon, 1993) pp.15-16.

12   By November 1993 216 enterprises had majority state holdings and in 125 the state retained a 'Golden Share'. The shares of 1,422 had been sold off in their entirety into private hands: *Ekonomika i zhizn'*, no.2, 1994, p.14 of supplement.

13   *Kommersant*, 25 December 1993, p.3.

14   There are those who claim vehemently that theory and practice point in the opposite direction. See, for example, the regular articles in *Ekonomika i zhizn'* from the Association of Enterprises with Workforce Ownership, and the comments of the head of the Russian Federal Property Fund in *Ekonomika i zhizn'* no.30, 1993, p.14.

15   *The Economist*, 3 July 1993, p.59.

16   *Finansovye Izvestiia*, 11-17 February 1993, p.2.

17   *Izvestiia*, 22 May 1992, pp.1-2; *Izvestiia*, 23 May 1992, pp.1-2.

18   *A Study of the Russian Privatisation Process*, pp.28-33.

19 *Delovoi mir*, 19 November 1993, p.4.
20 Although one should note a legal opinion that this refers only to the privatisation process itself. According to this view, once privatised enterprises can change their Statute to close the share register. *Ekonomika i zhizn'*, no.33, 1993, p.12 of supplement.
21 For example, *Rabochaia tribuna*, 10 July 1992, pp.1-2.
22 *Kommersant*, 9 December 1992, p.8.
23 *Business Central Europe*, February 1994, p.30. The point is made about Czech voucher investment funds, which have had a far greater role in privatisation than their equivalents in Russia.
24 *Izvestiia*, 30 November 1992, p.1. See also promises that privatised enterprises will not be discriminated against in the awarding of government contracts, a standard form of state subsidy: *Kommersant*, 28 November 1992, p.3.
25 For discussion of what is a more confused legal situation than is implied here, see *Khoziaistvo i pravo*, no.9, 1992, pp.104-11; *Khoziaistvo i pravo*, no.12, 1992, pp.81-4.
26 Giving units independent status down to a low level also reduces the opportunities for transfer pricing to protect poorly performing units, and so makes possible the imposition of a harsher budget constraint: *A Study of the Russian Privatisation Process*, p.28.
27 For an example of an enterprise maintaining production of a loss maker specifically in order not to lose skills, see *Rabochaia tribuna*, 22 September 1992, p.1.
28 *Izvestiia*, 7 July 1992, p.2. But for a report suggesting the failure of the Kirov's reprofiling efforts so far, see *Kommersant*, 18 December 1993, p.5. For other examples, see *Ekonomika i zhizn'*, no.3, 1992, p.13; *Izvestiia*, 22 May 1992, pp.1-2; *Izvestiia*, 11 June 1993, p.5; *Kommersant*, 24 December 1993, pp.1 and 10.
29 *Ekonomika i zhizn'*, no.22, 1993, p.5 of supplement. For other examples, see *Ekonomika i zhizn'*, no.20, 1993, p.19; *Delovoi mir*, 6 July 1993, p.1. The Moscow-based manufacture of the 'Moskvich' car, however, is going in the opposite direction, having recently received a large interest-free credit from the Moscow city government to build a new engine plant, in order to free it from dependence on the unreliable Ufa Engine Factory: *Kommersant*, 18 December 1993, p.5.
30 *EKO*, no.7, 1992, p.53.
31 In Russia 'joint venture' has confusingly come to refer only to firms in which there is mixed Russian-foreign ownership. I use the phrase more broadly here.
32 *Finansovye Izvestiia*, 14 January 1993, p.4; *Izvestiia*, 3 February 1993, p.5.
33 For examples additional to those cited above, see *Delovoi mir*, 21 December 1993, p.1; *Kommersant*, 23 December 1993, p.1; *EKO*, no.7, 1992, p.53.
34 Oliver E. Williamson, 'Comparative Economic Organization: The Analysis of Discrete Structural Alternatives', *Administrative Science Quarterly*, vol.36, no.2, June 1991, pp.269-296; Walter W. Powell, 'Neither Market nor Hierarchy: Network Forms of Organization', *Research in Organizational Behavior*, vol.12, 1990, pp.295-336; Andrew H. Van de Ven, 'The Emergence of an Industrial Infrastructure for Technological Innovation', *Journal of Comparative Economics*, vol.17, no.2, June 1993, pp.338-365.

35 *Ekonomika i zhizn'*, no.20, 1993, p.21; *Ekonomika i zhizn'*, no.29, 1993, p.9 of supplement; *Ekonomika i zhizn'*, no.30, 1993, p.14; *Ekonomika i zhizn'*, no.31, 1993, p.1.

36 For the expression of such views by top officials of the Higher Arbitration Court and the Russian Federal Property Fund, see *Ekonomika i zhizn'*, no.21, 1993, p.1; *Ekonomika i zhizn'*, no.30, 1993, p.14; *Ekonomika i zhizn'*, no.3, 1994, p.22. The Higher Arbitration Court's policy is set out in its document 'On some issues of the practice of resolving disagreements connected with the application of legislation on the privatisation of state and municipal enterprises'. *Ekonomika i zhizn'*, no.52, 1993, p.7 of supplement.

37 For a clear statement of the perceived impossibility of technologically related enterprises existing independently, see Sergei Glaz'ev in *Ekonomika i zhizn'*, no.38, 1992, p.22.

38 For an example, see *Ekonomika i zhizn'*, no.47, 1991, p.4.

39 *Sotsialisticheskaia industriia*, 27 September 1989, p.2; *Pravitel'stvennyi Vestnik*, no.17, 1989, p.9; *Kommersant*, 12 December 1992, p.4.

40 *Khoziaistvo i pravo*, no.11, 1992, pp.90-100.

41 *Kommersant*, 1 December 1992, p.4.

42 *Izvestiia*, 10 July 1992, p.5; *Ekonomika i zhizn'*, no.27, 1993, p.4.

43 *Izvestiia*, 3 April 1992, p.2; *Izvestiia*, 14 May 1992, p.2; *Izvestiia*, 22 September 1992, pp.1 and 3.

44 *Kommersant*, 11 November 1992, p.2; *Kommersant*, 24 December 1992, p.3.

45 *Ekonomika i zhizn'*, no.48, 1992, p.18.

46 *Sobranie aktov*, no.49, 1993, article 4766.

47 Chubais describes GKI's influence on the decree in *Kommersant*, 4 September 1993, p.3.

48 *Kommersant*, 4 September 1993, p.3; *Kommersant*, 15 December 1993, p.3.

49 For an example of such a view, see *Izvestiia*, 11 September 1992, p.2.

50 One notes in this regard the enthusiasm of one of the doyens of Western organisational economics, Alfred Chandler Jr, for the ob"edinenie movement of the 1970s. Although in its specifics that enthusiasm might be somewhat naive, his ability as an 'outsider' to stand outside the ideology of decentralisation is useful: Alfred D. Chandler, Jr., 'Organizational Capabilities and Industrial Restructuring: A Historical Analysis', *Journal of Comparative Economics*, vol.17, no.2, June 1993, pp.309-337.

7 From Soviet to Russian Foreign Policy

AMIN SAIKAL AND WILLIAM MALEY

Dean Acheson once commented of Great Britain that it had lost an empire without finding a role. The same could easily be said of Russia. The erosion of Communist Party dominance during the later years of Gorbachev's rule, culminating in the disintegration of the Soviet Union itself, both undermined the ideological basis of Moscow's foreign policy, and radically restructured the world within which the Russian Federation now lives. As a result, Russian foreign policy in a number of ways differs radically from that of the Soviet Union. However, there are continuities as well as discontinuities, not least among the personnel responsible for policy advising and implementation. Our aim in this chapter is to identify these points of continuity and discontinuity, and to show how they are shaping Russia's responses to some of the pressing international issues in the post-Cold War world.

At the outset, one must recognise that it is necessary to study 'Russian foreign policy' not simply as a set of formal doctrines, but also as a pattern of behaviour in specific situations. The idea of 'policy' is not nearly as straightforward as upon initial inspection one might suspect. Lasswell and Kaplan, by defining policy as 'a projected program of goal values and practices',[1] capture one important sense of the term, namely statements by actors about courses which they propose to follow. However, the term can also and more usefully be applied to the general pattern of outcomes which results when an actor, without explicitly stating a projected program of goal values and practices, nonetheless reaches consistent decisions with respect to a sufficient number of cases to justify the inference that a commitment so to decide is in place. Policy may simply emerge through trial and error, as in Braybrooke and Lindblom's model of policymaking through a process of 'disjointed incrementalism'.[2] Distilling the essentials of a state's foreign policy from its behaviour can, however be a difficult task. First, the domestic political structure of a state may allow a range of different forces to take actions with international implications, and there may be no overarching mechanism for ensuring that these actions are coherent rather than contradictory. Second, foreign affairs in a turbulent world of the kind that the collapse of bipolarity has helped produce[3] can cause unique problems, demanding responses for which there are no useful precedents.

The chapter is divided into three sections. The first examines the evolution of official debate about Russian foreign policy, noting the implications of the replacement of the Gorbachev-era doctrines of 'new thinking' with conceptual foundations for foreign policy based more directly on conceptions of Russia's role as a power, both in the wider world and with respect to specific areas of direct interest. Here we note the open conflict between a number of schools of thought about Russia's place in the world, which bears a loose resemblance to the familiar division in the nineteenth century Russian intelligentsia between Westernisers and Slavophiles. The second section addresses the ways in which the formulation of policy has changed with the disintegration of the Soviet Union. This requires an examination of the broader institutional context of the foreign policy making process, and of the adjustments in policy which have been prompted by national political developments in Russia, such as the unexpected rise of Zhirinovskii's neo-fascist Liberal-Democratic Party. The third section examines the tensions surrounding Russian policy towards some of the most important of these areas. We open by examining Russian relations with the United States, with the countries of NATO, and with China and Japan—all of them regions from which Soviet leaders at one time or another detected distinct threats. We go on to discuss the development of Russian relations with the Baltic States, and suggest that Russian rhetoric about the treatment of ethnic Russian minorities may reflect more an internal concession to the sensitivities of a recently-humiliated Russian military than a well-grounded concern about the situation of Russian speakers. We then discuss the complexities of Russia's relations with Ukraine, focussing on the management of Ukraine's inherited nuclear weapons capability, on the position of the Crimea, and on the resolution of the fate of the Black Sea Fleet. It will immediately be obvious that the Third World, a vital concern of Soviet policy over a number of years,[4] is not a central focus of this chapter. This mirrors the Third World's notably diminished status in Russian foreign policy—the main exceptions being India, and the states of the Middle East and West Asia.

The philosophy of Russian foreign policy

It is almost a constituting feature of the modern state that it seeks officially to define the appropriate character of its relations with the wider world. A state which could not do so would hardly merit the name. For the Soviet Union, this involved the application to international relations of propositions which could be related to the broader official ideology of Marxism-Leninism. The scope for pragmatic flexibility which this permitted should not be underestimated: the ambiguity of the canonical texts of this tradition, and still more the unchallengeable position of the Soviet leadership (however constituted) as authoritative interpreter of the canon, permitted diverse policy positions to be defended, ranging from the Stalinist proclamation of the inevitability of war given the threat of capitalist encirclement, to the Khrushchevian and Brezhnevite endorsements of 'peaceful coexistence' and then *détente*.[5] In this way, the twists and turns of Soviet behaviour could be both rationalised and justified.[6]

With the advent to office of Gorbachev, the Soviet philosophy of international affairs changed more radically. The ideology of 'new thinking' (*novoe myshlenie*) marked a break with the zero-sum view of the world ineradicably associated with Marxist theory.[7] It posited the importance of common security in an international system with a number of thermonuclear powers, placed reduced emphasis on military power as a guarantor of 'security', and endorsed 'national reconciliation' as a strategy for the resolution of Third World conflicts in which the superpowers were significantly involved, such as those in Cambodia and Afghanistan.[8] 'New thinking' had distinctly idealist overtones, and appeared to outline an agenda for international relations in which 'national interests' defined in narrowly 'realist' terms should be subordinated to wider global concerns.[9] The most striking casualty of 'new thinking' was the Brezhnev Doctrine, by which, under the guise of defending the common gains of socialism, the Soviet leadership had sought to justify the Warsaw Treaty Organisation invasion of Czechoslovakia in August 1968.[10] Together with the Soviet withdrawal from Afghanistan, the breaching of the Berlin Wall in 1989 signalled that a new era had indeed arrived in the Soviet Union's relations with the wider world.

Andrei Kozyrev, from 1974 to 1990 an officer of the International Organisations Directorate of the Soviet Foreign Ministry, became Foreign Minister of the Russian Federation on 11 October 1990—well before the collapse of the Soviet Union—and some of the most important features of Russian foreign policy date from this period, when the Russian Foreign Ministry was engaged in a process of 'product differentiation' in order to carve out its own sphere of activity.[11] Kozyrev fashioned a strongly pro-Western policy, and enjoyed the support of Boris Yeltsin—notably on the question of the continuation of Soviet aid to the communist regime in Afghanistan, a practice which Yeltsin denounced.[12] Until the August 1991 coup, both Yeltsin and Kozyrev were kept at arms length by the Bush Administration, which in spite of events such as the crackdown in the Baltic states in January 1991 continued to avoid moves that could be seen as raising doubts about US backing for Gorbachev.[13] However, all this changed with the coup, *inter alia* because USSR Foreign Minister Aleksandr Bessmertnykh and a significant number of his ambassadors equivocated in the face of the bid for power by the coup plotters.[14] From this point, Kozyrev's views came increasingly to the fore.

Perhaps the most important feature of these views was an emphasis not on *class* interests or *universal* interests, but *national* interests. 'The "supertask" of Russian diplomacy in all areas', he wrote in 1992, 'is to make the utmost, concrete contribution to the improvement of the everyday life of Russian citizens'.[15] This reorientation, while congenial to proponents of a realist view of world politics in which sovereign states are seen as fundamentally interest-driven, left largely unexplained both the substance of Russia's interests, and the power instruments by which the Russian government might seek to advance them. The result was a vigorous debate, confusingly mingled with debates going on in Russian domestic politics, as to the precise character of Russia's interests. In some respects, this paralleled the venerable conflict between Slavophiles and Westernisers which played such a large role in shaping the course of Russian thought in the last century.[16] The parallel was not perfect, as the earlier controversy was concerned centrally with cultural identity, but in each case the debate arose as a response to social turmoil and dislocation, and involved the presentation of alternative courses to follow in response to novel challenges. In the nineteenth century, the challenge was to cope with the criticism set out by the essayist Chaadaev, who painted Russia as a country without a history. In the late twentieth century, the challenge was to cope with the recent history of the loss of a country.

Russian intellectuals and foreign policy makers responded to this challenge with a range of answers. While the foreign policy elite was fragmented in its general orientations to politics, Kozyrev and a number of his associates opted for a perspective which emphasised the benefits of integration with Western Europe and the West more generally. Given the dire condition of the Soviet economy, this was hardly surprising, as the West was an obvious potential source of both economic aid and venture capital. This 'Atlanticist' perspective stressed the importance of social and institutional factors in determining the quality of interstate relations, and downplayed the significance of geography and primordial culture. This position did not long go uncontested. The most widely-discussed alternative was the 'Eurasian' perspective of Sergei Stankevich, who argued that the protection of the interests of ethnic Russians in the former republics of the Soviet Union should be the central task of Russian foreign policy.[17] While economic interests in time drove both schools of thought to recognise the value of cultivating the oil-rich Gulf States, and to endorse arms sales as a revenue-raising measure,[18] the differences between them were more than ones of emphasis. They assigned primacy to different 'circles' of focus in foreign policy,[19] and did not simply represent different *Weltanschauungen* applied uniformly across the range of foreign policy concerns.

Not surprisingly, the course of this debate could not be insulated from the developing struggle between Yeltsin and his parliamentary opponents, a number of whom were eager to assert that their patriotism exceeded that of the President and his Foreign Minister. The most powerful illustration of the ferocity of this struggle came on 14 December 1992, when Kozyrev, attending a meeting in Stockholm of European Foreign Ministers, delivered a speech, later revealed to have been a deliberate spoof, replete with Soviet-era cliches of the kind which he asserted could become commonplace if the President's domestic opponents were to triumph. Ironically, by 1994, the drift of Kozyrev's own pronouncements seemed asymptotically towards the position he parodied in December 1992, at least where the former states of the USSR—the so-called 'near abroad'—are concerned. With the broader retreat from reform in Russia, the tide has turned against Atlanticism, although the picture is not bleak on all fronts. To clarify why this is the case, it is necessary to explore in more detail the forces and institutions underpinning the making of foreign policy.

The formulation of Russian foreign policy

Policy formulation and implementation are notoriously difficult to study, especially if one must examine a range of discrete decisions in order to infer what a state's policy on some particular matter actually is. Processes may vary dramatically according to whether one is discussing routine decisionmaking, decisionmaking under stress, or crisis decisionmaking. To complicate matters still further, one must recognise that implementation may involve a large number of non-elite individuals, whose interests may differ markedly from those giving them their instructions, and whose scope to block the realisation of policy goals—either consciously or inadvertently—may be considerable. This is especially the case in a political system with a low level of institutionalisation. In such circumstances, the functional responsibilities of different agencies may be ill-defined, and policy may be the incoherent outcome of conflict and bargaining between different agencies, mediated through institutions dominated by politicians with little interest in the specific issues over which the conflict and bargaining takes place.

In Russia, there is strong evidence that differences in perspective on foreign policy are not merely articulated at the top of the elite by political figures such as Kozyrev and Stankevich, but are endemic *within* a range of foreign policy establishments, including the Foreign Ministry. Alexei Arbatov sees four groups 'affecting or trying to affect Russia's foreign policy': Pro-Western, Moderate Liberals, Centrist and Moderate Conservatives, and Neo-Communists and Nationalists.[20] On the basis of focus group interviews from June 1991, Judith Kullberg paints an even more complex picture, distinguishing seven categories: Westerniser, Liberal Moderate Reformer, Moderate Reformer, Conservative Moderate Reformer, Democratic Socialist, Communist, and Nationalist.[21] Beyond these differences of perspective, however, the politics of foreign policy is also complicated by antagonisms, not necessarily related to policy, between cliques and factions in different governmental agencies. While Kozyrev has successfully weathered a number of storms, there is ill-concealed hostility towards him and some of those he promoted[22] from some former officers of the Soviet Foreign Ministry and of the International Department of the Central Committee of the Communist Party of the Soviet Union.[23]

Differences *between* institutions are also apparent, and not in the least surprising. The most important schism is that between the Foreign Ministry and the Russian Ministry of Defence, and relates to the 'near abroad'. Russia is now obliged to conduct relations on a state-to-state basis with the other former Soviet republics, and the Foreign Ministry can claim no particular expertise in the language, cultures, or politics of these states. Before the disintegration of the USSR, inter-republican relations were deemed to be matters of domestic affairs, and were handled by the Communist Party, the KGB, and the Ministry of Defence, which deployed forces throughout the territory of the USSR. Thanks to the institutional arrangements establishing the Commonwealth of Independent States (CIS), Russia retained a military presence in CIS states from December 1991, as well as—far more controversially—in the Baltic States. In respect of certain regions of the former USSR, there is evidence that the military has sought to pursue political objectives quite different from those of the Foreign Ministry—notably in Tajikistan, and in Georgia, where Russian units were accused by Georgian Head of State and former Soviet Foreign Minister Eduard Shevardnadze of intervening on the side of Abkhazian separatists.[24] Doubts as to the motives and impartiality of the Russian military help explain the reluctance of Western governments to see these forces redesignated by the UN as 'peacekeepers' in the theatres within the former Soviet Union in which they are presently deployed.[25]

Given the salience of the armed forces in Russia, the tension between the Foreign and Defence Ministries is unlikely to diminish in the near future. Under the provisions of Articles 86 and 87 of the Constitution of the Russian Federation which came into force following the plebiscite of December 1993, the President of the Russian Federation 'takes the leadership of the foreign policy of the Russian Federation', and is 'Supreme Commander-in-Chief of the Armed Forces'. However, Article 114 provides that the Government of the Russian Federation 'takes steps to ensure the defence of the country, state security, and the realisation of the foreign policy of the Russian Federation',[26] which suggests that the grant of power in Articles 86 and 87 may prove illusory once informal processes define more clearly the roles of different actors within the Russian political system. Given that the Constitution also leaves room for the State Duma to influence foreign policy matters,[27] the power of the President may well come down—in Richard E. Neustadt's famous phrase characterising the power of a US president—to the 'power to persuade'.[28] And strategically-placed members of the armed forces may prove difficult to persuade on matters which lie close to their hearts. This is not to say that the armed forces dominate *politics* in Russia. From the purge of the Red Army in the 1930s to the Zhukov Affair, from the maladroit actions of Defence Minister Iazov in August 1991 to the retaking of the Parliament Building in October 1993, praetorianism has had a bad name amongst both civilians and the military.[29] However, in particular spheres of activity, the voice of the military is likely to ring strongly, and this is especially so in the realm of foreign policy, which in certain cases may be inextricably intertwined with security policy.

However, Yeltsin and the government are under pressure not simply from the military and the State Duma, but also from what they take to be public opinion. This is perhaps the respect in which the Russian foreign policy process differs most sharply from the Soviet, where popular opinion could be ignored in the short run, even though in the long run it may have had a role to play once filtered through the institutions of the ruling party. The importance of public opinion became evident in 1992 and 1993 when Yeltsin shifted towards a Eurasianist position over Tajikistan, probably to prevent the issue from being exploited to his disadvantage by his parliamentary opponents.[30] As Suzanne Crow has pointed out, the drift in Russian foreign policy preceded the rise of Zhirinovskii,[31] and a sensitivity on the part of Yeltsin and Kozyrev to the possibility of alienating public opinion may be one reason why this was the case. It may also help to explain the ambiguities and irresolution apparent in a number of areas of contemporary Russian foreign policy.

Issues in Russian foreign policy

Across a wide range of foreign policy issues, ambiguities and tensions are apparent in Russia's responses. The complexities of Russia's relations with Eastern Europe and with Central Asia are examined in detail in the later chapters by Leslie Holmes and Amin Saikal, and we therefore have put them to one side. In this chapter, we examine five broad areas which illustrate clearly the difficulties which Russia faces in trying to deal with the new world order which the disintegration of the Soviet Union helped to produce. We have chosen these areas partly because of their historical importance to Russia, but also because they have a symbolic importance which may outweigh their strategic significance. Put bluntly, Russian pressure on Estonia evokes unease of a kind that Russian pressure on Moldova does not.

US-Russian relations

Eileen Crumm and James N. Rosenau have recently argued that US-Russian relations 'will continue to become ever more ordinary'.[32] Russia's recent relations with the United States have been considerably shaped by Russia's loss of superpower status, but the effects of this development have been complex. 'A super power', one observer wrote in the 1970s, 'is one able to wreck half the world, and committed upon conditions to do so. Also, it must command the technology and economy to maintain into the foreseeable future the strategic forces needed for that destructive capacity'.[33] In the light of this definition it is clear why Russia is no longer a superpower (and for that matter why Ukraine and Kazakhstan did not become superpowers by inheriting parts of the USSR's strategic nuclear forces): the Soviet Union's decline as an economic power made the maintenance of its strategic capability increasingly costly in terms of other goods foregone, and the erosion of the communist power monopoly made the conditional commitment to wreck the international opponents of communism increasingly pointless. At one level, the loss of superpower status has made Russia more susceptible to sanctions—both positive and negative—from the United States. At another, however, it has prompted a sense of humiliation resulting in hypersensitivity to slights to Russia's status in fora in which Russia and the USA are formally equal—notably the United Nations Security Council, of which both the United States and the Russian Federation are permanent members with a right of veto under Article 27.3 of the UN Charter. Memories of humiliation could in some circumstances prompt a Russian drive to regain superpower status, in which case US-Russian relations might cease to be 'ordinary'.

A further important factor in shaping US-Russian relations has been the change of administration with the inauguration of President Clinton in January 1993. Whilst the achievements of the Bush Administration in aiding reform in post-communist Russia were unspectacular, the 1992 presidential election resulted in the replacement of a president whose main interest lay in foreign affairs with one with avowedly domestic interests, for whom foreign relations were an irritating distraction. Added to the familiar US problem of speedily filling senior bureaucratic offices in the wake of a change of president, this left Russia and its problems relatively marginalised. While President Clinton paid an official visit to Moscow in January 1994, the conciliatory joint declaration of 14 January in which Clinton and Yeltsin welcomed the arrival of a new stage in US-Russian relations marked by a 'mature strategic partnership based on equality, mutual advantage, and recognition of each other's national interests'[34] was swiftly overshadowed by the reported observation by Clinton's adviser Strobe Talbott, now US Deputy Secretary of State, that Russia needed 'less shock, more therapy'[35]—a remark regarded by a number of Russian liberals as a gratuitous and maladroit intervention in Russian domestic affairs at a time when it would have paid to tread delicately.

The net result of these factors, and of the apparent robustness of opponents of reform within Russia, has been a distinct cooling in US-Russian relations—not to anything like the temperature of the Cold War years, but appreciable when compared to the enthusiasm prevailing in 1990 and 1991. There is at mass level a residual suspicion of the United States which is open to exploitation by opponents of reform: 26% of respondents in a survey conducted in June-July 1993 identified the USA as a 'threat to peace and security' in Russia—compared to only 17% who spoke of Germany in such terms, and scarcely less than the 29% who saw China as a threat.[36] Furthermore, there are distinct forces at work in both the USA and Russia which counsel caution in the development of closer relations—either because of the threat which the end of the Cold War poses to their institutional interests, or as a result of genuine uncertainty as to what the future holds.[37] Even amongst reformers there is disillusionment—not merely with words, but also with a perceived lack of leadership from the US in the G7 forum in support of the reform process. Perhaps most importantly of all, there is a degree of mutual suspicion between the two powers arising from the ways in which they have responded to the great European crisis caused by the disintegration of Yugoslavia, and the resulting civil war in Bosnia-Herzegovina.

Russia and NATO

The North Atlantic Treaty Organization (NATO) was created in 1949 to address the threat from the Soviet Union which had become clear with the Berlin blockade, and to undercut in the process any justification for German resurgence. The Atlantic alliance remained the centrepiece of Western strategy to deter a feared Soviet assault on Western Europe through into the 1980s, and survived vocal domestic opposition in European countries to NATO measures such as the deployment of US Cruise and Pershing-II missiles in response to the deployment of Soviet SS-20 intermediate range ballistic missiles in the late 1970s.[38] With the disintegration of the Eastern Bloc and the end of the Cold War, the original rationale for NATO's existence appeared to have vanished as well, even prompting proposals that Russia should join NATO.[39] This did not come about, and the mood is now more sombre. This is partly because NATO's evolving role as a source of firepower to enforce *démarches* issued to the Bosnian Serbs is one which at least some Russians find distasteful, but also because of Russia's demand for a special status in the context of the 'Partnership for Peace' regime.

The carnage in the former Yugoslavia has been anguishing for the United States and the Western Europeans, and has created significant stresses within the alliance. Germany moved rapidly to recognise the separatist republics of the former Yugoslavia as independent states, a move which some analysts regard as having triggered the outbreak of civil war. The arms embargo imposed upon the warring parties in Bosnia-Herzegovina, while strongly supported by the British on the grounds that an uninterrupted flow of arms could only escalate the conflict and hamper humanitarian relief operations, was opposed by the Clinton Administration and wider circles in the US on the grounds that it punished the Bosnian Muslim victims of Bosnian Serb aggression carried out with weapons from the former Yugoslav Army. With a UN force, UNPROFOR, deployed in parts of the former Yugoslavia as well, on occasion further stresses were imposed by conflicting signals to the belligerents from NATO on the one hand, and from the Special Representative of the United Nations Secretary-General on the other. Russia entered the Yugoslav scene essentially as an independent player. With Vladimir Zhirinovskii openly seeking to mobilise support for Serbia, NATO's February 1994 ultimatum to the Bosnian Serbs to lift the siege of the Bosnian capital Sarajevo or face NATO bombing was potentially embarrassing for Russian moderates. The resulting Russian diplomatic intervention, patently directed at asserting a Russian right as a great power to be involved in the solution of the conflict, was followed by the lifting of the siege and the deployment of Russian peacekeepers. Yet while Russia's intervention was welcomed by the British and French, the United States had every reason to be less enthusiastic—and doubtless felt its scepticism to have been vindicated when Kozyrev in June 1994 reportedly stated that lifting sanctions against Bosnia could bring back 'the worst years of the Cold War'.[40]

It is in respect of the expansion of NATO, however, that relations between Russia and the NATO powers have been most strained. The 'Partnership for Peace' proposal amounted to an offer of enhanced opportunities for cooperation, falling short however of NATO membership, for members of the Conference on Security and Cooperation in Europe. It represented an attempt to reconcile a range of interests: the interest of the East European states in obtaining the protection of powerful allies in Western Europe, and the interests of both Russia and some existing NATO states in postponing—although for different reasons—full NATO membership for former Eastern bloc states.[41] By mid-1994, Poland, the Czech Republic and Slovakia, Hungary, Romania, Bulgaria, and Albania, as well as the three Baltic States and a number of other former republics of the USSR had all joined the Partnership. Russia, however, had not. Russian demands for special status within the partnership framework ran into resistance from NATO members, culminating in a summit meeting in Istanbul in June 1994 which was surrounded by rumours of stormy clashes between the Russian delegation and NATO. While Russia finally joined the Partnership in late June, the episode showed that the path to new security arrangements in Europe is strewn with obstacles.

Russia and North East Asia

The relations of the Soviet Union with both China and Japan were tense for much of the postwar period, although for very different reasons. While the USSR entered the war against Japan only after the bombing of Hiroshima, its involvement left a legacy of bitterness, as well as a territorial dispute, which remain to this day. This was aggravated by Soviet backing for North Korea during the Korean War from 1950 to 1953. Tension in relations with China also developed in the 1950s, following the advent to power in 1949 of the Chinese Communist Party led by Mao Zedong, and flared at the June 1960 meeting of fraternal communist parties in Bucharest. The Sino-Soviet dispute, which persisted until Gorbachev's visit to Beijing in 1989 restored formally correct 'party-to-party' relations, saw border clashes in the late 1960s between the two largest powers of the communist bloc, and fierce exchanges on ideological questions.

Russo-Japanese relations remain haunted by this legacy, and especially by the unresolved territorial dispute, which relates to sovereignty over the islands of Etorofu, Kunashiri, Shikotan, and the Habomai archipelago which were occupied by Soviet forces at the end of the Second World War.[42] While the 1956 Soviet-Japanese Joint Declaration committed the USSR to return Shikotan and the Habomai archipelago to Japan upon the conclusion of a peace treaty, this commitment was withdrawn by the USSR in 1960 and has been a point of contention ever since. While paths to a solution to the dispute can easily be foreshadowed,[43] in both Russia and Japan there are well-placed opponents of any strategy of concession to resolve the dispute, and as a consequence, the evolution of Russo-Japanese relations remains inhibited in other respects as well. Here again there is conflict between the Russian Foreign and Defence Ministries, with the former attaching less intrinsic significance to the disputed territories than does the latter.

Sino-Russian relations are far warmer than now than was the case for much of the Soviet era, and have received a great deal of attention from Russian policymakers. The reasons for this attention are obvious. Given the length of the land border between the two countries, each is in the position to pose a range of security threats to the other, and the costs of coping with them could be considerable. On a more positive note, as the most populous country in the world, China is an obvious export market for Russian goods as its economy grows: a great deal of private trade is already taking place between the two states.[44] Economic matters, notably marine transport, the protection of natural resources, and fisheries were the focus of discussion when Russian Prime Minister Chernomyrdin paid a four-day visit to China in May 1994.[45] On the other hand, constraints remain on the expansion of relations. China's unexpected June 1994 nuclear test was criticised by other thermonuclear powers, including Russia, and at a deeper level, Russia leaders are waiting anxiously to see in what direction China will move after the death of Chinese paramount leader Deng Xiaoping.

By contrast, Russia's relations with North Korea deteriorated sharply in the post-Soviet era, and during the mid-1994 crisis over a suspected covert nuclear weapons programme in North Korea, Russia made it clear that the 1961 Treaty of Friendship and Cooperation between the USSR and North Korea would not bind Russia rigidly to assist Kim Il-Sung's regime.[46] This was partly because of improvements in relations with South Korea, whose President, Kim Yong-Sam, paid a successful visit to Moscow in early June 1994, but more broadly because Russia had no interest whatever in coming to the aid of a hermit communist state.

Russia and the Baltic States

Relations between Russia and the Baltic States have been marked by very high levels of tension, fuelled by vivid recollections of the lives lost in the brutal crackdown of January 1991, and by a history of over five decades of repression of Baltic aspirations by Soviet occupiers before Estonia, Latvia, and Lithuania recovered their independence following the August 1991 coup.[47] For Balts, the continued presence of Russian troops on Baltic soil has been a painful reminder of that history. On the other hand, various Russian political figures have taken it upon themselves to challenge the treatment by the new Baltic governments of the Russian minorities within their frontiers, with Zhirinovskii in one interview proposing to bury nuclear waste on the borders of the Baltic States so that Lithuanians would 'die from diseases and radiation'.[48] In the light of his concluding remarks in the same interview—'Soon there will be no Lithuanians, Estonians, and Latvians in the Baltics. I'll act as Hitler did in 1932'—it is hardly surprising that Baltic leaderships have watched the drift away from Atlanticism in Russian foreign policy with undisguised concern. Muted versions of such views appear to be widely held within the Russian elite, with even Kozyrev reportedly stating that Russia 'would not sit still if the rights of Russian speakers in the Baltic States were violated'.[49]

The level of tension has been lowest in relations with Lithuania, for a number of reasons. First, at the 1989 All-Union Census, Russians made up only 9.4% of the Lithuanian population, with 79.6% being Lithuanian.[50] With no fear of being swamped by 'colonists', Lithuania was able to adopt a generous law of citizenship which in effect granted the opportunity to assume Lithuanian citizenship to all permanent residents. Second, the 1992 elections in Lithuania saw the return to office of the former communists under the leadership of Algirdas Brazauskas, which had a soothing effect on relations with Russia.[51] Third, after considerable sparring, the withdrawal of Soviet troops from Lithuania was completed on 31 August 1993. With Latvia and Estonia, on the other hand, Russian relations are poor. In 1989, these states had Russian minorities of 34.0% and 30.3% respectively, with the titular nationality making up only 52.0% of the population in Latvia and 61.5% in Estonia. Fears of a threat to indigenous culture as a result of the migration during the Soviet period which resulted in these proportions prompted the Estonian and Latvian Governments to take a more stringent attitude to the granting of citizenship, and florid charges from Moscow of human rights violations—charges used to justify the retention of Russian troops on Latvian and Estonian soil. In April 1994, agreements were finally concluded between Russia and Latvia providing for the withdrawal of most troops by the end of August 1994, and the balance by the year 2000. However, negotiations between Russia and Estonia remained stalemated over the issue of welfare benefits for Russian military retirees in Estonia.[52]

It is not, however, the case, that the degree of tension manifested between Russian and Baltic elites is mirrored at the mass level, even in Estonia.[53] On the contrary, when asked in late 1993 to describe ethnic relations between themselves and members of the titular nationality, 88% of Russian respondents in Lithuania, 74% in Estonia, and 62% in Latvia opted for 'good' or 'very good'. Only 31% of Russian respondents in Estonia, 29% in Latvia, and 9% in Lithuania felt non-citizens and minority nationalities were being badly treated. Nor is Russia particular attractive for such Russians: excluding those who expressed no opinion, 66% of Russian respondents in Estonia, 59% in Latvia, and 61% in Lithuania agreed or strongly agreed that 'conditions for people like me in Russia are worse than here'.[54] Baltic Russians also feel that a wide range of rights are better protected in the new Baltic systems than under the old Soviet system.[55] What all this suggests is that the intrusion of Moscow-based politicians into Baltic politics as self-appointed patrons of the Russian minorities may be counterproductive from the minorities' point of view, needlessly creating doubts as to their loyalty to their new homelands, and blocking the process of reconciliation at the microsocial level. Such meddling may be a source of ego gratification for figures in the Russian military who resented the advent of Baltic independence in the first place, but it hampers the emergence of a mature post-imperial foreign policy towards the Baltic region.

Russia and Ukraine

The Ukrainian referendum of 1 December 1991, at which 90.3% of those who voted endorsed the independence declaration of 24 August, was a bitter blow to those who aspired to hold the Soviet Union together, and led directly to the union's disintegration. The separation of Ukraine from Russia was bound to bring its traumas. With a population of over 51 million, independent Ukraine became one of the most populous countries of Europe. However, it contained within its borders a Russian minority of 22.1%,[56] and in the Crimea, ethnic Russians were a majority of the population. Furthermore, in contrast to the Baltic States, but like Belarus and Kazakhstan, it became a nuclear power by inheriting elements of the strategic nuclear capability of the USSR based on its territory— and this gave it a basis upon which to resist Russian pressure.[57]

Military issues have been a major source of friction in Russian-Ukrainian relations. Russia's extreme disquiet at having a nuclear-armed Ukraine on its doorstep was shared by Western powers, and considerable pressure was brought to bear on Ukraine to sign the START-1 Treaty and become a non-nuclear state. However, the Ukrainian Government predictably dragged its feet on this issue, plainly hoping to extract the most generous terms possible for relinquishing its nuclear arsenal. Finally, in January 1994, a Trilateral Agreement was signed by Yeltsin, Clinton, and Ukrainian President Leonid Kravchuk, which provided for Ukraine to receive approximately $1 billion worth of nuclear reactor fuel from Russia.[58] While the treaty specified only that warheads would be transferred to Russia for dismantling 'in the shortest possible time', a subsequent report suggested that approximately 60 warheads a month are being withdrawn, with a 3-4 year timetable for completion of the withdrawal.[59] The division of the Black Sea Fleet between Russia and Ukraine has proved just as intractable a problem. While the two states in 1992 agreed in principle to divide the Black Sea Fleet between them, the detailed negotiations of the division have been fraught with complexity, and much remains to be settled.[60]

In the political sphere, the position of the Crimea has severely aggravated bilateral relations between Russia and Ukraine. Historically part of Russia, Crimea was transferred to Ukraine on 26 April 1954. In the December 1991 referendum, 54.1% of those who voted in the Crimea supported Ukrainian independence.[61] However, in January 1994, Iurii Meshkov of the Republican Movement of Crimea was elected as Crimea's president. Once elected, he issued a decree (which Kravchuk declared *ultra vires*) ordering a referendum on the status of Crimea, at which substantial majorities supported greater autonomy for the Crimea, duel Russian-Ukrainian citizenship, and the force of law for decrees of the Crimean president. While Chernomyrdin and Kozyrev avoided statements which might give succour to Russian nationalists in the Crimea, other Russian politicians were less discreet, notably State Duma Speaker Ivan Rybkin and Yeltsin's aide Sergei Filatov.[62] Nevertheless, as in the Baltic States, there is evidence of greater moderation at mass than at elite level, with a significant point of consensus being 'the general feeling of goodwill expressed by both sides towards each other'.[63]

Relations between Russia and Ukraine are also liable to be influenced by Ukraine's relations with third parties, most importantly the USA. This is worth noting in the light of Zbigniew Brzezinski's recent recommendation of a grand strategy of 'the consolidation of geopolitical pluralism within the former Soviet Union', implying 'an even-handed treatment of Moscow and Kiev'.

For Brzezinski, 'without Ukraine, Russia ceases to be an empire, but with Ukraine suborned and then subordinated, Russia automatically becomes an empire'.[64] It is an open question whether such a policy will be adopted by Washington, but there is no doubt that the consequences of such a policy shift could be dramatic, with one Russian commentator already warning that a 'surge of anti-American feeling' in Russia could result.[65] A surge of anti-Ukrainian feeling could result as well.

Conclusion

This brief survey of some key issues in Russian foreign policy leaves many important issues untouched, but it does permit us to make a number of general concluding observations. There are clearly a range of interests, forces, and actors at work in the determination of foreign policy, and predicting outcomes of struggles over policy is extremely difficult given the relatively low level of institutionalisation of the Russian political system. Furthermore, a number of the foreign policy dilemmas which Russia faces are potentially explosive ones in domestic politics— none more so than the treatment of Russians in the 'near abroad'— and this may subordinate the demands for rational policy to the need to cut away the ground beneath the feet of dangerous populists. This leads us to perhaps the most troubling conclusion. While the Cold War is over, it may be premature to conclude that another cannot emerge in its place. Russia remains a great power, and under different leaders than Yeltsin and Kozyrev, its foreign policy could become far more assertive. If this were to happen, the optimistic joint declaration of Clinton and Yeltsin might appear no more than a latter-day version of the 1925 Treaty of Locarno, which promised so much and delivered so little.

Notes

1 Harold Lasswell and Abraham Kaplan, *Power and Society* (New Haven: Yale University Press, 1950) p.71. The recently-released 'Foreign Policy Concept of the Russian Federation' is an obvious example of policy in this sense.
2 See David Braybrooke and Charles E. Lindblom, *A Strategy of Decision: Policy Evaluation as a Social Process* (New York: The Free Press, 1963) pp.81-110.
3 On the concatenation of circumstances contributing to this turbulence, see Robert H. Jackson, *Quasi-States: Sovereignty, International Relations, and the Third World* (Cambridge: Cambridge University Press, 1990); James N. Rosenau, *Turbulence in World Politics: A Theory of Change and Continuity* (Princeton: Princeton University Press, 1990); Joseph A. Camilleri and Jim Falk, *The End of Sovereignty?: The Politics of*

a *Shrinking and Fragmenting World* (Aldershot: Edward Elgar, 1992); Zbigniew Brzezinski, *Out of Control: Global Turmoil on the Eve of the 21st Century* (New York: Scribner's, 1993); Paul Kennedy, *Preparing for the Twenty-First Century* (New York: Random House, 1993); Kenneth N. Waltz, 'The Emerging Structure of International Politics', *International Security*, vol.18, no.2, Fall 1993, pp.44-79.

4 See Daniel S. Papp, *Soviet Perceptions of the Developing World in the 1980s: The Ideological Basis* (Lexington: D.C. Heath, 1985); Jerry F. Hough, *The Struggle for the Third World: Soviet Debates and American Options* (Washington DC: The Brookings Institution, 1986); Roy Allison, *The Soviet Union and the Strategy of Non-Alignment in the Third World* (Cambridge: Cambridge University Press, 1988).

5 For further discussion of Soviet ideology of international relations, see William Zimmerman, *Soviet Perspectives on International Relations 1956-1967* (Princeton: Princeton University Press, 1969); Vendulka Kubálková and A.A. Cruickshank, *Marxism-Leninism and theory of international relations* (London: Routledge & Kegan Paul, 1980); Vendulka Kubálková and A.A. Cruickshank, *Marxism and International Relations* (Oxford: Oxford University Press, 1985); Allen Lynch, *The Soviet study of international relations* (Cambridge: Cambridge University Press, 1987); Margot Light, *The Soviet Theory of International Relations* (Brighton: Wheatsheaf, 1988).

6 For an overview of Soviet foreign policy, see Alvin Z. Rubinstein, *Soviet Foreign Policy Since World War II: Imperial and Global* (New York: HarperCollins, 1992).

7 For more detailed discussions of 'new thinking', see Anatolii Gromyko and Vladimir Lomeiko, *Novoe myshlenie v iadernyi vek* (Moscow: Mezhdunarodnye otnosheniia, 1984); Vendulka Kubálková and A.A. Cruickshank, *Thinking New About Soviet "New Thinking"* (Berkeley: Institute of International Studies, University of California, 1989); Robert F. Miller, *Soviet Foreign Policy Today: Gorbachev and the New Political Thinking* (Sydney: Allen & Unwin, 1991); Jeff Checkel, 'Ideas, Institutions, and the Gorbachev Foreign Policy Revolution', *World Politics*, vol.45, no.2, January 1993, pp.271-300.

8 See William Maley, 'Regional Conflicts: Afghanistan and Cambodia', in Ramesh Thakur and Carlyle A. Thayer (eds.), *Reshaping Regional Relations: Asia-Pacific and the Former Soviet Union* (Boulder: Westview Press, 1993) pp.183-200.

9 See Peter Shearman, 'New political thinking reassessed', *Review of International Studies*, vol.19, no.2, April 1993, pp.139-158.

10 On the Brezhnev Doctrine, see Robert A. Jones, *The Soviet Concept of 'Limited Sovereignty' from Lenin to Gorbachev: The Brezhnev Doctrine* (London: Macmillan, 1990). On events in Czechoslovakia, see H. Gordon Skilling, *Czechoslovakia's Interrupted Revolution* (Princeton: Princeton University Press, 1976); Karen Dawisha, *The Kremlin and the Prague Spring* (Berkeley & Los Angeles: University of California Press, 1984).

11 See John Löwenhardt, 'The Foreign Policy of the Russian Federation', Paper prepared for the Tokyo/Kanazawa International Symposium, 25-27 November 1991; Nikolai Kosolapov, 'Vneshniaia politika Rossii: problemy stanovleniia i politikoformiruiushchie faktory', *Mirovaia ekonomika i mezhdunarodnye otnosheniia*, no.2, 1993, pp.5-19; Mark Webber, 'The Emergence of the Foreign Policy of the Russian Federation', *Communist and Post-Communist Studies*, vol.26, no.3, September 1993, pp.243-263.

12 William Maley, 'Soviet-Afghan Relations after the Coup', *Report on the USSR*, vol.3, no.38, 20 September 1991, pp.11-15.

13 For an analysis of US-Russian relations during this period, see Michael R. Beschloss and Strobe Talbott, *At the Highest Levels: The Inside Story of the End of the Cold War* (Boston: Little, Brown & Co., 1993), especially pp.347-350.

14 See Sallie Wise, 'Foreign Ministry Adrift', *Report on the USSR*, vol.3, no.36, 6 September 1991, pp.28-30; Suzanne Crow, 'Reforming the Foreign Ministry', *Report on the USSR*, vol.3, no.40, 4 October 1991, pp.8-10.

15 Andrei Kozyrev, 'Russia: A Chance for Survival', *Foreign Affairs*, vol.71, no.2, Spring 1992, pp.1-16 at p.10.

16 On this, see Andrzej Walicki, *The Slavophile Controversy: History of a Conservative Utopia in Nineteenth-Century Russian Thought* (Oxford: Oxford University Press, 1975).

17 Sergei Stankevich, 'Russia in Search of Itself', *The National Interest*, no.28, Summer 1992, pp.47-50. See also Alexander Rahr, '"Atlanticists" versus "Eurasians" in Russian Foreign Policy', *RFE/RL Research Report*, vol.1, no.22, 29 May 1992, pp.17-22.

18 For more detailed discussion of Russian policy towards Iran and the other states of the Middle East, see Amin Saikal, 'Russian Policy towards West Asia and the Middle East', in Peter Shearman (ed.), *Russian Foreign Policy* (Boulder: Westview Press, forthcoming).

19 Peter Shearman, 'Russia's Three Circles of Interests', in Ramesh Thakur and Carlyle A. Thayer (eds.), *Reshaping Regional Relations: Asia-Pacific and the Former Soviet Union* (Boulder: Westview Press, 1993) pp.45-64.

20 Alexei G. Arbatov, 'Russia's Foreign Policy Alternatives', *International Security*, vol.18, no.2, Fall 1993, pp.5-43 at pp.8-14.

21 Judith S. Kullberg, *The End of New Thinking?: Elite Ideologies and the Future of Russian Foreign Policy* (Columbus: The Mershon Center, The Ohio State University, 1993).

22 On Kozyrev's restructuring of the upper echelons of the Foreign Ministry, see Jeff Checkel, 'Russian Foreign Policy: Back to the Future?', *RFE/RL Research Report*, vol.1, no.41, 16 October 1992, pp.15-29 at pp.24-26.

23 The International Department was almost certainly the single most important bureaucratic agency involved in foreign policy formulation in the USSR: see Leonard Schapiro, 'The International Department of the CPSU: key to Soviet policy', *International Journal*, vol.32, no.1, 1976-77, pp.41-55.

24 On Tajikistan, see Sanobar Shermatova, 'Suppression or conciliation?', *Moscow News*, no.12, 25-31 March 1994, p.4. On Georgia, see Elizabeth Fuller, 'Eduard Shevardnadze's Via Dolorosa', *RFE/RL Research Report*, vol.2, no.43, 29 October 1993, pp.17-23 at p.21.

25 On Russian forces as 'peacekeepers', see Suzanne Crow, 'The Theory and Practice of Peacekeeping in the Former USSR', *RFE/RL Research Report*, vol.1, no.37, 18 September 1992, pp.31-36.

26 'Konstitutsiia Rossiiskoi Federatsii', *Izvestiia*, 10 November 1993, pp.3-5 at p.4.

27 Jan S. Adams, 'Who Will Make Russia's Foreign Policy in 1994?', *RFE/RL Research Report*, vol.3, no.6, 11 February 1994, pp.36-40.

28 Richard E. Neustadt, *Presidential Power: The Politics of Leadership* (New York: John Wiley & Sons, 1964) p.23.

29 On civil-military relations in the Soviet era, see Timothy J. Colton, *Commissars, Commanders, and Civilian Authority: The Structure of Soviet Military Politics* (Cambridge: Harvard University Press, 1979); Thomas M. Nichols, *The Sacred Cause: Civil-Military Conflict over Soviet National Security, 1917-1992* (Ithaca: Cornell University Press, 1993). For discussion of more recent developments in civil-military relations, see John W.R. Lepingwell, 'Soviet Civil-Military Relations and the August Coup', *World Politics*, vol.44, no.4, July 1992, pp.539-572; Robert Arnett, 'Russia after the Crisis: Can Civilians Control the Military?', *Orbis*, vol.38, no.1, Winter 1994, pp.41-57; Brian D. Taylor, 'Russian Civil-Military Relations After the October Uprising', *Survival*, vol.36, no.1, Spring 1994, pp.3-29; Stephen Foye, 'Civilian and Military Leaders in Russia's "New" Political Arena', *RFE/RL Research Report*, vol.3, no.15, 15 April 1994, pp.1-6.

30 See William Maley, 'The Future of Islamic Afghanistan', *Security Dialogue*, vol.24, no.4, December 1993, pp.383-396 at pp.393-394.

31 Suzanne Crow, 'Why Has Russian Foreign Policy Changed?', *RFE/RL Research Report*, vol.3, no.18, 6 May 1994, pp.1-6.

32 Eileen Crumm and James N. Rosenau, 'From Superpower Deadlock to Ordinary Relationship: Materials for a Theory of U.S.-Russian Relations', in Manus I. Mislarsky, John A. Vasquez, and Peter V. Gladkov (eds.), *From Rivalry to Cooperation: Russian and American Perspectives on the Post-Cold War Era* (New York: HarperCollins, 1994) pp.126-144 at p.141.

33 A.L. Burns, 'Introduction', in Carsten Holbraad (ed.), *Super Powers and World Order* (Canberra: Australian National University Press, 1971) pp.xi-xxi at p.xi.

34 Suzanne Crow, 'Russian-American Moscow Declaration', *RFE/RL News Briefs*, vol.3, no.4, 10-21 January 1994, p.6.

35 *The Economist*, 29 January-4 February 1994, p.29.

36 Richard Rose, Irina Boeva, and Viacheslav Shironin, *How Russians are Coping with Transition: New Russia Barometer II* (Glasgow: Studies in Public Policy no.216, Centre for the Study of Public Policy, University of Strathclyde, 1993) p.45.

37 Andrei Kozyrev, 'The Lagging Partnership", *Foreign Affairs*, vol.73, no.3, May/June 1994, pp.59-71 at p.60.

38 See Philip Towle, Iain Elliot and Gerald Frost, *Protest and Perish: A Critique of Unilateralism* (London: Institute for European Defence & Strategic Studies, 1982); Clive Rose, *Campaigns Against Western Defence: NATO's Adversaries and Critics* (London: Macmillan, 1985); Philip A.G. Sabin, *The Third World War Scare in Britain* (London; Macmillan, 1986); Ferenc Fehér and Agnes Heller, *Doomsday or Deterrence? On the Antinuclear Issue* (New York: M.E. Sharpe, 1986).

39 Coral Bell, 'Why Russia Should Join NATO", *The National Interest*, no.22, Winter 1990, pp.37-47.

40 John Lepingwell, 'Kozyrev on Bosnia Sanctions', *RFE/RL Daily Report*, 14 June 1994.

41 On the background to the 'Partnership for Peace' proposal, see Michael Mihalka, 'Squaring the Circle: NATO's Offer to the East', *RFE/RL Research Report*, vol.3, no.12, 25 March 1994, pp.1-9.

42 On the dispute, see Leszek Buszynski, 'Russia and Japan: the unmaking of a territorial settlement', *The World Today*, vol.49, no.3, March 1993, pp.50-54; Richard deVillafranca, 'Japan and the Northern Territories Dispute: Past, Present, Future', *Asian Survey*, vol.33, no.6, June 1993, pp.610-624; Yakov Zinberg and Reinhard Drifte, 'Chaos in Russia and the Territorial Dispute with Japan', *Pacific Review*, vol.6, no.3, 1993, pp.277-

284; Tsuyoshi Hasegawa, 'Japan', in Ramesh Thakur and Carlyle A. Thayer (eds.), *Reshaping Regional Relations: Asia-Pacific and the Former Soviet Union* (Boulder: Westview Press, 1993) pp.101-123;

[43] See, for example, Graham Allison, Hiroshi Kimura, and Konstantin Sarkisov, *Beyond Cold War to Trilateral Cooperation in the Asia-Pacific Region: Scenarios for New Relationships Between Japan, Russia, and the United States* (Cambridge: Strengthening Democratic Institutions Project, Harvard University, 1992), which identifies sixty six different scenarios for solving the issue.

[44] Eugene Bazhanov and Natasha Bazhanov, 'Russia and Asia in 1993', *Asian Survey*, vol.34, no.1, January 1994, pp.87-97 at pp.90-91.

[45] Stephen Foye, 'Chernomyrdin winds up visit to China', *RFE/RL News Briefs*, vol.3, no.23, 30 May-3 June 1994, p.2.

[46] Suzanne Crow, 'Yeltsin on North Korea', *RFE/RL News Briefs*, vol.3, no.23, 30 May-3 June 1994, p.5.

[47] For background, see William Maley, *The Politics of Baltic Nationalisms* (Canberra: Working Paper no.1990/6, Department of International Relations, Research School of Pacific Studies, Australian National University, 1990); Kristian Gerner and Stefan Hedlund, *The Baltic States and the End of the Soviet Empire* (London: Routledge, 1993); Anatol Lieven, *The Baltic Revolution: Estonia, Latvia, Lithuania and the Path to Independence* (New Haven: Yale University Press, 1993).

[48] Vera Tolz and Elizabeth Teague, 'Is Russia Likely to Turn to Authoritarian Rule?', *RFE/RL Research Report*, vol.1, no.4, 24 January 1992, pp.1-8 at p.3.

[49] Suzanne Crow, 'Kozyrev Tough on Critics', *RFE/RL News Briefs*, vol.3, no.4, 10-21 January 1994, pp.3-4.

[50] These and subsequent 1989 census figures are presented in *The Baltic States: A Reference Book* (Tallinn: Tallinn Book Printers, 1991) p.16 (Estonia), p.92 (Latvia), p.176 (Lithuania).

[51] Saulius Girnius, 'The Parliamentary Elections in Lithuania', *RFE/RL Research Report*, vol.1, no.48, 4 December 1992, pp.6-12.

[52] Dzintra Bungs, 'Russia Agrees to Withdraw Troops from Latvia', *RFE/RL Research Report*, vol.3, no.22, 3 June 1994, pp.1-9.

[53] See Andrus Park, 'Ethnicity and Independence: The Case of Estonia in Comparative Perspective', *Europe-Asia Studies*, vol.46, no.1, 1994, pp.69-87.

[54] Richard Rose and William Maley, *Nationalities in the Baltic States: A Survey Study* (Glasgow: Studies in Public Policy no.222, Centre for the Study of Public Policy, University of Strathclyde, 1993) p.56.

[55] Rose and Maley, *Nationalities in the Baltic States: A Survey Study*, pp.39-40.

[56] For population data, see Bohdan Krawchenko, 'Ukraine: the politics of independence', in Ian Bremmer and Ray Taras (eds.), *Nations and Politics in the Soviet Successor States* (Cambridge: Cambridge University Press, 1993) pp.75-98 at p.85.

[57] Ukraine inherited 176 ICBMs with 1,240 warheads: see Karen Dawisha and Bruce Parrott, *Russia and the New States of Eurasia: The Politics of Upheaval* (Cambridge: Cambridge University Press, 1994) p.261.

[58] See John W.R. Lepingwell, 'The Trilateral Agreement on Nuclear Weapons', *RFE/RL Research Report*, vol.3, no.4, 28 January 1994, pp.12-20.

[59] John Lepingwell, 'All nuclear warheads out of Ukraine in 3-4 years', *RFE/RL News Briefs*, vol.3, no.21, 16-20 May 1994, p.8.

60 For an overview, see Ustina Markus, 'The Ukrainian Navy and the Black Sea Fleet', *RFE/RL Research Report*, vol.3, no.18, 6 May 1994, pp.32-40.

61 Bohdan Nahaylo, 'The Birth of an Independent Ukraine', *Report on the USSR*, vol.3, no.50, 13 December 1991, pp.1-5 at p.2.

62 John Lepingwell, 'Russian politicians on Crimean Crisis', *RFE/RL News Briefs*, vol.3, no.22, 24-27 May 1994, p.6.

63 Ian Bremmer, 'The Politics of Ethnicity: Russians in the New Ukraine', *Europe-Asia Studies*, vol.46, no.2, 1994, pp.261-283 at p.280.

64 Zbigniew Brzezinski, 'The Premature Partnership', *Foreign Affairs*, vol.73, no.2, March/April 1994, pp.67-82 at pp.79, 80.

65 Alexei K. Pushkov, 'Russia and America: The Honeymoon's Over', *Foreign Policy*, no.93, Winter 1993-94, pp.76-90 at p.90.

8 RUSSIA'S RELATIONS WITH THE FORMER EXTERNAL EMPIRE

LESLIE HOLMES

In analysing the relationships between Russia and those countries formerly described as the Soviet Union's East European empire[1] (that is, Bulgaria, Czechoslovakia, the German Democratic Republic, Hungary, Poland, Romania), this chapter will adopt two principal and closely related themes.

First, it is argued that the numerous bilateral and multilateral relationships in one sense reflect the domestic politics and relationships of communist and post-communist systems. Thus, during the communist era, the systems were more authoritarian, hierarchical, simple and stable. Conversely, the post-communist systems are more pluralistic, egalitarian (in some ways), complex and unstable. In addition, the current domestic scenes are typified by a plethora of new organisations (for example political parties) that are still crystallising; similarly, the international scene is typified by a multitude of new organisations, and changing relationships that are still crystallising.

Second, and intimately connected with the first point, both the domestic scene and international relations are in a state of flux and contradictoriness. There is the tension between desire and resistance—for instance, in the sense of the east European states simultaneously wanting to move closer to Western Europe, yet also wanting to retain their only recently gained independence of other, more powerful states. Then there is the tension between theory and reality. On the domestic front, for instance, this is reflected in the abstract commitment to marketisation and democratisation on the one hand, and the fears many post-communist politicians have of the destabilising effects the implementation of these two policies are bound to have. In the area of international relations, many in both east and west are now realising that, for all its ideological rancour and sabre-rattling, the Cold War era had a certain stability which, as memories of its worst features fade, can appear increasingly attractive to some.[2] In both the domestic and international scenes, centrifugal and centripetal forces are operating simultaneously at present.

Certainly, one cannot begin to understand the complexity of Russia's relations with its former Warsaw Pact allies and Council for Mutual Economic Assistance partners simply by analysing a series of bilateral relations—or even the relationship between

Moscow and what was Eastern Europe as a bloc. In addition to these, one must attempt to make sense of and incorporate the changing international context—as well as Russia's relations with the so-called 'near-abroad' (that is, the other former republics of the USSR). This last set of relationships, especially within the Commonwealth of Independent States (that is, excluding the Baltic States), is particularly interesting, since it does not fit neatly into either domestic politics or international relations. Perhaps there is a need for a new intermediate category of politics for this—for relationships less close than in a federal system, yet closer than between genuinely sovereign states. However, this point having been made, the focus here is not on that particular set of relationships.

There are a number of different types of relationship to be examined before one can attempt to draw any conclusions about the current situation in a general sense. First, there are formal diplomatic relations; these are not generally of great significance, and will be addressed only tangentially in this chapter. Second, there are political and ideological relationships; whilst these will not constitute a major part of the present analysis either, they must at least be identified in any attempt at comprehensive analysis. Third, there are the military/strategic relationships —which are important. Finally, there are the all-important economic relations; although one must always be wary of excessive reductionism, this is probably the single most important determinant of the general climate within which relations operate.

Before exploring the various dimensions just outlined, it is necessary to point out that the relationships are developing within specific contexts. For our purposes, at least two major contexts can be identified. The first is that in which the post-communist states were born. In a book published by the present author in 1993, the events of 1989-1991 in Eastern Europe and the USSR were described as the 'double-rejective revolution'.[3] The two rejections were of communism as a power system (with its emphasis on democratic centralism, the centrally-planned economy and teleologism) and of Soviet hegemony.[4] This clearly had major implications for the kinds of decisions foreign policy makers in the various countries were likely to make. Most obviously, they were unlikely to choose options that either appeared to be too similar to the policies of the communist era, or that might render them overly-dependent on individual major foreign powers.

The second context was that of instability and growing global recession. The reasons for the instability of the transitional countries of post-communism are obvious. Most generally, the extent of change intended in as short a time-frame as was hoped for was almost certainly without precedent. Not only were political and economic systems undergoing wide-ranging and rapid change, but there was also a need for a profound change of political culture—for instance, in terms of attitudes towards officialdom, the nature and role of ideology, and social structure. Somewhat less obvious was the instability of the West, especially Western Europe. Yet the problems were several and significant. They included those arising from the unification of Germany; the tensions within the European Community (recently renamed the European Union)[5] revealed by the difficulties of having the Maastricht Treaty adopted or in the *de facto* collapse of the Exchange Rate Mechanism; the increasing inability of opinion pollsters to predict the likely outcome of forthcoming elections, that in turn reflected the growing volatility of the electorate in many countries; the growing racial tensions and neo-Nazi activities in several countries (to some extent exacerbated precisely by ramifications of the instability of the post-communist world). All these testified to the fact that the West was itself in a period of greater uncertainty than it had been for many years. The growing recession in the West was intimately connected to—and helps to explain—these manifestations of instability. The West was becoming more introspective and self-protective. The question of whether this instability in the West is merely a short-term phenomenon—a temporary aberration—or reflective of a more serious instability throughout Europe, will be addressed later in the chapter.

Political and Ideological Relations

During the communist era, there was a remarkably high level of similarity between the structures and even policies of the communist states of Europe. In most cases, the constitutions closely emulated the Soviet Union's. Despite the differences between, say, the German Democratic Republic's New Economic System and Hungary's New Economic Mechanism, the economic reforms of the 1960s and 1970s in Eastern Europe and the USSR were mostly variations on the same basic themes. And to ensure limits on the level of diversity in the communist world, the Soviets would often involve themselves in one way or another in leadership politics—particularly leadership changes—in their various satellites. There was also a comparatively high level of ideological uniformity in the communist era, with the official stress on Marxism-Leninism, socialist internationalism, and a peculiar brand of official nationalism.

Turning to the post-communist era, the relative homogeneity just described has been replaced by a heterogeneous situation. In terms of constitutions, the recent framers of these have tended to look to their own country's pre-communist past or to the West, especially Germany, to a lesser extent France. In the area of economic policy, the role-models have tended to be the West, Latin America and the Newly Industrialising Economies of East Asia—although the post-communist states have largely had to devise their own approaches to privatisation, for example the various voucher or coupon systems.[6] On the ideological front, there has been a widespread rejection of grand theories in the post-communist world. It might be objected that nationalism has replaced Marxism-Leninism as the all-encompassing ideology of at least many of these countries. But nationalism is at most a partial ideology: most obviously, it has no inherent commitment to a given type of political or economic system. This puts it into a quite different category from, for instance, liberalism or socialism.

Far from Russia dictating or inspiring the political and ideological systems of the post-communist world, it is—at least to some extent—emulating much of the practice of the countries to its west that are two to three years further down the post-communist track. In short, there has to some extent been a role reversal.

Military-Strategic Relations

During the communist era, the Warsaw Treaty Organisation was perceived by some as primarily a tool of Soviet hegemony. With the invasion of Czechoslovakia in 1968 and the subsequent emergence of the Brezhnev Doctrine, there were good grounds for accepting the argument that the Warsaw Treaty Organisation existed more to exercise Soviet control over the countries of Eastern Europe than to act as a counterweight to NATO.[7]

Gorbachev's unambiguous abandonment of the Brezhnev Doctrine and adoption of the so-called Sinatra Doctrine (that is, the notion that each communist state should find its own way, without external interference) at the end of the 1980s is justifiably seen as one of the major factors explaining the collapse of East European communist power. However, it would be wrong to infer that Gorbachev wanted or intended to dissolve the Warsaw Treaty Organisation altogether. Rather, he appears to have accepted that the Warsaw Treaty Organisation's days as an instrument of military coercion were over—but still believed that it should and could continue to play a role as an agency of political cooperation.

But signs of a major reconceptualisation were evident by June 1990 at the latest. At the Warsaw Treaty Organisation summit held that month, major changes were agreed in principle—and observers were quick to identify signs of a possible total dissolution.[8] Another clear indication that the putative *raison d'être* of the Warsaw Treaty Organisation was now in doubt was the announcement by both NATO and Warsaw Treaty Organisation spokespersons at the Paris summit in November 1990 of the Conference on Security and Cooperation in Europe that the two organisations no longer regarded each other as enemies.

Further serious questioning of the Warsaw Treaty Organisation came at the meeting of Czecho-Slovak, Hungarian and Polish Foreign Ministers held in Budapest in January 1991. At this, all three countries—which were by this stage being described by the Soviets as the 'troika'[9]—agreed to cease cooperating with the Warsaw Treaty Organisation from July 1991 at the latest.[10] But Hungary opted to go even further; at about the same time as the Foreign Ministers' meeting was being held, the Hungarian parliament almost unanimously voted to accept a NATO offer of associate (non-voting) membership of the North Atlantic Assembly. Thus, one member of the Warsaw Treaty Organisation was not merely rejecting the organisation, but was actually proposing to enter what had for years been regarded as perhaps the ultimate symbol of the enemy camp. The Northern Tier countries were not alone in their position: both the Romanian and Bulgarian leaders declared the Warsaw Treaty Organisation to be an anachronism in January and February respectively.

But Gorbachev had still not accepted that the Warsaw Treaty Organisation would disappear altogether, and was attempting to retain at least a rump organisation. Thus he wrote to the leaders of the troika in mid-February, recommending the liquidation of just the military structures by 1 April 1991.[11] This was followed on 25 February by the signing by all Foreign and Deputy Foreign Ministers of the Warsaw Treaty Organisation states (excluding the German Democratic Republic, which had ceased to exist in October 1990) of a protocol cancelling the validity of all military agreements and structures of the Warsaw Treaty Organisation with effect from 31 March 1991. At the same time, and despite reluctance on the part of most of the east Europeans, agreement was reached temporarily transforming the political structures into a purely voluntary consultative organisation. But the reluctance to agree to even this highly diluted version of what the Warsaw Treaty Organisation had been until so recently testified to the enormous gap that had now become so visible between the USSR and its erstwhile allies. The USSR wanted a political counterpart to NATO at least until the conclusion of important Conference on Security and Cooperation in Europe talks; the east Europeans were barely able to accede even to this request. They wanted the total dissolution of the Warsaw Treaty Organisation.

The dissolution came in July, with the signing of a protocol in Prague. This document advocated a gradual shift towards pan-

European security structures, on the basis of agreements reached at the November 1990 Conference on Security and Cooperation in Europe summit. Although the protocol was not technically in force until the six member-states' parliaments had ratified it, the Warsaw Treaty Organisation had now *de facto* ceased to exist.

Yet there remained a number of other important issues to resolve in terms of Russia's military-strategic relationship with its former allies. Top of the list was the question of the Soviet troops still in eastern Europe. This did not pertain to Bulgaria or Romania, since there had been no permanent Soviet troops in those countries for several years. In the cases of Hungary and Czecho-Slovakia, the issue was resolved at about the same time as the Warsaw Treaty Organisation was dissolved; the last Soviet troops withdrew from the two countries on 19 and 30 June 1991 respectively. The Polish case was far more difficult. As of mid-1991, there were still approximately 50,000 Soviet troops stationed in Poland, which the Polish government wanted removed before the end of the year. But the USSR did not plan to withdraw the last of its troops until the end of 1993. Polish-Soviet negotiations on this in July 1991 did not properly resolve this; as of January 1993, for instance, there were still more than 4,000 Russian troops on Polish territory. Not until August 1993 did the Russians finally commit to a withdrawal of the remaining troops by 1 October 1993—three months early by Russian reckoning, but much later than the Poles had wanted.

Although the issue of Soviet-Russian troops had been resolved, there were still important ramifications of this 'occupation' to be sorted out. Perhaps the most important was the matter of compensation. For instance, Hungary claimed the equivalent of US$1700 million from the USSR or its successor for environmental damage caused by Soviet troops since the 1956 uprising and for other aspects of the military presence. Much of this issue was subsequently resolved; in June 1993, for example, President Goncz visited Russia, and agreed to cancel approximately US$800 million of the debt in return for 28 MiG-29 fighter jets. And in September 1993, Russia agreed to transfer all of its property in Poland to the Polish state, in return for which Poland agreed to drop all claims for compensation for environmental clean-ups necessitated by the Soviet military presence.

Other aspects of debt and pecuniary claims will be examined later; for now, the focus will remain on aspects of military alliances. In November 1991, NATO and the former members of the Warsaw Treaty Organisation joined together to form the North Atlantic Cooperation Council. This included all the former Soviet republics except Georgia. Given that both NATO and the Warsaw Treaty Organisation had until so relatively recently perceived the other as its number one enemy, the establishment of this council was one of the most visible symbols of the end of the Cold War and the dramatic change in the East-West relationship. The Council set up a High-Level Working Group, which first met in January 1992, primarily to discuss the ratification and implementation of the Conventional Forces in Europe Treaty.

Another sign of the dramatic change in military attitudes and policy—and of the move towards a pan-European approach to defence and military issues—was the signing in March 1992 by 51 states of the Conference on Security and Cooperation in Europe 'Open Skies' agreement, to be effective from 1993. The idea behind this policy dates back to 1955, when President Eisenhower proposed the concept. It was another American president—George Bush—who resurrected it, at a NATO summit held in May 1989. Following a number of hiccoughs, serious negotiations on the 'open skies' concept commenced just a few weeks after the establishment of the North Atlantic Cooperation Council, in December 1991, under the auspices of the Conference on Security and Cooperation in Europe. The negotiations resulted in a formal agreement in March 1992, and became a reality in July 1993, when Hungary permitted the USA to run test-flights over its territory. This open skies agreement has been described as the first major arms control agreement of the Post-Cold-War era.

At the same time as the former Eastern and Western blocs as a whole were coming together, new sub-groupings began to emerge amongst the former Warsaw Treaty Organisation allies. In the military sphere, perhaps the most significant example was an agreement between what was at that time known as the 'Visegrad Three' (Czecho-Slovakia, Hungary and Poland—known as the 'Visegrad Four' since the formal division of Czecho-Slovakia at the very end of 1992) on an 'open barracks' policy. In one sense, this reflected the growing integration of these countries, and their further distancing from what had by now become the Commonwealth of Independent States.

But the whole situation in Europe was changing at a rapid pace in the early-1990s. Whereas most of the West had been delighted at the collapse of communism, and had initially appeared to be willing to welcome the countries of the former Soviet external empire with open arms, a mood of cautiousness had become obvious by 1992, as the effects and ramifications of recession, German unification, and war in parts of the former USSR and Yugoslavia became increasingly tangible in so many West European countries. One clear sign of this were the statements by the Secretary-General of NATO, Manfred Woerner, during visits to Poland and the Baltic States in March 1992, to the effect that, even though NATO was committed to ensuring that no security vacuums would emerge in eastern Europe, it would be able to offer neither formal security guarantees nor membership to the countries of the region in the foreseeable future.

Nevertheless, it had become clear by 1993 that some of these countries were very keen to join NATO. This was particularly true of the Visegrad Four. At first, President Yeltsin indicated that Russia had no major objections to the notion of its former military allies joining what had been its number one enemy. Already by 1991, Russia had dropped earlier demands that there should be a clause in all new bilateral treaties with its former military allies that would have prevented them from entering any alliance that Russia might interpret as threatening. In August 1993, Yeltsin gave a clear indication that he had no objection to Poland, the Czech Republic or Hungary joining NATO.[12]

Following the closure of the Russian parliament, however, Yeltsin changed his line dramatically. At the very end of September, the Russian President wrote to various Western leaders, warning them against any expansion of NATO eastwards. Following this, the so-called 'power ministries' (notably defence and the security police) became very vocal in their criticism of the attempts by the Visegrad Four to acquire membership of NATO. In late November 1993, the director of Russia's foreign intelligence services, Evgenii Primakov, made it very clear at a press conference that 'Russia' was feeling threatened by the notion of an expanded NATO right on its Western frontiers: 'This expansion would bring the biggest military grouping in the world, with its colossal offensive potential, directly to the borders of Russia ... If this happens, the need would arise for a fundamental reappraisal of all defence concepts on our side, a redeployment of armed forces and changes in operational plans'.[13] This was of particular concern because Primakov went on to argue that ' ... irritation in military circles might emerge that is not in the interests of the political or military leadership of Russia or the country in general'.[14] Primakov's warnings were duplicated—and amplified— during the electoral campaign that preceded the Russian parliamentary elections of December 1993, in particular by the quasi-fascistic Zhirinovskii and his misleadingly named Liberal Democratic Party. Traditional Russian imperialistic arguments were finding increasing resonance amongst many citizens—almost certainly more so than would have been the case had the post-communist Russian economy been performing better than it was.

By 1993, some of the applicants for membership of NATO— notably Poland and Slovakia—were stating publicly that they would not be intimidated by a renewed Russian aggressiveness. On the other hand, they initially appeared to accept the fact that most Western governments were unenthusiastic about admitting former members of the Warsaw Pact into NATO too rapidly.

But the success of Zhirinovskii—with his calls to reconstitute the former Russian empire—encouraged leaders such as President Walesa to strengthen their calls for admission to NATO. At the same time, other countries now made their first formal bids for membership—again largely as a reaction to the relatively impressive showing of Zhirinovskii in the December 1993 elections. Thus Lithuania's President Brazauskas made the first formal request for membership from a former Soviet republic in early January 1994, shortly before the NATO summit that was held later that month in Brussels. Clearly, developments within Russia were instilling fear in its former allies, and were encouraging more of them to work harder to gain access to the one military alliance that could realistically be expected to be able to contain future Russian attempts at expansionism.

Yet the West remained apprehensive about admitting the formerly communist states—or even providing security guarantees. Despite the pleas from Walesa, Brazauskas, Slovakian President Kovac and others, President Clinton continued to push his limited 'Partnership for Peace' proposal at the January summit. Under this, which NATO eventually adopted, the former Warsaw Treaty Organisation applicants would be permitted to participate in some NATO exercises and formally to express security concerns to NATO—but little else. Only time will tell whether or not the USA was justified in arguing at the time of the summit that this was not an appeasement of the extremists in Russia, but rather a way of reducing their attractiveness to Russian voters by neither overreacting to them nor appearing to be the very threat Primakov and Zhirinovskii had warned against.[15]

Despite the recent tensions between Russia and its former allies, a number of treaties of various kinds have been signed and ratified since the collapse of communism and the USSR. For example, Russia now has Friendship and Cooperation Treaties with Bulgaria, ratified in April 1993, and the Czech Republic and Slovakia, signed in August 1993. Even military cooperation agreements have been signed (for example with Poland, in July 1993)—although it should be borne in mind that several east European countries have also signed such agreements with Germany, for example Hungary in April 1993 and Poland in June 1993, so that the significance of the agreements with Russia should not be exaggerated or seen out of context. Indeed, Russia itself signed a military cooperation agreement with Germany in April 1993, before the marked increase of nationalist and military influence within Russia in the latter part of 1993.

Economic and Trade Relations

During the communist era, economic and trade leverage was often seen as another way in which the USSR exercised domination over its East European partners—although it should be noted that the Soviets often appeared to be paying an economic price for their political influence.

The principal formal mechanism through which the USSR conducted trade with, and exercised influence over the domestic economic policies of, its East European partners was the Council for Mutual Economic Assistance. This was a larger organisation than the Warsaw Treaty Organisation, in that it included three countries beyond Europe (Cuba, Mongolia, and Vietnam). As happened with the Warsaw Treaty Organisation, the emergence of post-communism soon led to a fundamental questioning of the Council for Mutual Economic Assistance.

Perhaps the most significant indication of this came at the January 1991 meeting of the Council for Mutual Economic Assistance Executive Committee, held in Moscow. At this, the Executive announced its approval of ' ... proposals for the radical overhaul of the system of economic cooperation by member states, including a draft charter for a new organisation'. In essence, it was agreed to disband the Council for Mutual Economic Assistance and to replace it with a new body, the Organisation for International Economic Cooperation. Yugoslavia and Albania were to be invited to join this. The Organisation for International Economic Cooperation was to be based in Budapest, and to have as one of its principal tasks the solution of the ownership wrangle over the two major jointly-owned Council for Mutual Economic Assistance institutions, the Bank for Investment and the Bank for Economic Cooperation. The January 1991 meeting agreed on a six-month budget, although this was directed more to the closing down of the Council for Mutual Economic Assistance than to the establishment of the Organisation for International Economic Cooperation.

But the decision to establish the Organisation for International Economic Cooperation was taken within days of the introduction of compulsory hard-currency trading between members of the Council for Mutual Economic Assistance. This replaced the system of conducting transactions in transferable roubles, which were now abolished. The transfer to the new system meant that the Council for Mutual Economic Assistance countries now needed to generate far more hard currency than previously—and this almost necessarily had the effect of encouraging the formerly communist states to look westwards rather than eastwards. Typical was the Hungarian parliament, which voted within days of the establishment of the Organisation for International Economic Cooperation to seek closer ties with both the Council of Europe and the European Community. Given this westward imperative—plus the ramifications of the 'double rejective revolution'—it is hardly surprising that the Organisation for International Economic Cooperation soon faded. In its place, former member-states of the Council for Mutual Economic Assistance have tended to opt for one or both of two main paths.

First, many of them have been forming regional economic groupings, of differing levels of integration; some of these comprise exclusively or overwhelmingly formerly communist states, whilst others include a number of Western states. So many of these have been formed in the early-1990s that it would take too much space to attempt a comprehensive listing here. However, among the more significant have been the Central European Initiative (originally consisting of Austria, Czecho-Slovakia, Hungary, Italy, Poland, Slovenia and Croatia—formed in 1992 on the basis of what started life as the Danube-Adria Group in November 1989); the Black Sea Economic Cooperation Project (including Bulgaria, Romania and Russia—formed in February 1992, on the basis of a 1989 Turkish proposal); the Council of Baltic States (which incorporates ten states in the Baltic region, including Poland, the three Baltic States and Russia—established in March 1992 following a German-Danish initiative); the Carpathian Euroregion (involving Hungary, Ukraine and Poland, with Slovakia as an associate member and Romania as an observer—created in February 1993); the Estonian-Latvian-Lithuanian Free Trade Agreement, signed in September 1993; and the Central European Free Trade Agreement (formed on the basis of the Visegrad Four in December 1992, although other countries, such as Ukraine, have expressed an interest in joining).[16] Some of these organisations (for example the Council of Baltic States, the Central European Free Trade Agreement) had as one of their primary aims the facilitation of linkages with the European Community/European Union, invariably with the ultimate goal of full membership of this.

Second, both individual and groups of post-communist countries have also made concerted efforts to move closer to Western European economic groupings. Thus the European Free Trade Association signed Free Trade Agreements with Bulgaria and Hungary in March 1993, following similar agreements with Czecho-Slovakia in March 1992 and with Poland and Romania in December 1992.[17] Although the Free Trade Agreements invariably contain exclusion clauses, they symbolise a commitment on both sides to much freer trade in the future. There have also been looser Declarations on Cooperation between the European Free Trade Association and some of the other post-communist countries, for example Slovenia in May 1992 and Albania in December 1992. However, for most, possibly all, European post-communist states, the European Free Trade Association is not as important in the long run as the European Union. Progress has been made here, too, in the 1990s. Thus Association Agreements with the European Community were signed by Czecho-Slovakia, Hungary and Poland in December 1991, by Romania in February 1993 and by Bulgaria in March 1993. Looser Trade and Economic Cooperation Agreements—under which the European Community agreed to reduce a number of import quotas, and to render development assistance—were signed with Albania and the Baltic States in May 1992, and with Slovenia in April 1993. Although there is no question that the European Union is perceived by the post-communist states as being more important in the long run than the European Free Trade Association, the formation of the European Economic Area in March 1993 has meant that closer cooperation with the European Free Trade Association can be a back-door entry to closer integration with the European Union.

The last few paragraphs strongly suggest a move by the former East European members of the Council for Mutual Economic Assistance away from Russia and towards the West. But it seems clear that Russia has itself been moving rapidly away from its former Council for Mutual Economic Assistance partners, as implied by the following trade statistics. In 1980, 49.0% of Soviet exports went to Council for Mutual Economic Assistance partners, while 48.2% of Soviet imports came from them. The respective figures for 1989 were 55.2% and 56.3%. But in the first half of 1992, only 21.2% of Russian exports went to its former Council for Mutual Economic Assistance partners, and a mere 15.4% of imports were from these countries. In the first half of 1993, the figures had dropped even further, to 18.6% and 12.9% respectively. Although it is difficult to compare data directly because they refer to money value (and are thus affected by exchange rates, and the conversion to hard-currency transactions within the Council for Mutual Economic Assistance at the beginning of 1991), there can be little doubt that the above statistics reflect an unambiguous reorientation in Russian foreign trading practices.

Despite the above developments, the growing reservations of the West that were identified in the section on military relations are also very visible in the economic and trade area. There are, in short, problems for the east European states in their endeavours to move closer to the West; these could have long-term implications for relations with Russia.

One of the most obvious signs of and reasons for these difficulties is the strengthening 'fortress Europe' mentality within the European Union. The difficulties the European Community experienced in having the Maastricht Treaty adopted by individual member-states were serious enough with only twelve members; as the European Union expands to fifteen or sixteen members by the mid-1990s, the potential for differences to emerge becomes even greater. The 'fortress' mentality has almost certainly been further exacerbated by the recession that has hit Europe in the 1990s. With the exception of the United Kingdom, it appeared at the beginning of the 1990s that Europe might escape the economic troubles that, most notably, the USA was experiencing. But as the USA appeared to be pulling out of its slump—by 1993—so Europe slid increasingly into one. Of nowhere was this truer than of the powerhouse of Europe, Germany. As economic problems increased, so did social ones; the recession must unquestionably be seen as one of the major reasons for the marked increase in racism and race-related violence in Europe in the 1990s. In such a climate, it is hardly surprising that West European governments are less outward-looking and welcoming than they might otherwise be; this, too, is part of the explanation for the 'fortress Europe' phenomenon.

This attitude has manifested itself in a number of tensions between the European Union and the east European states. Perhaps the best-known case is that of the meat dispute of 1993. On 8 April, the European Community banned the import of meat, live animals and dairy produce from all the countries of Central and Eastern Europe. This was a response to the discovery in Italy of animals that had been imported from Croatia, without the appropriate documentation, and which had foot-and-mouth disease. On the following day, Hungary and Poland retaliated by imposing their own bans on a number of imports from the European Community. Over the next few days, Bulgaria, the Czech Republic and Slovakia followed suit. On 28 April, the European Community lifted the bans on Bulgaria, the Czech Republic, Estonia, Hungary, Romania, Slovakia and Slovenia, after all these countries had accepted a number of conditions. But the ban on Polish imports—from the largest country in the region—was not lifted until mid-July, following protracted and sometimes heated negotiations. Even then, the European Community imposed a minimum price for Polish cherries in West European markets, which the Poles claimed was above the average market price; the Poles believed, with some justification, that the European Community was engaging in unfair competition at their expense.

The 'Polish cherries affair' was but one more example of a deeper underlying tension between the countries of eastern

Europe and the European Community. Despite the various trading agreements between these two groups, a number of sensitive items, including steel and textiles, were excluded. Understandably, several east European states complained about West European protectionism—yet another manifestation of the 'fortress Europe' mentality. What had by 1993 become particularly galling for many east Europeans was the fact that the trade imbalance between their own countries and the European Community was running heavily in the latter's favour. Moreover, whilst exports from the European Community to eastern Europe increased in 1992 by approximately 20% in comparison with 1991, exports in the other direction were up 'only' 11%. Whilst this is to be expected when less developed economies seek rapid modernisation and technological upgrading, it can also be readily appreciated why this would rub salt into the already sore wounds of the early post-communist states.

The European Community/European Union is not the only major Western institution to have irritated some of the east European states in the early 1990s because of what the latter perceive to be either unfair treatment or excessive interference in their internal affairs. Both the IMF and the World Bank have also had altercations with several of these states. In October 1991, for instance, Poland's extended credit facility was suspended. In January-February 1993, an IMF delegation spent two weeks in Hungary, at the end of which it refused to lift a temporary ban on a previously agreed credit arrangement, on the grounds that the Hungarian government was permitting what the IMF considered to be too large a deficit. And in July 1993, an IMF delegation to Romania also censured the Romanian government for inadequate progress in restructuring state enterprises and lowering inflation.

The above examples help to explain why the 'turn to the West' by so many post-communist states has proven to be more problematical than they had expected. If one adds to this the fact that former communists are increasing their influence in several of these states,[18] it might appear likely that there will be at least a partial return to the *status quo ante* in terms of the relations between Russia and its former allies/partners.

Conclusions

At the beginning of this chapter, two contextual aspects of the relations between Russia and its formerly communist neighbours— the 'double-rejective revolution', and global recession and instability—were identified. Whereas the first of these might initially lead to the inference that the post-communist states of eastern Europe would do everything possible to distance themselves from Russia, it should not be overlooked that Russia itself is no longer either communist or the centre of an empire. Elements of both the communist legacy and the imperialistic past still exist, of course—as borne out clearly in the December 1993 parliamentary elections—but it would be premature to argue that they have now become dominant within Russia. It is perhaps more obvious why the second contextual variable would lead one to question the 'obvious' notion that the countries of the former external empire would do anything to distance themselves as much as possible from Russia. After all, when one looks beyond ideological and nationalistic rhetoric, it becomes clear that there are sound reasons why the post-communist states of Europe need at least to maintain a *modus vivendi* with Russia. The latter is one of the world's richest countries in terms of resources, even if the extraction and distribution of these is presently being seriously hampered by Russia's political instability. Many of the post-communist countries could in the future find that Russia would be the best source of extracted products and energy.

A second reason for the continuation of some sort of relationship is the fact that Russia represents a huge consumer market. Again, the current (serious) problems within Russia can blind observers to the fact that sooner or later Russia is going to 'turn the corner' economically. When it does, it will need to import all sorts of goods, both manufacturing and consumer. Given the lower labour costs in eastern Europe, the fact that a number of factories there are being re-equipped to the latest international standards, and the mutual knowledge of each other's way of conducting business, it is quite likely that the post-communist states will find Russia a willing purchaser of their export goods.

This all said, there are also reasons for arguing that the former external empire might become increasingly marginalised—effectively excluded not only from Western markets if the latter become increasingly *de facto* inward-looking and protectionist, but also from the Russian market. One reason this could happen is because the Russians are almost certainly more concerned with what used to be called their 'internal empire' (that is the states that used to comprise the USSR—all of which, except for the Baltic States, are currently members of the Commonwealth of Independent States) than with the former external empire. Moreover, in the longer term, the West could well feel that Russia, and the Commonwealth of Independent States, are more important than the former external empire, if a choice has to be made. This again relates to Russia's natural resources and the size of its market. But it also relates to the fact that Russia is still a major nuclear power, and could again become a threat to the West.

This last issue leads on to another important point—namely that Russia and the various parts of Europe are currently at a potentially dangerous crossroads. Clearly, Russia remains in a highly volatile state; ironically, the December 1993 elections could result in even worse conflicts between the Presidency and Parliament than those that resulted in the bloody events of October 1993. The parliamentarians (members of the new State Duma and the Council of the Federation) could justifiably argue that they are far more legitimate than were the members of the old Congress of People's Deputies and Supreme Soviet—and that the Russian president therefore has even less justification in attempting to overrule them or even shut them down when they disagree with him. Moreover, whilst there can be no question that some of the manifestations of nationalism in the former external empire are both nasty (racist) and threaten neighbours, the fact is that the resurgence of an aggressive, expansionist Russian nationalism is potentially far more dangerous to the world order. Yeltsin's change of policy towards membership of NATO by former members of the Warsaw Treaty Organisation almost certainly reflects, on one level, his greater dependence on the Russian military since September 1993. Given that the Russian military has been so humiliated and demoralised in recent years, many officers may now feel that the time has come to reassert both themselves and their country on the world stage. If Yeltsin will not at least partially accommodate them, then some may well be attracted to Zhirinovskii. The dangers inherent in such a development are clear.

At the same time as Russia is unstable, the West is showing signs of confusion over how best to deal with the tensions and contradictions of the post-communist world generally. The January 1994 NATO decision to grant Eastern European countries only very limited connections with the alliance (via the Partnership for Peace policy) can be interpreted from this perspective. The West does not wish to appear to be taking sides too clearly in the conflicts between Russia and its former allies; as mentioned above, several of the latter have felt themselves to be under a far greater threat from Russia than was the case before the Russian elections. Given their avowed expansionist aims, the fact that the State Duma was prepared to give Zhirinovskii's party the chair of a committee for 'geopolitical' affairs in January 1994 makes it clear just why these fears cannot be too readily dismissed. Whether the West will be able to continue to sit on the fence indefinitely remains to be seen.

The last few paragraphs have tended to focus on the more pessimistic scenarios of Russia's relations with its former external empire, and the position of both in Europe and the world. But not to refer to some of the more optimistic developments of recent times would be to paint a distorted picture.

One of the potentially most encouraging signs was the agreement on the GATT, eventually adopted on 15 December 1993 after more than seven years of the Uruguay round of negotiations. If this is indeed implemented, it should give a boost to the economies of eastern Europe, and even—eventually—to Russia and the Commonwealth of Independent States.[19] Another encouraging sign is the fact that Poland and the Czech Republic, at least, now seem to have reversed the downward economic trend that marked the early stages of all the post-communist states. If these two can maintain this trend, and if they are joined by others, this could provide ammunition for those in Russia wanting to accelerate and deepen economic reform. If their policies are implemented and help to improve Russian economic performance, this will almost certainly weaken the position of both the communists and the nationalists within Russia—which will bring some relief to eastern Europe. Finally, the fact that the US economy seemed by early 1994 to be continuing the modest but definite growth it had been experiencing since 1992-1993 suggested that the global recession might really be over. If one bears in mind that several Asian economies were also showing strength, this impression is heightened. This is not to deny that there was a real recession and signs of instability in many parts of Europe; but if other significant economies are improving, there is reason for cautious optimism that Europe will begin to pull out of its economic trough in the relatively near future and, as a corollary, become politically more stable.

None of these potentially positive variables should lead to a feeling of complacency. The current situation in Russia is cause for real concern, not only for the east Europeans. On the other hand, it would at this point still be premature to assume that the current relationship between Russia and its former external empire is in essence not too dissimilar from that between Nazi Germany and various central European countries in the late-1930s. The West must do everything possible to avoid such a similarity arising.

Notes

I would like to thank the members of the Department of Political Science, University of Western Australia—in particular Campbell Sharman, Bob Dowse, Jeremy Moon and Sara Gomm—for having provided me with both computing facilities and a very pleasant working environment during January 1994 in Perth, where work on the final version of this chapter was carried out.

1   For stylistic reasons, this article refers to the 'former external empire'. In fact, the chapter deals exclusively with the European part of that empire as it was by the 1980s; there is no consideration here of Vietnam, Mongolia, Cuba or any other country that might once have been considered part of that empire (for example Albania until the 1960s). In this chapter, 'Eastern Europe' refers to the former communist states in the eastern part of Europe, excluding all parts of the USSR, whereas 'eastern Europe' refers to the same countries—or their successors—in the post-communist era. I have opted not to use the term East Central Europe, *inter alia* because, by some definitions, this excludes the Balkan states. An alternative term to 'external empire' is 'outer empire'; for an example of this usage, plus an analysis of the breakdown of this empire from the mid-1980s, see Alex Pravda (ed.), *The End of the Outer Empire: Soviet-East European Relations in Transition, 1985-90* (London: Royal Institute of International Affairs and Sage, 1992).

2   On the ending of the Cold War see for example John Lewis Gaddis, 'Toward the Post-Cold War World', *Foreign Affairs*, vol.70, no. 2, Spring 1991, pp.102-122; William Pfaff, 'Redefining World Power', *Foreign Affairs*, vol.70, no. 1, 1991, pp.34-48; Michael J. Hogan (ed.), *The End of the Cold War: Its Meaning and Implications* (Cambridge: Cambridge University Press, 1992).

3   See Leslie Holmes, *The End of Communist Power: Anti-Corruption Campaigns and Legitimation Crisis* (New York: Oxford University Press, 1993), especially pp.xi and 21-22.

4   It should be noted that the rejection within the USSR was mainly of Russian hegemony. Although Russia itself did not experience the second rejection in the same way as the other countries, it did lose a role—that of being an imperial power. In this sense, there was a double transition, even if it was not identical to that elsewhere.

5   In this paper, I shall refer to the European Community for matters pertaining to the period up to, but not beyond, November 1993; to the European Union for matters pertaining to the period since November 1993; and to the European Community/European Union for matters that straddle both periods.

6   For one of the most accessible and concise overviews of privatisation see M. Valencia and P. Frankl, 'Power to the People?', *Business Central Europe*, vol.1, no.5, October 1993, pp.60-62. For more detailed analyses, see for example R. Frydman, A. Rapaczynski, J. Earle *et al*, *The Privatization Process in Central Europe* (London: Central European University Press, 1993) and Anders Åslund and Richard Layard (eds.), *Changing the Economic System in Russia* (London: Pinter, 1993), especially pp.89-124.

7   See Robin Alison Remington, *The Warsaw Pact: Case Studies in Communist Conflict Resolution* (Cambridge: The MIT Press, 1971).

8   On the death of the Warsaw Treaty Organisation and the orientation of some of the east European states towards NATO see Alfred A. Reisch, 'Central and Eastern Europe's Quest for NATO membership', *RFE/RL Research Report*, vol.2, no.28, 9 July 1993, pp.33-47.

9   See for example *Pravda*, 25 January 1991, p. 4.

10 *Izvestiia*, 23 January 1991, p. 5.

11 *Pravda*, 18 February 1991, p. 5.

12 On Yeltsin's visits to some of the Central European states in August 1993 see Jan B. de Weydenthal, 'Russia Mends Fences with Poland, the Czech Republic and Slovakia', *RFE/RL Research Report*, vol.2, no.36 10 September 1993, pp.33-36.

13 See *International Herald Tribune*, 26 November 1993, pp.1-2.

14 *International Herald Tribune*, 26 November 1993, p.2.

15 By March 1994, 14 post-communist states had signed the Partnership for Peace agreement. Russia itself had by this stage indicated its intention to join. However, there were clear signs of disagreement on this issue at the top of the Russian political system, and it remains to be seen (as of early April 1994) whether or not Russia actually will sign.

16 For listings and analysis of these organisations see for example Douglas L. Clarke, 'Europe's Changing Constellations', *RFE/RL Research Report*, vol.2, no.37, 17 September 1993, pp.13-15; Alfred A. Reisch, 'The Central European Initiative: To Be or Not To Be?', *RFE/RL Research Report*, vol.2, no.34, 27 August 1993, pp.30-37; Milada Anna Vachudova, 'The Visegrad Four: No Alternative to Cooperation?', *RFE/RL Research Report*, vol.2, no.34, 27 August 1993, pp.38-47; G. Bakos, 'After COMECON: A Free Trade Area in Central Europe?', *Europe-Asia Studies*, vol.45, no.6, 1993, pp.1025-1044.

17 It should be noted that Czechia and Slovakia signed similar agreements individually in April 1993.

18 See for example D. Meth-Cohn, P. Simpson, C. Woodard and S. Biswas, 'The New Left', *Business Central Europe*, vol.1, no.6, November 1993, pp.7-9.

19 For a detailed analysis of the position of the post-communist states vis-a-vis GATT see L. A. Haus, *Globalizing GATT: The Soviet Union's Successor States, Eastern Europe and the International Treaty System* (Washington DC: The Brookings Institution, 1992).

9 RUSSIA AND CENTRAL ASIA

AMIN SAIKAL

In the short space of time since the collapse of the Soviet Union in late December 1991, Russia's policy towards Central Asia has come full circle. After an initial period of transitional neglect, during which certain regional powers, namely Turkey, Iran, Saudi Arabia and Pakistan, and some Western powers, especially the United States, attempted to fill the power vacuum created by the breakup of the USSR, Russia has lately made a concerted effort to regain some of the lost ground in the former Soviet Muslim republics. In an attempt to deter other powers from filling the gap, Russia has taken a series of firm steps which point to an increasingly assertive foreign policy and which lay the foundations for what could crystallise as Russia's Central Asia policy. Whatever the domestic pressures behind this development, President Boris Yeltsin and his Foreign Minister Andrei Kozyrev have personally been obliged to support this change, realising that no matter how much Russia needs closer ties with the West, practical political and security considerations may require that it seek to maintain a determining influence in Central Asia.

Obviously a variety of factors have motivated them in this direction, but perhaps none more so than their growing concern about a perceived threat from two sources: ethnonationalism and Islamic radicalism. In the process, they have supported recycled ruling communist groups in most of the Central Asian republics as the best instruments through which to achieve their objectives. Yeltsin's suppression of his parliamentary opponents in September-October 1993 and the outcome of the subsequent December election for a new parliament have created more pressure on him to maintain his reassertive efforts. Whereas the first act made Yeltsin excessively beholden to the military, which had been unhappy about Russia's loss of control over Central Asia, the election enabled the ultra-nationalist 'Liberal Democratic' Party of Vladimir Zhirinovskii to emerge with the largest number of votes for a party list, with an avowed aim to restore Russia's rule over former Soviet territories and combat Islamic radicalism in all its forms. The danger is that while the Yeltsin leadership may be committed to democratising Russia, its policy approach to Central Asia aims at contrary objectives in that region.

This chapter has a three-fold purpose: the first is to look at the chaos which engulfed Russian policy towards Central Asia in the wake of the disintegration of the USSR; the second is to outline some of the developments which point to the shape of a Russian

Central Asian policy; and the third is to evaluate the two main factors of concern which have motivated Russian behaviour towards Central Asia, and to examine Russia's responses to such perceived threats. 'Central Asia', as the expression is used in this chapter, refers to the five Muslim republics of the former USSR—Kazakhstan, Uzbekistan, Turkmenistan, Kyrgyzstan, and Tajikistan—as well as Afghanistan, still striving to recover from the traumas inflicted by the USSR's decade-long military presence.

Policy disarray

The initial disarray in Russia's foreign policy in general and in its behaviour towards the Central Asian Muslim states in particular, was easily discernible and explicable. It stemmed partly from a state of general confusion and a lack of direction which not surprisingly beset Moscow in the wake of the USSR's disintegration, but largely from a divide between two rival groups which had become active ever since the dying days of the Soviet Union and now sought to control Russian foreign policy: the 'Atlanticists' and 'Eurasianists'.

In general, the 'Atlanticists', led by Yeltsin and Kozyrev, emphasised the significance of Russia's democratic and capitalist transformation, and its identification with the North and partnership with the West as a necessary condition for this transformation and for Russia's effective participation in the creation of a new world order. As such, they felt that Russia's conduct of its relations with the South should be premised upon these imperatives. In this scheme of thinking, the 'Atlanticists' did not ignore the importance of the Central Asian states, especially given their awareness of the presence of various but substantial Russian minorities in those republics. They simply eschewed any policy of reassertiveness which could possibly undermine their efforts to achieve their wider goal of partnership with the West. They seemed to rely on the organic links of the states with Russia and on the presence of the Russian forces in them from Soviet days to maintain a necessary degree of influence in the region as a whole.

On the other hand, the 'Eurasianists', whose initial main spokesman emerged in the person of Russian State Counsellor Sergei Stankevich, opposed the idea of exclusive alliance with the West and criticised 'Atlanticists' for abandoning the South. They argued that Russia's natural and traditional allies were in the South rather than in the West. They warned against alienating China, the Muslim world—more importantly its Middle Eastern component—and India, and urged that Russia should develop its relations with the South on the basis of its own assessment of political developments, that is, independently of Western perceptions, in that part of the world.[1] Thus, they attached greater importance to the need for Russia to remain actively involved in Central Asia, which they saw as significant to Russia's security and economic links to Asia and the Middle East. Further, they called for a more subtle approach, distinct from that of the West, to handling relations with the new states. Various versions of this vision subsequently gained currency among the opponents of Yeltsin inside and outside the Supreme Soviet, including Vice-President Aleksandr Rutskoi and Parliamentary Chairman Ruslan Khasbulatov, as they attempted to exert greater legislative control over foreign policy.[2]

The struggle between these competing visions, which soon found supporters in the foreign, defence and trade ministries, laid an important foundation for diversity in Russia's policy approach. As the struggle intensified, however, Yeltsin and Kozyrev found it necessary to embrace some of the formulations of their opponents by emphasising the need for 'adaptation in the world community', with the maintenance of Russia's status as 'a great power', 'with global and regional interests', and good relations with both East and West on the basis of what best served "Russian national interests" as 'the only ideology of ... foreign policy'.[3] What as a consequence emerged to govern Russia's process of policy formulation towards Central Asia was a blend of these competing visions, underlined by a considerable degree of confusion and inactivism.

At first, the Yeltsin leadership failed to formulate a clear policy towards Central Asia. While showing from the start a preference for bonding the former Soviet republics within the broad framework of the Commonwealth of Independent States (CIS) under Russia's leadership, it could not adopt firm steps to fill the vacuum that the collapse of Soviet power created for the Central Asian republics. The fact that it initially sought to build the CIS on the basis of an alliance with nuclear and mainly Slavic Ukraine and Belarus, and a nuclear and demographically Russian-driven Kazakhstan caused the leaderships of Tajikistan, Turkmenistan, Uzbekistan, and to some extent Kyrgyzstan to feel that thenceforth Russia would focus more on those ex-Soviet republics which would ethnically and strategically serve Russia's new broader goal of internal democratisation and external partnership with the West, particularly the United States.

This confronted these leaderships—which (except in Kyrgyzstan) were dominated either by communists or reformed communists—with serious dilemmas as to how to overcome their ideological vacuum, on the one hand, and cope with problems normally associated with transition to independence and with redefinition of national identity, on the other. Worried about their lack of domestic legitimacy—as few of them had been elected on a popular, democratic basis—and lack of resources to meet the cost of transition to independence as well as the rising expectations of their populations for better living standards and for more appropriate definition of their national identities, especially in relation to Islam, they adopted what subsequently emerged as a two-pronged approach, although varying in character from state to state. First, with the exception of Kyrgyzstan to a degree, they continued to maintain essentially their iron-fisted communist political systems, though in different garbs, and clung on to remnants of Soviet military and security power in their territories as a major source of protection.[4] Yet, second, in order to meet their non-military needs and impress upon their populations that they were now dedicated not to communist but democratic principles, they found themselves with little choice but to give a liberal slant to their ideological rhetoric and open up to the outside world.[5]

This, in interaction with the factor of the power vacuum, immediately exposed the republics to regional power rivalries and Islamic influences. Of the regional powers, Iran, Turkey, Pakistan, and Saudi Arabia now found a new arena where they could promote their rival regional interests. With the victory of the *Mujahideen* over the Soviet-installed government of Najibullah in Afghanistan in April 1992, this rivalry raised the spectre of what some of the Russians had feared. That was the threat of the spread of Islamic radicalism—or what is generally referred to in the West as 'Islamic fundamentalism'—from Iran and Afghanistan into the Central Asian states and to Russia's own restive Muslim minorities, especially in Tatarstan. It is important to be reminded that it may have been a perception of such a threat which also figured as a factor behind the December 1979 Soviet invasion of Afghanistan.

Meanwhile, there was a highly publicised upsurge in the US concern under President George Bush about what was called the growth of 'Iranian-backed Islamic fundamentalism' in the Middle East and the vulnerability of the former Soviet Muslim republics to it. This entailed two important results. First, it enabled Washington and its allies, particularly Israel, to amplify on their demonisation of the Iranian Islamic regime, with certain presidential aides warning against the possibility of the growth of an Islamic confederation, stretching from Pakistan to Central Asia to Iran to Turkey, against Western and by implication Russian interests in the region.[6] The Bush Administration promptly established diplomatic missions in all of the five Central Asian republics, with Secretary of State James Baker making a well-publicised tour of the republics in early 1992, urging their leaders to look to Turkey for the best model of development rather than to Iran, which he declared to be an 'outlaw state'.[7] Second, it affected the balance in the foreign policy debate in Moscow. While causing the Yeltsin camp to became more concerned about the potential for Islamic radicalism in Central Asia, it played into the hands of the military and opposition forces to increase pressure on Yeltsin to shift to a policy of reassertion towards Central Asia.

However, the events which proved most instrumental in pushing the Yeltsin camp further towards this shift were the enlargement of old and advent of new ethnonationalist conflicts in the Caucasus, particularly in the Muslim republic of Azerbaijan, and the eruption by mid-1992 of a serious conflict in Tajikistan. The latter quickly became a venue for a fierce power struggle between the ruling communist government of President Nabiev and the opposition, led by an alliance of Islamists and democrats. In September 1992, the alliance wrested power from the communists in Dushanbe and the Chairman of the Tajik Supreme Soviet, Akbar Shah Iskandarov, became Acting President, with the commitment to create the necessary conditions for a democratically elected government. The Islamic regimes of Iran and Afghanistan (especially that of the latter from where certain *Mujahideen* groups had provided some help to their Tajik counterparts) naturally not only voiced support for the new Iskandarov government but also privately applauded the role of the Islamists in the development.[8]

A policy begins to take shape

This development marked a turning point. It alerted the Yeltsin camp to the possibility that Russia was losing influence fast in favour of other powers in Central Asia, that it could no longer rely on the residue of Soviet power and mechanisms of control to arrest this situation; and that if it failed to take concrete steps to stem the rise in the tide of political Islam it could face a serious threat to its national security and integrity. The Tajikistan conflict also sent alarming signals to the leaderships of the neighbouring Muslim republics, especially Uzbekistan, where President Islam Karimov has continued to maintain a communist dictatorship, with little sign of willingness to tolerate any form of opposition.[9] Supported to some degree by the other Muslim republics, Karimov adopted two firm intertwined policy measures: (1) to help the Tajik communists to regain power and to neutralise any Islamic influence from Afghanistan; (2) to reinforce Russia's fear of a radical Islamic-driven instability in Central Asia, stimulating it to take on more active responsibility for the defence of its former Muslim republics.

While providing prompt direct military assistance to the Tajik communists, including authorising the Uzbek air force to bomb various parts of Tajikistan in December 1992 and participating in 'mopping up operations' in the following January after they had wrested power, Karimov publicly blamed the Afghan *Mujahideen* for the Tajikistan conflict and warned against the Islamic threat from Afghanistan. Addressing the United Nations General Assembly in March 1993, he asserted that 'the slightest attempt against the inviolability of the borders of Tajikistan will be treated as a direct menace to the sovereignty of all Central Asian states'.[10] Taking advantage of the *Mujahideen*'s factional fighting, he welcomed the former Afghan Uzbek communist warlord, General Rashid Dostam, who had secured a strong enclave among Afghanistan's Uzbek minority in the vicinity of the country's northern city of Mazar-i-Sharif,[11] bordering Uzbekistan, Tajikistan and Turkmenistan, as a fraternal ally against cross-border attacks on Tajikistan by Afghanistan-based Tajik *Mujahideen*. The two sides also reportedly 'agreed to create a buffer state between Kabul and the Afghan border with Tajikistan and Uzbekistan'.[12]

It is worth noting that it was Dostam's initial defection to Ahmad Shah Massoud, the celebrated Tajik commander of the moderate *Mujahideen* group, the *Jamiat-i Islami Afghanistan*, that had led to the overthrow of Najibullah. However, from early 1993, Dostam cooled off his relations with Massoud and sought closer ties with Massoud's Pushtun arch-rival, the renegade radical Islamic 'Prime Minister' in the *Mujahideen* government, Gulbuddin Hekmatyar—although the latter had used the Uzbek warlord's initial defection to denounce Massoud as a traitor and to rocket Kabul intermittently in pursuit of his longstanding goal to become the absolute ruler of Afghanistan. Supported by many former leading Afghan communists, including Babrak Karmal, the first Soviet-installed President of Afghanistan (1979-1986) who from 1992 frequently used Uzbekistan as a haven, Dostam forged an alliance with Hekmatyar, who was supported by Pakistan's military intelligence (ISI). Dostam did so in spite of the fact that the Uzbeks culturally share more in common with the Tajiks— historically the second largest ethnic group in Afghanistan, than with the traditionally largest, but highly tribalised, Pushtuns.[13]

The extent of the Hekmatyar-Dostam alliance became fully evident when the two sides launched a massive attack on Kabul on 1 January 1994 to topple President Burhanuddin Rabbani's Islamic government, of which Massoud is the supreme military leader. Although unsuccessful in their attempt, they inflicted a protracted war on the already battle-ravaged capital, causing horrendous human and material losses, and confronting the dwindling Kabul citizens for the first time in the fifteen-year long Afghan conflict with a distinct possibility of massive starvation. In the fight for Kabul, Dostam has reportedly enjoyed increased logistic and material support from Uzbekistan, including provision of base facilities at the Termez airport for the section of the Afghan air force that Dostam inherited in the wake of the collapse of Najibullah's regime. Despite its repeated initial denial, Karimov has lately made the admission that Uzbekistan supplies electricity and energy to Dostam.[14] The whole development has been a clear illustration of Karimov's determination to protect the rule of recycled communists in Central Asia and ensure that Afghanistan remains embroiled in domestic fighting, so that it will be unable to provide inspiration to Islamic forces either in Tajikistan or in any of its neighbours.[15]

However, Karimov's interventionist efforts would not have gained strength if it had not been for the fact that they were in tune with the changing policy thinking in Moscow. While echoing Karimov's allegation of Afghan involvement in the Tajikistan conflict, the Yeltsin leadership, with pressure from the military and KGB, in October 1992 ordered a reinforcement of Russian forces both inside Tajikistan and on the border of Tajikistan with Afghanistan, to intervene on behalf of the fallen Tajik communists, and ensure the inviolability of the Afghan-Tajik border. This Russian intervention, coordinated with that of Uzbekistan, proved instrumental in enabling the communists to regain power under the leadership of Imamali Rakhmanov, who immediately banned all forms of opposition activity and moved with all dictatorial powers necessary to establish his rule.

Russia assumed a key role as the protector of Rakhmanov's government. In early 1993, Russia augmented its forces in Tajikistan—Foreign Minister Kozyrev later quoted a figure of 15,000 Russian troops in Tajikistan, and urged that 'several thousands more' should be sent[16]—and declared, with the support of other Muslim republics, the Tajik-Afghan border as the border of the CIS and therefore within the legitimate right of Russia to protect it. It carried out numerous cross-border air operations against Afghanistan either in retaliation for alleged Afghan help to Tajik Islamists or in hot pursuit of the latter who fled Rakhmanov's suppression. As a result, hundreds of Afghans were killed and many more displaced, not to mention some 60,000 Tajiks who sought refuge in the war-torn Afghanistan. Ironically, some traditionally pro-Russian analysts still seek to depict these Russian actions as non-interventionist, designed mainly to 'to protect fleeing Russian civilians and evacuate refugees rather than to seek to change the political map. Although these were undeniably "colonial" operations, they were part of a general strategic withdrawal. They were not intended to preserve an empire which Russians recognized was finished'.[17]

Although both Afghanistan and Tajikistan subsequently declared a willingness to normalise relations, neither is the Tajikistan problem resolved, nor is there any sign of Russia's reducing its level of direct military involvement in the country. Furthermore, in a vein similar to that of Tashkent, Moscow has accorded increased recognition to Dostam and maintained a large consulate in the warlord's stronghold of Mazar-i-Sharif, serving as a major outlet for expanding ties with him and his organisation, especially since the closure of the Soviet embassy in Kabul. It has also maintained close contacts with some of the other senior members of the former Afghan communist governments, including most importantly Babrak Karmal. While failing to endorse the Dostam-Hekmatyar offensives, in early February 1994 it received one of Dostam's senior aide, General Faizullah, on what was described as 'a secret business' mission. In an interview, Faizullah condemned the Rabbani government as source of a serious Islamic threat to Central Asia, and intimated that the purpose of his mission was to further cooperation between Dostam and Russia.[18] This was despite Moscow's public assertion that it was supportive of a resolution of the Tajikistan problem through dialogue between Rakhmanov and his Islamic opponents, and that it had no interest in interfering in the Afghan conflict.

Meanwhile, to contain further the Tajikistan problem and prevent a repetition of it elsewhere in Central Asia, Russia has adopted a more interventionist posture with an increased effort to reintegrate Central Asian and Russian security within the institutional context of the CIS's collective security, and a series of bilateral security arrangements with individual Central Asian states. It has increasingly sought to give structure and substance to the Treaty on Collective Security which it signed with Tajikistan, Uzbekistan Kazakhstan, Kyrgyzstan, and Armenia in Tashkent on 15 May 1992. This Treaty is a significant one, for articles 1 and 4 make it clear that an aggression on one of the member states will be regarded as an aggression against all the Treaty participants, and that no Treaty participant is allowed to enter any alliance or engage in any action which may be directed against another participating state.

Further, it has sought to reinforce this overall treaty with a number of bilateral security agreements that it reached with the individual Central Asian states following the conclusion of the Treaty on Collective Security. While casting Russia in the role of the security guarantor of the Muslim states, they have included the following. First was the security agreement with

Turkmenistan, signed on 10 June 1992, in whose negotiation the Russian Defence Minister Pavel Grachev was personally involved, and which envisioned the formation of a national army for Turkmenistan under joint command. Although out of deference to Iran, Turkmenistan since then has declared a policy of neutrality, this has not seriously affected its close defence cooperation with Russia, to which the Turkmen leadership has repeatedly looked as guarantor of its security. Second was the security agreement with Tajikistan, signed on 21 July 1992, which the ruling Tajik communists and Russia have subsequently expanded and relied upon to justify Russia's substantial, active military involvement in the republic. Third was the Treaty of Friendship, Cooperation and Mutual Assistance with Kazakhstan, signed on 25 May 1992, which was reaffirmed by Presidents Yeltsin and Nazarbaev on 26 February 1993, with a commitment to enhance it by a decision to sign a 'treaty on military cooperation in order to set up a united defence space and make joint use of military capabilities'. Fourth was the Treaty on the Fundamentals of Interstate Relations, Friendship and Cooperation with Uzbekistan, signed on 30 May 1992, and a number of subsequent agreements in support of implementing this treaty and ensuring full Russo-Uzbek military cooperation as an important pillar of security in Central Asia, as was underlined by Pavel Grachev during his visit to Uzbekistan in February 1993. Fifth was the Friendship and Cooperation Treaty with Kyrgyzstan, signed on 10 June 1992, under which Russia subsequently reaffirmed its position as the guarantor of Kyrgyzstan's security.[19]

Ethnonationalism and Islamic radicalism

A question which needs to be asked at this point is: is the threat from ethnonationalism and Islamic radicalism of the extent to warrant the degree of security involvement that Russia has sought in Central Asia? There is no denying that the potential is there for both of these factors to play major roles. All of the states, without exception, suffer in one form or another from deep-seated ethnic, linguistic, sectarian and territorial differences within and between each other, as well as from problems of political legitimacy and infrastructure development, and a host of other difficulties arising from the process of transition to independence and a market economy. Given this and the countries' geographical and colonial links with Russia on the one hand, and their historical-cultural links with West Asia-Middle East and Turkey on the other, it would be less than realistic to underestimate the potential in the region for instability or for that matter Russia's security concerns about it.

Equally, the region is marked by attributes that make it quite vulnerable to Islamic radicalism, stimulated by forces from within and outside. Of course, the Iranian and Afghan Islamic regimes have a vested interest in enhancing the cause of Islamism in the region, although from varying approaches and with different sectarian objectives; they cannot pretend otherwise, given their ideological commitment to Islam.

The Iranian regime regards Central Asia as an important part of its region of security and interests. It therefore wants to be a vital player in the region and possibly beyond. To this end, Tehran has been quick off the mark to establish full diplomatic relations with the newly independent Muslim states, to seek close bilateral and regional cultural and economic ties and cooperation. 'It has offered the republics outlets and pipelines for shipping their energy products, as well as overland rail routes and prospective port connections for improving their international trade.' It has also played an important role in organising the Economic Cooperation Organisation (ECO) as 'the first step towards an Islamic political and economic alliance in South West Asia'.[20] Further, it has been eager to develop, if possible, ideological links with Islamic groups and movements in those states. It has actively sought to fashion its approach as an extension of its wider support for groups such as the *Hezbi Wahdat* (or Party of Unity) in Afghanistan or the Islamic National Front in the Sudan or the Islamic Salvation Front (FIS) in Algeria; and of its geopolitical intrigues in competition with rival regional powers, most importantly Saudi Arabia, Turkey and, to some extent, Pakistan.

Similarly, given Afghanistan's extensive cross-border ethnic-linguistic and sectarian ties with Tajikistan, Uzbekistan and Turkmenistan, the Afghan Islamic regime cannot sit passive in the face of events in these republics. Thus, the regime has sympathised with the Tajik Islamists and provided humanitarian and some logistic help to those of them who have fled to Afghanistan. Certain *Mujahideen* groups have also given some military training and light arms to the Tajik *Mujahideen*. Even if the government were not involved in such activities, the people of northern Afghanistan, a majority of whom are of Tajik origins, would have organised their own assistance.

However, it is important not to exaggerate the potential for ethnonationalist conflicts and Islamic radicalism in Central Asia. For a start, the situation varies from republic to republic. For example, whereas in Kazakhstan the almost equal division of the population between native Kazakhs and Russians protects the republic to a considerable extent from national conflict, especially if President Nazarbaev continues to maintain the balance and move in the direction of institutionalising it,[21] in other republics the native populations possess a sufficient degree of numerical dominance and interdependence with their respective national minorities to enable them to avoid serious internal eruptions. This would of course be contingent upon their leaderships acting prudently and promoting the types of political and economic reforms which would minimise the scope for internal dissension and interstate conflicts, as well as for manipulation of their domestic settings and external postures by outside powers for wider ends. Given the fact that all of the republics have limited individual military capacity, even if an interstate conflict does arise it could easily be limited in scope and therefore quickly prove manageable.

As for the factor of Islamic radicalism, it is erroneous to assume that Iran (or Afghanistan) is responsible for the rise in Islamic activism in Tajikistan and for the emergence of Islamic movements in some of the other republics, especially Turkmenistan and Uzbekistan. The Islamic movements that have emerged have had indigenous roots and have been responding to varying national conditions in the region. Political Islam has come to prominence largely because after seventy years of communist suppression, the Muslim majorities in some of these republics have wanted to rediscover the roots of their identity. In the absence of any acceptable state ideology, the only recourse left to the public has been to go back to their religion as one of the strongest identity references. This of course has differed from state to state. Islam's reemergence as source of identity in Tajikistan,[22] is unlikely to be replicated in Kyrgyzstan, where Islam was introduced on the mass level only in the sixteenth century and more recently has had limited success either in eclipsing pre-Islamic Kyrgyz traditions or undermining the effects of the country's seven-decade long process of Sovietisation. In Tajikistan, the leading Islamic figure, Qazi Akbar Turadjanzadeh, was a product of the official Islamic establishment, and has pronounced himself in favour of a secular state. While Islam in Turkmenistan and Uzbekistan is weaker than in Tajikistan as an identity reference, Kazakhstan falls behind all of them. The Kazakhs experienced greater secularisation and attitudinal change away from Islam under the Soviet rule than probably any of their neighbouring Muslim republics.[23] Ultimately, it is important to note that Islam in all of the republics, with the exception of Tajikistan to some extent, has had more of cultural than religious grip, and this does not augur well for future of radical Islamic groups in pursuit of dominating politics in those states. Even so, the varying degree of Islamic resurgence which has swept the republics cannot be attributed to the Iranian or the *Mujahideen* activities; it could have happened irrespective of whether or not there were Islamic governments in Iran and Afghanistan.[24]

Further, it must be stressed that today the forces of political Islam are as divided as the Muslim world. Sectarian, cultural and political differences have kept them apart, and constantly rendered 'the unity of the Muslim world' a hollow proposition. What exist presently are a variety of political Islamic movements or what some Western writers have called 'Islamic fundamentalisms',[25] with few of them emulating the Iranian leadership but a majority of them pursuing courses of their own according to the demands of the places of their origins. This is illustrated not only by divisions which exist between the Iranian and Afghan Islamic regime, but also between them and the Islamic movements in the Central Asian republics.

It is also a mistake to assume that Afghanistan and Iran in their present conditions are wealthy enough to offer more than a symbolic amount of assistance to the Islamic forces in Central Asia. After a decade of devastating Soviet occupation, Afghanistan today is one of the most socioeconomically dislocated and impoverished countries in the world. It can hardly look after itself, let alone enjoy the capacity to engage in a foreign policy adventure in Central Asia. It is because of this that the Afghan government under President Rabbani has constantly sought to play down the Tajikistan conflict and maintain normal relations with the Central Asian republics. In 1993, he visited both Tajikistan and Uzbekistan to stress his government's desire for good neighbourly relations, and mutual non-interference in each other's internal affairs, as well as for a peaceful resolution of the Tajikistan problem. In return, he welcomed President Rakhmanov on a visit to Kabul, with both sides undertaking to work out their differences peacefully. As far as Rabbani is concerned, it is not in his interest to engage in a foreign policy adventure, which could divert resources from repulsing his opponents and consolidating his regime. This is not to claim that no assistance has been extended from Afghanistan to the Tajik *Mujahideen*. What it does suggest, however, is that the amount of arms delivered to the Tajiks has been of a light type and small in quantity. And even so, many of these arms may have been transferred by Rabbani's rivals, most likely Hekmatyar, who has been keen to drag the government into a conflict in the north, assisting his own objective of seizing power in Kabul.

Although Iran is not in a situation comparable to Afghanistan, its present economic position undermines its capacity to act as an exporter of 'Islamic revolution'. The country's poor economic situation strongly demands that Tehran should do its best to end its international isolation. Since the advent of the Islamic regime in 1979, the country has experienced a steady rise in its national consumption but decline in its national productivity. While its population has grown from some 34 million to nearly 60 million, its oil income has fallen from a pre-revolution level of some $20 billion to $12 billion per annum in 1991 and the shortfall has not been met from any other source. Although official figures put the inflation rate at 18 percent and do not clarify the rate of unemployment, according to unofficial data, Iran's inflation in 1991 was at about 50 percent and unemployment at 30 percent; and its per capita income half of what it was just before the revolution.[26]

Faced with a US policy of containment and Arab policy of limited ties, the country is in dire need of foreign investment and foreign borrowing. Despite an effort by President Rafsanjani it has not been able to reduce its international isolation to the extent to be able to attract more than a very limited amount of capital. In contrast to other oil-rich Gulf states, especially Saudi Arabia, Iran does not have the necessary non-human resources either to engage in large-scale military modernisation or to provide substantial aid to receptive states and movements for regional influence. In spite of the Pentagon's repeated warning about Tehran's military build-up, Iran continues to remain one of the low spenders in the region.[27] This has in fact been instrumental in the Iranian Islamic regime's constant desire to have close ties with Russia as a major source of arms and technological supply. The regime cannot afford but be pliable to Russia and this precludes it from engaging in destabilising actions in Central Asia which could undermine its friendship with Moscow. According to one Russian scholar, 'In the economic aspirations of the reviving Russia, Iran may occupy a truly exceptional place as a linking chain between Russia and that part of the Third World that has not yielded completely to the American dictatorship'.[28]

Conclusion

Most of the conflicts which have occurred so far in Central Asia have been of a political nature. They have stemmed mainly from the problem of political legitimacy which is common to most of the new states in various degrees. Obviously, the country where this has caused the greatest political eruption is Tajikistan. This has been largely due to the fact that the Tajik leadership, at first under Nabiev and subsequently under Rakhmanov, has stubbornly refused to accompany the transition to independence with a substantial move towards political pluralism and creation of a legitimate government. Should this refusal persist, the appeal of Islamism in the republic is likely to grow in stature and popularity as an ideology of resistance, reassertion and salvation. The way forward is to encourage the development of political pluralism and provide for institutionalised processes of legitimation and participation.

The present Russian policy approach to Central Asia has three negative dimensions. First, it is geared towards protecting those forces which remain very much attached to autocratic communist methods of governance and therefore opposed to democratic processes of change and development in the region. In so doing, it undermines the process of free self-determination and democratisation in the area. Second, it is interventionist, not simply for the reason of safeguarding the rights of Russian minorities in the Central Asian states, but going beyond that to create a type of regional geopolitical map which would be highly conducive to the strengthening of Russia's position as an influential player—a position which leaves it wide open to the suggestion that while its empire has collapsed, an imperial mentality still guides its regional behaviour. Third, it rests on a need to exaggerate the threat from Islamic radicalism. It gives more credence to a fear of what the political forces of Islam are capable of achieving than the reality of the situation actually justifies. If Moscow is not careful, Russia's approach could prove counterproductive by fundamentally fostering rather than diminishing the conditions for insecurity and instability in the region, as has been the case with American policy towards West Asia and the Middle East for decades.

Notes

1 For a succinct discussion of these two schools of thinking, see Alexander Rahr, '"Atlanticists" versus "Eurasians" in Russian Foreign Policy', *RFE/RL Research Report*, vol.1, no.22, 29 May 1992, pp.17-22.

2 For a more detailed discussion of schools of foreign policy debate, see Alexei G. Arbatov, 'Russia's Foreign Policy Alternatives', *International Security*, vol.18, no.2, Fall 1993, pp.5-43.

3 See BBC *Summary of World Broadcasts*, SU/1524/A1/3-4, 29 October 1992.

4 For details see Bess Brown, 'Central Asian States Seek Russian Help', *RFE/RL Research Report*, vol.2, no.25, 18 June 1993, pp.83-88.

5 See Bess Brown, 'Regional Cooperation in Central Asia?', *RFE/RL Research Report*, vol.2, no.5, 29 January 1993, pp.32-34.

6 A leading exponent of this idea was the US Republican Senator Larry Pressler. For his relevant remarks, see *India Abroad*, vol.22, no.16, 17 January 1992, pp.1, 12.

7 See Amin Saikal, 'The West and post-Khomeini Iran', *The World Today*, vol.49, no.10, October 1993, pp.197-200.

8 For a detailed account of the Tajikistan conflict, see Keith Martin, 'Tajikistan: Civil War without End?', *RFE/RL Research Report*, vol.2, no.33, 20 August 1993, pp.18-29.

9   See Yalcin Tokgozoglu, 'Uzbek Government Continues to Stifle Dissent', *RFE/RL Research Report*, vol.2, no.39, 1 October 1993, pp.10-15.

10 *Komsomol'skaia pravda*, 19 March 1993.

11 The Uzbeks in Afghanistan constitute no more than 1 million of the country's estimated 15-17 million population.

12 Martin, 'Tajikistan: Civil War without End?', p. 26.

13 It is important to remember that although prior to the Soviet invasion of Afghanistan in December 1979 the Pushtuns, who themselves have been divided along various tribal and sub-tribal lines, made up about 50 percent of the Afghan population, the conflict since the invasion has changed Afghanistan's demographic structure. With more Pushtuns being killed and forced into exile than Tajiks in the war, one can no longer safely claim that the Pushtuns still possess their pre-invasion numerical strength. See Amin Saikal and William Maley, *Regime Change in Afghanistan: Foreign Intervention and the Politics of Legitimacy* (Boulder: Westview Press, 1991) pp.136-137, 157.

14 *Reuters*, 28 February 1994.

15 See Ahmed Rashid, 'Push for Peace: Neighbours gear up to broker a Tajik Settlement', *Far Eastern Economic Review*, 3 February 1994.

16 Bess Brown, 'More Russian Troops to Tajikistan', *RFE/RL News Briefs*, vol.2, no.37, 6-10 September 1993, p.8.

17 Jonathan Steele, *Eternal Russia: Yeltsin, Gorbachev and the Mirage of Democracy* (London: Faber & Faber, 1994) p.151.

18 See *Komsomol'skaia pravda*, 3 February 1994.

19 For a full discussion, see Mohiaddin Mesbahi, 'Russian foreign policy and security in Central Asia and the Caucasus', *Central Asian Survey*, vol.12, no. 2, 1993, pp.181-215.

20 Stephen Blank, 'Russia and Iran in a New Middle East', *Mediterranean Quarterly*, vol.3, no.4, Fall 1992, p.121. The Economic Cooperation Organisation (ECO) is now comprised of Iran, Pakistan, and Turkey, as well as Azerbaijan and the five Central Asian Muslim republics of Kazakhstan, Uzbekistan, Turkmenistan, Tajikistan and Kyrgyzstan; Afghanistan has been invited to join.

21 See James Critchlow, 'Kazakhstan: The Outlook for Ethnic Relations', *RFE/RL Research Report*, vol.1, no.5, 31 January 1992, pp.34-39.

22 For details on the position of Islam, see Muriel Atkin, *The Subtlest Battle: Islam in Soviet Tajikistan* (Philadelphia: Foreign Policy Research Institute, 1989).

23 Bess Brown, 'Kazakhstan and Kyrgyzstan on the Road to Democracy', *RFE/RL Research Report*, vol.1, no. 48, 4 December 1992, p.20-22 at p.22.

24 For a discussion of the role of Islam, see Dale F. Eickelman (ed.), Russia's *Muslim Frontiers: New Directions in Cross-Cultural Analysis* (Bloomington: Indiana University Press, 1993) pp.49-97.

25 For a comprehensive discussion, see James Piscatori, *Islamic Fundamentalisms and the Gulf Crisis* (Chicago: American Academy of Arts and Sciences, 1991).

26 For an assessment of the Iranian economic situation see Elaine Sciolino, 'Iran Struggles to Attract Investors', *The New York Times*, 30 April 1992; Carlyle Murphy, 'Iran: Reconciling Ideology and a Modern State', *The Washington Post*, 28 April 1992; Peter Waldman, 'Clergy Capitalism: Mullahs Keep Control of Iranian Economy With an Iron Hand', *The Wall Street Journal*, 5 May 1992. For a more critical assessment of the Iranian position, see Hazhir Teimourian, 'Iran's 15 years of Islam', *The World Today*, vol.50, no.4, April 1994, pp.67-70.

27 For a survey of military expenditures in the region, see *The Military Balance 1992-1993* (London: Brassey's for the International Institute for Strategic Studies, 1992) p.102-138.
28 *Literaturnaia Rossiia*, 30 April 1993, p.6.

10 CULTURE IN RUSSIA AND RUSSIAN CULTURE

SERGEI SEREBRIANY

The word 'culture'—undoubtedly one of the most important words in modern European languages, including Russian[1]—is also, to cite Professor T.H. Rigby's phrase, 'in wide, if inconsistent use among social scientists and historians'.[2] For the purposes of this chapter, I distinguish at least three meanings which are nowadays more often attached to this word in scholarly discourse. These three meanings are different enough among themselves, but also in many ways interconnected; therefore they may be intentionally mixed or unintentionally confused.

Strangely enough—or perhaps, on the contrary, naturally enough—standard dictionaries of the English language do not adequately reflect or register all the meanings of the word 'culture' that I am going to define and use. It is only as my starting point that I can take one of the definitions in the *Oxford English Dictionary*: 'The training, development, and refinement of mind, tastes, and manners; the condition of being thus trained and refined; the intellectual side of civilisation'.[3] In this chapter I will but rarely use the word 'culture' as defined in the first two parts of this definition. The third part, rather opposed to the rest, is more important for my purposes, but also the least satisfying and accurate. What may be accepted is that the word 'culture', in one of its meanings, designates a certain part of that *whole* which here is called 'civilisation'. But why only the 'intellectual' part? Should we not rather say, using the terms of this very definition: that *part of the whole* which is connected, or perceived as being connected with 'the training, development, and refinement of mind, tastes, and manners'? Beside 'intellectual' should we not put 'imaginative', 'artistic', 'creative'?

If so changed, extended, amplified, the third part of the *Oxford English Dictionary* definition would yield the meaning in which the word 'culture' is now most widely used in mass media as well as in scholarly texts. By its very nature, this meaning can hardly be defined more exactly and specifically, because it is open to various interpretations. But it can be described either through enumeration or through subtraction. In the former case we may say that 'culture' comprises literature, music, the art of painting, theatre, cinema, in short, the arts in general. In certain contexts education and scholarship—the humanities—would be added. Some would say that religion is also part of 'culture', though others would claim, on the contrary, that 'culture' is—or should be—part of religion. In the latter case—a description by subtraction—'culture' is what remains after subtracting from the *whole* those parts that have other names and are not perceived as belonging to 'culture' in this sense: economics, politics domestic and international, law, social relations. This is how 'culture' seems to be defined in this volume.

I will call this meaning of the word 'culture' the 'narrow' one, because another meaning of the same word refers to that *whole*, of which 'culture' in the 'narrow' sense designates only a part. We may call this meaning 'comprehensive' or 'cultural-anthropological' because it comes from (and is most widely, though not at all exclusively, used in) the discipline of cultural anthropology. This meaning is said to have been brought into the English language from German, by E.B. Tylor in his famous book *Primitive Culture*, and almost till today to be looked upon by many, though not in America, as an alien element.[4]

The classical definition of Tylor—'Culture or civilisation, taken in its wide ethnographic sense, is that complex whole which includes knowledge, belief, arts, morals, law, custom, and any other capabilities and habits acquired by man as a member of society'[5]—has by now developed into two interrelated concepts. The first one, designated by the word 'culture' as an uncountable noun, refers to what is considered to be the essential nature (characteristics) of any human community just as a community of humans. As the late Soviet ethnographer R.F.Its[6] once put it, 'culture means all that which has been created by man as different from that which has been created by nature'.[7] Or, to quote the American anthropologist A.L. Kroeber, 'Culture is the special and exclusive product of men, and is their distinctive quality in the cosmos'.[8] In its countable variety, '*a* culture' refers to a particular manifestation, within a particular human community, of this universal human characteristic. Thus T.S. Eliot wrote: 'By culture ... I mean first of all what the anthropologists mean: the way of life of a particular people living together in one place. That culture is made visible in their arts, in their social system, in their habits and customs, in their religion'.[9] In this sense '*a* culture' is sometimes interchangeable with '*a* civilisation'. It is also worth stressing that, for an anthropologist or a sociologist, the word 'culture' in its countable variant is not tied up to any particular kind of human community and does not at all predetermine the size or 'type' of the community to which it might be applied. As Claude Lévi-Strauss writes, 'what is called a "culture" is a fragment of humanity which, from the point of view of the research at hand and of the scale on which the latter is carried out, presents significant discontinuities in relation to the rest of humanity'.[10] Thus we may speak about Russian culture—the culture or civilisation of Russia—as a whole, or about the culture of a particular village in the Moscow Oblast', or about the culture of Russian emigrés in France during the 1920s and so on.

All the meanings of the word 'culture' described above are important enough for the discussion of today's situation in Russia and the prospects for the future. In what follows I will try, as a rule, to differentiate between these meanings, so that my statements were unambiguous. But in certain contexts such differentiating may be impossible or unnecessary and the ambiguity unavoidable or indeed welcome. Rather than present only my own views, I will refer in this paper to a number of recent Russian publications which, to my mind, well represent the gamut of feelings and ideas in today's Russia. The Russian words *kul'tura* and *tsivilizatsiia* I will translate with the English words 'culture' and 'civilisation'. But it should be borne in mind that these two Russian words may have as many different meanings as their English counterparts, and probably even more, because in Russian there overlap influences of English, French and German, as is the case with many other 'international' words.

Now I am neither a professional analyst of current affairs—political, social or cultural—nor a professional expert on Russia. My main justification for writing this chapter is just my belonging to Russia: I was born and have been living all my life in this country, have been conditioned by her culture, and now experience all the changes that take place there. My chapter is not an attempt at a systematic analysis—which would hardly be possible given the skills of the author, the size of the chapter and the complexity and fluidity of the matter—but rather a mosaic of impressionistic notes from 'inside' which should convey my perception of the problems involved.

The changing role of culture

After the ill-fated *perestroika* and the disintegration of the Soviet Union, Russian culture now lives through a period of crisis and painful changes. To this statement hardly anybody would object. But opinions strongly differ when it comes to analysing the present crisis, to explaining its causes and foreseeing its possible results.

In 1934 Osip Mandel'shtam wrote the famous line: *My zhivem pod soboiu ne chuia strany* ('We live not feeling our country underfoot'). Strange as it might sound, this line has retained its relevance till today. Of course, one of the most publicised changes in Russia since 1985 has been the evolution from a 'closed' society towards an 'open' one. But 'opening' a 'closed' society is not like opening a closed box. In the Soviet system the production and circulation of information was deliberately and consistently blocked in many ways (which in the end proved to be suicidal for the system itself). And now, in spite of all the achievements of *glasnost'*, we still do not have any established and reliable mechanisms of producing and distributing objective information—knowledge—about our country and society, about the processes that go around us. Hence, among other things, the recent shock of the December 1993 elections and the unexpected success of Vladimir Zhirinovskii.

The peoples of Russia are still, to a very considerable extent, an unknown quantity, both to themselves, to the more articulate elites within the country, and I dare say to outside observers. The peoples may not be exactly silent (as in the final scene of A.S. Pushkin's *Boris Godunov*), but neither is there a clear and unequivocal *vox populi* which could be taken as a basis for decisions and actions. As for the more articulate elites themselves, they conspicuously fail to articulate such an analysis of the situation and such plans for actions which would rally and mobilise the whole of the country. Probably not only the elites are to blame, but also the ambiguous situation itself and, to repeat, the lack of reliable means to know and analyse the situation. A lot of strong opinions are expressed from different sides, especially by politicians and politically engaged people, but those voices sound more authentic and convincing—for me at least—which honestly admit that they do not have ready-made answers to urgent questions of today. Thus, the editorial board of the weekly *Ogonek*, in the first issue of 1994, addresses the readers with a 'letter' which says: 'So far we have not found approaches to many problems, to new phenomena of our life, and we honestly admit this today'.[11] The writer Fazil Iskander in an interview published by the weekly *Stolitsa* ('The Capital City'), says: 'Today those who think are awfully oppressed with the impossibility to understand what is one's duty, what one should apply one's energy to'.[12]

Indeed, even if one tries just to describe the 'mere facts' of the present situation in Russian culture ('wie es eigentlich ist', as von Ranke might have said), one encounters a kind of persistent ambiguity or, in other words, a kind of shaky balance between the negative and the positive. To put it briefly: liberated from the oppressive care of the state, culture by now has found itself 'liberated' also from its habitual material support and has been mercilessly thrown into the elements of a market economy, so that its fate seems to depend mostly on how soon new agencies of non-state support will develop. Thus, 'old'—formerly state-owned—publishing houses often go bankrupt unless they start publishing some 'marketable' trash, but there appear new publishing houses, some of them rather promising. The cinema production in Russia, they say, soon may stop altogether, but now and then we see on the TV our cinema people celebrating their achievements—not to mention the fact that now we can see on our TV a lot of great foreign films, that formerly we could only read about; true, we are shown a lot of foreign rubbish too. Libraries do not have money to get new books and to repair their buildings, but now a lot of books that had been kept in 'special stores' have been 'liberated'. I could go on and on with these pros and contras.

The economic problems of various branches of culture are indeed very urgent, and must be analysed and faced specifically in their own right, but here I would like to stress that the present plight of culture in Russia not only reflects the present economic plight of the country and the attitudes of those in power, but is also a sign of more important changes in Russian culture, that is, civilisation. Under the Soviet regime culture—in the 'narrow' sense—occupied a very important place in public life. But for several reasons and in several ways this importance was, so to say, disproportionate and artificial. On the one hand, the rulers rightly considered culture as one of the important levers of their power and control over the people. So they fostered those kinds and forms of culture that, in their perception, were the most useful for their purposes. But of course, hard though they tried, the rulers could not control and regulate the whole of culture, once they allowed it to exist at all. And, as other ways of expressing non-official views and attitudes were mostly forbidden, the sphere of culture became also the most natural channel of expressing such views and attitudes.[13] Real and publicly observable events in political or economic spheres were rare and far between. So cultural events very often filled the vacuum and were perceived as the most important events—which in fact they could really be—both by the establishment, by its opponents and by foreign observers. The publication (or banning) of a novel or a poem, the issuing (or not issuing) of a film, the opening (or closing) of an exhibition could become an event of the first order, if only because such an event was taken as a sign of some invisible processes in the Soviet Union or as a convenient pretext for a propaganda campaign. Under Gorbachev we had a kind of transitional period in this respect. Some visible political events started to happen, but cultural events still were sometimes felt to be almost as important. I may recall, for instance, the famous film *Pokaianie* by Tengiz Abuladze (which was, in a way, a kind of political gesture by Gorbachev's group of reformers) or the novel *Deti Arbata* by Anatolii Rybakov. This novel is hardly a piece of great literature, but I remember how avidly it was read in 1987 and what a significant event it was taken to be.

Now, since about 1989 or 1990, we have had so many formidable political and economic events that culture has been, so to say, cut down to size. Books go on to be written and even published, films shot and even sometimes shown, theatre performances produced, exhibitions opened, and such cultural events may be very remarkable in their own right, but all this cannot any longer compete, as far as the impression on the people and the dramatic quality is concerned, with the current political and economic events: the coup d'etat of August 1991 and the subsequent disintegration of the Soviet Union, the storming of the 'White House' in October 1993, the wars in Moldavia, Georgia, Tajikistan and elsewhere, the collapse of the economy and the galloping inflation—to recall only some of the most striking ones.

This relative decline of state and public attention paid to culture probably indicates the direction of further and more lasting developments. Various branches of culture in Russia may more or less successfully overcome the present economic difficulties. But if, as I hope, Russia is indeed going to transform herself, the sphere of culture too will have to undergo changes that now may look, to some, too drastic and unwelcome.

To be more specific, let me consider the case of literature. Traditionally, literature occupied a very important place in Russian culture. Rather recently, if I am not mistaken, there was coined a new word 'literaturocentrism' to describe this peculiarity of Russia. But it was observed long ago that literature in Russia had to play the roles and meet the demands that in other countries were played and met by other kinds of activities. Evgenii Evtushenko expressed this in a memorable line: 'A poet in Russia is more than a poet ...'. In the 18th and19th centuries literature in Russia was a means, a medium—sometimes almost the only one—of expressing social, political, philosophical and even religious ideas. It was even a kind of imperfect counterpart of political opposition in more democratic societies. Literature was called and taken to be 'a teacher of life'. After 1917 this tradition, in a way, persisted.[14] Aleksandr Solzhenitsyn is a recent example of a Russian writer who has become much more than a mere writer (at least in the modern European sense) and who, following the tradition, aspired to be 'a teacher of life' for his readers. But probably he is also the last eminent Russian writer of this type.

Now, it seems, literature in Russia may become 'just' literature and writers 'just' the authors of novels and short stories. Social, political, philosophical and religious thoughts now will have, as in the West, their own proper means of expression. It remains to be seen what consequences this situation will have for Russian literature.[15]

The future of Russian culture

As I have already said, opinions strongly differ when it comes to analysing the causes of the present situation in Russian culture. Some, like the well known theatre director Roman Viktiuk, while admitting that the very existence of culture—in his case, the theatrical culture—in Russia is endangered, explain this as a 'natural' result of political and economic changes: culture has proved to be unprepared for the kind of freedom that it suddenly got.[16] Another kind of opinion is forcefully expressed, for instance, by the eminent film director Stanislav Govorukhin in his book *Velikaia kriminal'naia revoliutsiia*: 'One cannot help seeing how persistently (*tselenapravlenno*) is being destroyed the culture of our fatherland!'.[17]

Govorukhin's book was written in 1993 and finalised after the so-called 'events of 3-4 October' in Moscow. Soon after those 'events' Govorukhin ran for election to the new State Duma on the list of the Democratic Party of Russia headed by Nikolai Travkin. So his book was probably also a kind of election manifesto of the author. This apparent political purpose of the book, in my perception, diminishes to some extent its credibility. But on the whole it reads as a very sincere and heartfelt outcry of a person, who had greeted and supported *perestroika* and even Boris Yeltsin—at least up to August 1991—but later was strongly disappointed with the developments of 1992-1993. Govorukhin believes that *perestroika* has proved to be a fraud and that now 'in the country there takes place a criminal revolution ... It is nearing its completion. The victory of this revolution will bring about the final establishment of a criminal-mafiosal state (*okonchatel'noe postroenie ugolovno-mafioznogo gosudarstva*)'.[18] In the chapter titled 'Has Russia a future?', Govorukhin, referring to the well known author Aleksandr Zinoviev, claims with him that Russia has been betrayed by the 'ruling idiots'. 'Russia is doomed for a disgraceful future, writes Govorukhin. She will become—is already becoming—a colony'.[19] According to the author, there takes place a forceful and crude 'westernisation' (*zapadnizatsiia*) of Russia, a mere 'aping' (*obez'iannichan'e*) of the West. 'We may say that Russia has made her choice.[20] She has agreed to her own death ... So Russia is finished'.[21]

Govorukhin's book cannot be easily dismissed as just a piece of propaganda written by a person who had thrived under the *ancien régime* and was dispossessed by the new one. The book contains a lot of very disturbing first hand information and conveys the genuine feeling of pain and despair experienced by many (especially of the older generations) who placed their hopes on the changes that started in 1985.[22]

I may refer in this connection to another book, also published in 1993, which is probably less sincere that Govorukhin's, but more sophisticated and far-going in its arguments. The book, by Sergei Kara-Murza, is titled *Chto proiskhodit s Rossiei? Kuda nas vedut? Kuda nas privedut?*[23] According to the author, 'The essence (*sut'*) of the crisis experienced by Russia is not political or even social. As in 1917, it is a confrontation of civilisations'.[24] Kara-Murza asserts that 'Russia was one of the major world civilisations, that survived the expansion of Western civilisation in the 16th-19th centuries. And now there takes place an attempt at destroying all the bases of Russian civilisation (*popytka sloma vsekh opor rossiiskoi tsivilizatsii*), as allegedly the 'dead branch' (*tupikovaia vetv'*) of mankind'.[25] Elsewhere Kara-Murza writes about 'destroying the cultural nucleus' (*demontazh kul'turnogo iadra*)[26] and 'the persistent undermining of the spiritual bases ... of the Russian people' (*tselenapravlennyi podryv dukhovnykh osnov ... russkogo naroda*).[27] In the present developments Kara-Murza sees not only 'the disintegration of Russia' (*raspad Rossii*)[28] and of her economic life (*raspad khoziaistva*),[29] but 'the disintegration of the soul (*raspad dushi*) in the considerable part of the Russian people. It is indeed a disintegration, not a transformation into a soul of a 'civilised human being'.[30]

Kara-Murza's book, demagogical to a certain extent though it clearly is, cannot possibly be dismissed either as just a figment of a biased imagination, because it reflects the moods and feelings that must be quite widely shared in today's Russia. Moreover, I believe that these two books also reflect, though probably in somewhat perverted ways, the real historical fact: Russia, Russian culture—civilisation—as a whole now crosses one of the most important watersheds in her history, which eventually may bring about considerable mutations in the very identity of Russia.

The present changes in Russia are often compared with various critical periods in her and the world's past history: with the revolution of 1917, with the reforms of Aleksandr II and with those of Peter I, with the so-called 'Time of Troubles' at the beginning of the 17th century and so on.[31] All such comparisons may have some heuristic value, but hardly any single one of them can do justice to the immensity of today's problems, can exhaust the contents of the present crisis. Nor do they help much in mapping possible future roads for Russia's development. For that matter, I would not risk here suggesting any list of scenarios for Russia's future. There are too many variables involved. What I will try and do is to describe analytically the major problems which, in my opinion, Russian culture faces now at the present watershed of her history.

To begin with, the present crisis of Russia may be conveniently described—using a fashionable expression—as 'a crisis of identity'. I discern three dimensions or interrelated constituent parts of this 'identity crisis': first, the disintegration of the Soviet Union and the emergence of the Russian Federation as a separate state; second, the new openness of Russia to the rest of the world —as well as to herself, to her own past and present—after the long period of isolation and 'closedness'; third the collapse of the former 'Soviet' or 'Communist' official ideology and, as a result, the appearance of what is often called an 'ideological or spiritual vacuum'. All these combined have given a new urgency to some old questions: What actually is—should be, might be—Russia? What is—should be, might be—her place or role in the world? In what ways is she different from other countries, cultures, civilisations, first of all from the West?

It would be difficult to say to what extent these questions are really relevant for the peoples of Russia at large, to what extent the common people are (or may be) consciously concerned with such questions. This should be a matter of special research work. It is of course mostly in the 'upper strata' that such questions are raised and discussed. It may well be that the future of Russia will be determined not at all through these discussions and their results. But here I may be permitted not to go into the problems of the interrelations between ideas and historical processes; I will consider ideas about Russia and her culture without any concern about their possible historical effectiveness.

To show the variety of opinions in the 'upper strata' on 'what is Russia', I will refer to a recently-published collection of interviews entitled *Rossiia v poiskakh budushchego*. When asked: 'What is Russia for you?', those interviewed give a number of different answers. For the politician Viktor Alksnis, Russia means the Russian Empire.[32] He stresses that he has always been against the 'Russian idea' (*russkaia ideia*), but for the 'idea of Russia, the Empire'(*ideia rossiiskaia, imperskaia*).[33] Another well known politician, Sergei Baburin is of a similar opinion.[34] A more complicated and sophisticated answer is given by the mathematician Igor' Shafarevich. He says that Russia should be compared not with some European country like France, but rather with the West European civilisation as a whole.[35] He seems to imply that for him Russia means both Russia proper (inhabited by ethnic Russians) and the former USSR, that is, the former Russian Empire.[36] Stanislav Terekhov, the president of the 'Officers' Union', says: 'First of all, we see our state (*nashe gosudarstvo*) within those borders within which it existed. Within the borders of the Soviet Union'[37] It looks like he is ready to give up the name 'Russia'. And for the philosopher Al'bert Sobolev, 'Russia' is almost synonymous with 'Eurasia' .[38] Iurii Boldyrev, another politician, is less definite and more cautious. When asked: 'What is Russia for you? What does it mean for you personally to be Russian?', he says: 'Your question for me is one of those, answering which you are bound to doubt every word you utter'[39] and actually evades any definite answer (in a very Gorbachevian way). Nikolai Travkin, the leader of the Democratic Party of Russia, has his own ways of evasion. He retorts abruptly: 'Let us not talk mythologically. Now the disintegration (*raspad*) of the USSR is a reality'.[40] Very telling are the answers of two persons outside politics. The writer (and former 'dissident') Evgenii Popov is asked: 'How would you define the borders of your motherland?'. After some hesitation and circumlocution ('The devil knows where these borders are ...'[41]) he says that he 'would mark the borders of the motherland by ... the definite notion: Russia. I do not consider my motherland the country called 'Azerbaijan', whose name it is so difficult for some to pronounce'.[42] Then, rather thoughtlessly, Popov leaves it to politicians to define the actual borders of his motherland, that is Russia. Sergei Chesnokov, a mathematician, musician and philosopher, is also asked: 'What is Russia now, geographically and socially?'. And he says: 'I simply do not know. Now various things are designated by this name, but for me they are mostly phantoms. Territory ... people ... But I know only those people whom I know. Russia means this very house, this place, where we are talking now. The people whom I know, with whom I am connected by intimate and friendly ties. The people about whom I know. The language which I use and the possibility of mutual understanding through this language. Nothing else'. This attitude may be taken as rather typical for a considerable part of the intelligentsia in Russia today.

The diverse opinions just cited are only part of the endless 'discourse on Russia' that quite intensely goes on now in this country. There are various dimensions in this discourse, and here I will try and consider some of them.

For some people Russia is first and foremost a state (*gosudarstvo*), a power (*derzhava*). Others may be either indifferent to this 'powerness' (*derzhavnost'*) or even positively hostile to it, identifying for themselves Russia with something else—with the people or the nature or the culture. Within the mainstream of the classical Russian culture there is a strong tradition of such attitudes towards *derzhavnost'*. We all learned at school the poem 'Motherland' (*Rodina*) by Mikhail Lermontov: *Liubliu otchiznu ia, no strannoiu liubov'iu* ... ('I love my fatherland, but with a strange kind of love ...'). In this poem one of the greatest poets of Russia actually opposes the ideal of Russia as a 'great' and 'glorious' power, to which he proclaims his indifference, and the reality of Russian landscapes and Russian peasant people, to which he proclaims his love—though, it is true, a kind of 'love from afar'. Lev Tolstoi, another great figure of Russian culture, by the end of his life became vehemently hostile to the whole establishment of the Russian Empire, including its ideological underpinning, Orthodox Christianity. In fact it may be argued that there has always been a more or less overt antagonism between Russian culture, in more than one sense of the word, and Russian statehood, though, probably, it was exactly this antagonism that has also been one of the most important formative factors of Russian culture itself.

This thesis may be applied to the Soviet period of Russian history too, though, I am afraid, the Soviet regime has destroyed much more than it helped, willingly or unwillingly, to create. Those who lived under that regime could feel very acutely the discrepancy and, in a way, incompatibility of the state establishment, which claimed to represent and 'care for' the people of Russia, and the culture of Russia at its best. Now, in 1994, in spite of all the dramatic changes, it seems that we are still quite far from the time when the political culture in Russia, the culture of its statehood, would be worthy of her culture as a whole.[43]

This makes one wonder whether or not it might be better for the future of Russian culture if Russia developed not as one huge state, which is too prone to do harm to its own people, but as several separate political bodies—provided of course they do not wage wars against each other. If indeed, as Shafarevich tells us, Russia is a whole civilisation, then it must be quite natural for her to exist in the form of a 'concert of states'. Such a kind of pluralism may contribute to the richness of Russian culture. One may recall in this connection that the English speaking culture by now for some time has been developing within several political entities, which fact undoubtedly has made this culture richer and more powerful. One may also refer, *mutatis mutandis*, to the examples of the French-speaking, German-speaking, Portuguese-speaking, and Spanish-speaking cultures. In fact, even under today's political borders we already have more than one political entity where Russian culture is bound to remain and develop one way or another. I may mention Ukraine, Belarus and Kazakhstan in the first place, where the Russian, or at least Russian speaking, population is considerable and the presence of Russian culture cannot possibly be wished away. Even in Latvia and Estonia (and probably in Lithuania too), when the present anti-Russian (basically, I believe, anti-Soviet) feelings calm down, there may remain Russian minorities which will develop their peculiar contributions to the common treasure house of Russian culture.

There are also such special cases as the Crimea and the so-called Pridnestrovye, territories in Ukraine and Moldova respectively, where Russian culture has rather deep roots.

The disintegration of the Russian Empire—alias the USSR—may of course be compared with the disintegrations of other European empires in the 20th century. But one of the most obvious peculiarities of the Russian case is that it has been very difficult to neatly cut out the 'metropolia' from the 'colonies'. Baburin calls the present Russian Federation the 'Leninist-Stalinist stump' (*leninsko-stalinskii obrubok*[44])—and not without reasons. More academic analysts compare the present borders between the states of the CIS with the borders between independent African states: the latter were drawn arbitrarily by European colonisers; the former, sometimes no less arbitrarily, by 'Communist' rulers. But there is hardly any 'objective', non-arbitrary way of drawing the borders of Russia proper, demarcating her from what is not Russia (and the same is true, I believe, for Russian culture as a whole), because, in the past, the borders of Russia have been ever changing and, at present, not at all everywhere are there clearcut watersheds between the Russian population and the non-Russian ones. But he who is concerned more with the future of Russian culture rather than with the fate of Russia as a great power, should not, I believe, attach too much importance to the problems of contingent political borders. Indeed these spatial aspects of Russia's identity are hardly the most important or the most complicated ones. Now Russia has to define herself anew not only in terms of her geographical borders, but also in many less tangible—cultural—respects. The need for such a redefinition has been brought about by the collapse of the 'Soviet ideology' and the concomitant opening of the country to the rest of the world.

I would not try and give here a detailed analysis of the 'Soviet ideology'. Suffice it to say that it was a phenomenon with many layers, meant for various kinds of consumption. Above or apart from more or less demagogic layers, there was also a more intellectual one with which even people who wanted to be honest with themselves could more or less successfully coexist, and whose influence on Russian minds may prove to be more lasting than that of other parts of the defunct ideology. To this intellectual layer there belonged a particular philosophy of history, technically known as historical materialism, which was a schematised and dogmatised kind of unilinear evolutionism inherited from the 19th century. This philosophy of history was mostly concerned with what might be called macrohistorical and macrosocial schemes. It did recognise the empirical existence of such entities as individual peoples (nations) with their particular cultures (ways of life), but considered various cultures (civilisations) first and foremost as varieties of more general patterns (and the emphasis was always on the general pattern rather than on the particular differentia) and, second, as historically passing, contingent phenomena. Thus, Russia and Russian culture were recognised to a certain, sometimes very considerable, extent as something of their own kind, but their 'peculiarities' were considered less important than their obeying the 'general laws of historical development'. The 'Soviet ideology' as such would probably have been not as harmful, had it not been accompanied by the 'closedness' of the country, that is, by the rather strict control over the information and ideas that were allowed to come in, to be produced and circulated in the society. Of course, this control could not be as strict under Brezhnev as it had been under Stalin, but still the breakthrough under Gorbachev and later for many 'Soviets' had an effect of a revelation—or rather too many revelations one after another. Again, the effects of these revelations must have been different for different kinds of people—depending on age, level of education and previous knowledge—and so 'ideological needs' now must also vary. But, assuming that the country and the people as a whole need a kind of comprehensive self-image, from which different persons may take different parts, I will try and sketch the main aspects of this 'imaginative' (that is, 'cultural') self-redefining that Russia is bound to undertake now.

One of the most important and painful processes is to come to terms with Russia's own past, both before 1917 and especially after 1917, in the context of world history. Many people of the older generations now living sincerely believed that their country was the champion of all the best in the world, had the best possible, the most progressive, social system and was doing her best to benefit the rest of mankind with her inspiring example as well as with material support. Many such people refuse to believe that all this was just a great lie and that they have lived their lives in vain. It is more natural for them to think that the Soviet Union has been destroyed through some sinister conspiracy—and there are enough demagogues to exploit such beliefs. But even for those who did not blindly believe in the 'Soviet myth', there may be some problems. The mere amount of new information and new ideas that have become available and must be consumed is enormous, and the digestion of this new food is bound to take some time. This applies not only to Russian history, but to the world at large that now is indeed open for us as it has not been for several generations. Among other things, the ex-Soviet Russians must learn and absorb one way or another the culture of the three—at least—waves of emigration that took from the mother country some of her most energetic and talented children.

This new and drastic 'openness' to the rest of the world after a long period of being 'closed' justifies the comparison of the present critical situation with the time of Peter I. Among other things, now, as then, our language is invaded by many foreign (mostly English) words, because either we do not have Russian words for new things and ideas or are too much in a hurry to find an appropriate Russian word. Now, as then, many 'conservatives' are appalled and believe that the 'Holy Russia' is being destroyed by an 'Antichrist'. But we may recall that after the reforms of Peter I, savage as they no doubt often were, there came what we now call the classical age of Russian culture. This consideration should in no way justify the savage aspects of today's reforms, if reforms they are, but may at least give some hope for the future.

The reforms of Peter I in Russia may be, and often are, considered a particular local variety of the global process of 'Europeanisation' or 'Westernisation' that has been going since the 16th century. In fact Russia was, in a way, both the object—the 'victim'—and the active promoter of this process. But her own several attempts at 'Westernisation' were mostly misconceived or at least miscarried.[45] The present 'reforms' may be interpreted as one more attempt, so far not too successful and inspiring, to appropriate the achievements of Western civilisation, to transplant them to Russia. And so again, as in the 19th century, between the Westernisers and the Slavophiles, the arguments go on about the possibility, or desirability, or permissibility, of borrowing this or that aspect of Western culture and about whether Russia should first of all strive to preserve its *samobytnost'* (roughly 'identity') or whether there should be some other priorities. In today's world similar debates are conducted in many non-Western countries which face the problems of 'modernisation'. Unpleasant as it must be for many Russians, in this respect Russia looks like many other 'developing' countries.

Now one of the specifically Russian and most delicate problems is the place of Orthodox Christianity within Russian culture. Some, sincerely or not, would claim that Russian culture is—must be, is bound to be—Orthodox Christian, that being Russian just means being Orthodox Christian. Others would point to the fact that there were and are Old Believers, Protestants (Baptists and others) and even some Catholics who were and are no less Russian. Yet others would point out that Russia, for good or for bad, has already tasted the post-Christian culture and for many Russians there is hardly any way back to traditional Christianity, Orthodox or otherwise. Even Orthodox Christianity now is divided within itself and must solve a lot of internal problems. Some people hoped, or were afraid, that after the collapse of the 'Soviet ideology' it would be precisely traditional Orthodox Christianity (or some kind of its mixture with 'Marxism') that would fill the vacuum. But so far this has not happened and does not look like ever happening. Rather it seems that Russia will have to evolve and live with a kind of ideological pluralism that she has hardly ever had in her past history.

The ethnic pluralism of the Russian Federation will also have to be taken in earnest. In the former Soviet Union in this respect, as in many others, there was a great discrepancy between the ideology and the reality. The relations between different peoples and their different cultures did not develop in a healthy way, which has brought about so many conflicts in recent years. Now in the Russian Federation the ethnic Russians constitute a considerable majority, about 80% of the population. But there are also non-negligible ethnic and cultural minorities whose interests should be carefully considered: the Tartars and the Ukrainians, the Chuvashs and the peoples of Dagestan, the Bashkirs and the Mordvinians, the Belorussians and the Russian Germans, the Chechens and the Ingushs, the Ossets and the Yakuts, the Buryats and the Kalmyks ...[46] The Russian Federation as a whole is bound to develop a kind of genuine multiculturalism which would accommodate all the minorities.[47]

To conclude, the Russia and the Russian culture that emerge after the present critical and transitional period may indeed be very different from what they used to be in the past.[48] But, for that matter, the whole of the world lives now through a critical and transitional period and, if it manages to survive, we may have, must have, as a result a very different world. So the changes in Russia are part of—and are very much conditioned by—the changes in the world at large.

Russia in the river of human affairs

There is one more dimension in the 'discourse about Russia' which points beyond history—though not in Fukuyama's sense— and beyond culture as the human way of life, the human condition. The 'Soviet' period of our history was not just one period among others, as bad and as good as other periods. There are reasons to think that it was rather exceptionally bad, qualitatively different from whatever had preceded. Well known is the term *raskulachivanie* ('dekulakisation') which in fact meant a kind of merciless crushing of the peasantry in Russia and other parts of the Soviet Union. Less known (even in Russia) are such terms (and processes) as *raskazachivanie* ('dekazakisation', that is, abolishing Cossacks as a peculiar ethno-social group) and *ras-shamanivanie* ('deshamanisation', that is, abolishing shamans as a group with a certain social role among the indigenous peoples of

Siberia). In general, what the domestic politics of the 'Soviet' regime amounted to may be justly called *raschelovechivanie* ('dehumanisation'), and in this sense *raskul'turivanie* ('deculturation') too. Not that the regime fully succeeded in this task, but it tried hard.

Now the world at large knows something about it from the writings of Aleksandr Solzhenitsyn. But even more revealing, though evidently less known, are the writings of another former prisoner of the GULAG, Varlam Tikhonovich Shalamov, first of all his *Kolymskie rasskazy*. They make difficult reading, almost physically torturing. They show that the texture of culture (civilisation), that we tend to take for granted, is very fragile, and that human beings can be easily reduced to inhuman ways of existence and eventually to death. I would not claim that in this respect Russia's experience in the 20th century was absolutely unique. Most probably it was not. According to Fazil Iskander, the message of Shalamov's book is this: ' ... Mankind can very easily and very soon perish. Disappear. Like the prisoners of Kolyma. Mankind has not yet developed powerful enough defence fortifications for the struggle against evil ... *Kolymskie rasskazy* is a book not about the fortuity of what has happened in Russia, but about the fortuity of the fact that mankind is still alive ... One should not be surprised with those heinous crimes that have been committed in Russia in the 20th century. One should rather be gladly amazed that it has not happened in the whole of the world'.[49] But Fazil Iskander warns his fellow citizens of Russia that it is they who first of all must take the lesson of the *Kolymskie rasskazy*: 'In three to four years Kolyma may become again a topical theme, in the most simple sense of the word. The *Kolymskie rasskazy* are not only a recollection about the Kolyma of the past, but a warning about the Kolyma of the future. They may be compared with the Apocalypse'.[50]

And yet this Abkhazian, who considers himself (and rightly so) a Russian writer, says: 'I believe that in the whole of our spiritual culture there must emerge today a new depth, commensurate with that abyss by which we are standing'.[51]

Let me finish my chapter with this note of hope.

Notes

1 Compare *Kultur und Zivilisation* (Munich: Max Hueber Verlag, 1967).
2 T.H. Rigby, 'Societies: A Historical-Analytical Outline', *Political Theory Newsletter*, vol.3, no.2, September 1991, pp.133-151 at p.133. One might add: 'and among scholars in other branches of the humanities'.
3 *The Oxford English Dictionary* (Oxford: Oxford University Press, 1971) Vol.II, p.1248.

4 Compare *Kultur und Zivilisation*, pp.146, 188-195, 265-268. It is only in the Supplement to the *Oxford English Dictionary* (Vol.I, 1972) that this 'anthropological' meaning of the word 'culture' is registered (though not adequately defined) under the number '5b'. The more recent edition of the *Oxford English Dictionary* is not so far available to me in Moscow.

5 E.B. Tylor, *Primitive Culture: Researches into the Development of Mythology, Philosophy, Religion, Language, Art, and Custom* (London: J. Murray, 1891) Vol.I, p.1.

6 The term 'Soviet' is deliberately used here as an apt epithet. Rudolf Ferdinandovich Its (1928-1990) was a son of an Estonian communist who worked in Russia and was executed there in 1937. Professor R.F. Its himself studied and worked in Leningrad: see *Etnosy i etnicheskiie protsessy. Pamiati R.F.Itsa* (Moscow: Nauka, 1993). His writings (in Russian of course), valuable as they are, have been inevitably conditioned by the Soviet ideology. It is all the more remarkable that this interpretation of the term 'culture' has found its way into his book. But in Russian, as in English, this meaning of the word remains rather technical.

7 R.F. Its, *Vvedeniie v etnografiiu* (Leningrad: Izdatel'stvo Leningradskogo universiteta, 1974) p.40. Here and further all translations from Russian are mine.

8 A.L. Kroeber, *Anthropology: Race, Language, Culture, Psychology, Prehistory* (New York: Harcourt, Brace & World, 1948) p.8. Compare *Kultur und Zivilisation*, p.195. See also: A.L. Kroeber and Clyde Kluckhohn, *Culture: A Critical Review of Concepts and Definitions* (Cambridge, Harvard University 1952).

9 T.S. Eliot, *Notes Towards the Definition of Culture* (London: Faber & Faber, 1962) p.120. Compare *Kultur und Zivilisation*, p.209. Compare also the definition of the *Random House Dictionary of the English Language* (New York: Random House, 1966) p.353: 'the sum total of ways of living built up by a group of human beings and transmitted from one generation to another'.

10 Claude Lévi-Strauss, *Structural Anthropology* (Harmondsworth: Penguin Books, 1977) p.295.

11 *Ogonek*, no.1, 1994, p.2. Compare further in this 'letter': '... people find it more and more difficult to understand and accept the new reality, to have a common language with it'.

12 *Stolitsa*, no.5, 1994, p.26.

13 Compare also the opinion of Hans Magnus Enzensberger, the German poet. In an interview with *Literaturnaia gazeta* he remarked that in the West people are constantly 'pressed' by the need to achieve or at least to keep afloat, while in the Soviet Russia 'where this pressure was not there, where the need for taking initiative was much less felt, where newspapers were boring and life poor in events, the only sphere of freedom was culture. The creative potentials of people were the monopoly of culture ... Now the situation has changed' (H.M. Enzensberger, 'Kul'tura—udel men'shinstva', *Literaturnaia gazeta*, no.24, 16 June 1993, p.7).

14 Dmitrii Prigov (born in 1940), an eminent poet and artist, formerly of the 'underground', said in a recent interview: 'Why literature [in Russia and in the USSR] acquired such an influence? [Because] other spheres of intellectual activity were not developed. Neither sociology, nor law. Literature combined everything in itself, it was both philosophy, and theology , and anthropology... It was the only representative of the human community before the power that be. It articulated the problems

of the society for those in power... And, conversely, transmitted the ideas of those in power into the people. That is why it has got such a strange role of a universal voice. It was everything'. The quotation is taken from a volume by Vasilii Agafonov and Vladimir Rokitianskii, *Rossiia v poiskakh budushchego* (Moscow: 'Progress'—'Kul'tura', 1993) p.208. This book is a collection of interviews taken by the two authors, mostly in June of 1992, from twenty five representative persons in Russia.

15 Compare a remark by Iurii Arabov, the poet and prose writer: '...Now literature, as a force that has the power over minds, is not there': *Nezavisimaia gazeta*, 25 November 1993, p.7.

16 *Rossiia v poiskakh budushchego*, p.73.

17 Stanislav Govorukhin, *Velikaia kriminal'naia revoliutsiia* (Moscow: 'Andreevskii flag', 1993) p.46. Compare a slightly different opinion of Valerii Turchin: 'Blow after blow is delivered on culture in Russia. From various sides and, as a rule, with a great force (*naotmash*). This child, withering before our eyes, (during a thousand years he did not manage to come of age) will probably soon utter his farewell 'a-u' and die ... Nobody will ever be able to help. In Sweden the art has died because of satiety, here because of dystrophy: both economical, and political, and spiritual. It is the end of it': Valerii Turchin, 'Kto vinovat? Krizis khudozhestvennoi kul'tury, o kotorom tak mechtali, nastal', *Nezavisimaia gazeta*, 29 December 1993, p.7.

18 Govorukhin, *Velikaia kriminal'naia revoliutsiia*, p.34.

19 Govorukhin, *Velikaia kriminal'naia revoliutsiia*, p.62.

20 The chapter from which the quotation is taken is titled *Vybor Rossii* which points, of course, to the 'election block' headed by Egor Gaidar.

21 Govorukhin, *Velikaia kriminal'naia revoliutsiia*, p.118-119. Govorukhin then quotes a poem by Maksimilian Voloshin ('Mir', written on 23 November 1917), which begins with the words: *S Rossiei koncheno ...* ('Russia is finished ...').

22 This despair was dramatically emphasised by two suicides that are mentioned by Govorukhin at p.67: that of the woman poet Iulia Drunina (in 1992) and that of the prose writer Viacheslav Kondrat'iev (in 1993). Both belonged to the 'war generation'.

23 Sergei Kara-Murza, *Chto proiskhodit s Rossiei? Kuda nas vedut? Kuda nas privedut?* (Moscow: 'Bylina', 1993). The author is a 'publicist' who writes for the newspapers *Pravda* and *Den'* (after October 1993 renamed *Zavtra*) and for the journal *Nash sovremennik*.

24 Kara-Murza, *Chto proiskhodit s Rossiei?*, p. 3.

25 Kara-Murza, *Chto proiskhodit s Rossiei?*, p.3.

26 Kara-Murza, *Chto proiskhodit s Rossiei?*, p.53.

27 Kara-Murza, *Chto proiskhodit s Rossiei?*, p.28.

28 Kara-Murza, *Chto proiskhodit s Rossiei?*, p.20.

29 Kara-Murza, *Chto proiskhodit s Rossiei?*, p.46.

30 Kara-Murza, *Chto proiskhodit s Rossiei?*, p.63. Both Govorukhin at p.121 and Kara-Murza at p.5 quote the dictum of Aleksandr Zinoviev: *My tselili v kommunizm, a popali v Rossiiu* ('Our target was communism, but we have hit Russia').

31 M.N. Gromov, the philosopher, writes: 'The disintegration (*raspad*) of the USSR is in the line of the disintegrations of the great empires of the past. By an external comparative criterion it may be put beside the sunset of the British empire, but by the intrinsic eschatological meaning it may be compared with the fall of Rome in the IVth and the

fall of the Byzantium, as the "new" or "second" Rome, in the XVth century' (M.N. Gromov, 'Vechnye tsennosti russkoi kul'tury: k interpretatsii otechestvennoi filosofii', *Voprosy filosofii*, no.1, 1994, p.54-55).

32 *Rossiia v poiskakh budushchego*, p.20. Alksnis was born in 1950.

33 *Rossiia v poiskakh budushchego*, p.17.

34 *Rossiia v poiskakh budushchego*, p.26. Baburin was born in 1959.

35 *Rossiia v poiskakh budushchego*, p.297. Shafarevich was born in 1923.

36 *Rossiia v poiskakh budushchego*, pp.297-298.

37 *Rossiia v poiskakh budushchego*, p.239. Terekhov was born in 1955.

38 *Rossiia v poiskakh budushchego*, p.219. Sobolev was born in 1936. He is a scholar who studies the legacy of the so-called *evraziitsy* of the 1920s and 1930s. But now the idea of Russia as 'Eurasia' is demagogically used by the newspaper *Zavtra* and by the Moscow journal *Elementy*, four issues of which were published in 1992-1993. This bizarre journal deserves a special study.

39 *Rossiia v poiskakh budushchego*, p.50. Boldyrev was born in 1960.

40 *Rossiia v poiskakh budushchego*, p.252. Travkin was born in 1946.

41 *Rossiia v poiskakh budushchego*, p.185. Popov was born in 1946.

42 A hint at Mikhail Gorbachev who could never properly pronounce the word 'Azerbaijan'.

43 Compare the pathetic remark of the playwright Edvard Radzinskii, *Ogonek*, no.1, 1994, p.5: '... In Russia everything has changed. And nothing has changed. She has become incredibly different. And has remained the same ... The essence does not change: there are both energy and laziness, the thirst for activity and inactivity; absolute freedom, on the one hand, and, on the other hand, the absolute all-powerfulness of the bosses—of exactly the same bosses (*polneishee vsevlastie nachal'stva—sovershenno togo zhe nachal'stva*)'.

44 *Rossiia v poiskakh budushchego*, p.26. Elsewhere the expression *leninsko-stalinsko-khrushchevskii obrubok* can be met, which emphasises the fact that it was Nikita Khrushchev who 'presented' the Crimea to Ukraine.

45 Compare the interview with Alexei Kara-Murza (not to be confused with Sergei Kara-Murza above) in the *Obshchaia gazeta* no.7/32, 1994, p.7, very tellingly titled *Pochemu, vzyskuia 'grada Kitezha', my poluchaem 'gorod Glupov'?* ('Why, seeking the "city of Kitezh", we get the "town of Glupov"? The reference is to the famous *History of a Town* by Saltykov-Shchedrin). Alexei Kara-Murza and Leonid Poliakov have prepared a book called *Sotvorenie Rossii: Labirinty natsional'nogo samosoznaniia*, which is an analytical and historical presentation of the views that Russians have had about Russia.

46 Probably Jews should also be mentioned in his context. But those Jews who have remained and will remain in Russia must be considered, in my opinion, not so much a non-Russian ethnic minority as a sub-cultural minority within the Russian ethnos itself (the dividing lines being often very much blurred). Much has been written about the (problems of) the emigration of Russian Jews to (or via) Israel. But from the point of view of Russian culture probably not less important is what will happen to those Russian Jews who, rather than go 'home' (*ha-baita*) to Israel, choose to remain 'at home' in Russia.

47 Compare *supra* on the prospects of pluralism in Russian culture proper, now that it is divided between several political entities. The Russian language has already registered the change in public consciousness.

The adjective *rossiiskii* and the noun *rossiianin* are now much more widely used than before. While *russkii* means ethnically (or culturally) Russian, *rossiiskii* and *rossiianin* both mean 'one belonging to Russia, though not necessarily ethnically Russian'. Until quite recently both words, especially the latter, had rather an archaic ring and would have been used more naturally in poetry rather than in political discourse. I remember a line by the Bashkir poet Mustai Karim, written probably in the 1960s: *Ne russkii ia, no rossiianin* ... ('I am not Russian, but belong to Russia ... '). Then it sounded very high style, now it is the language of newspapers.

48 Compare the passage from N.A. Berdiaev's book *Russkaia ideia*, in the text published in *Voprosy filosofii*, no.1, 1990, p.79: 'For Russian history discontinuity (*preryvnost'*) is characteristic ... In Russian history there are already five periods which present different images [of Russia]. There are the Russia of Kiev, the Russia of the time of the Tartar yoke, the Russia of Moscow, the Russia of Peter and the Soviet Russia. And probably there will be a new Russia. The development of Russia has been catastrophical ...'.

49 *Stolitsa*, no.5, 1994, p.28.

50 *Stolitsa*, no.5, 1994, p.28.

51 *Stolitsa*, no.5, 1994, p.28.

11 RECONSTRUCTION, DECONSTRUCTION AND THE RESTORATION OF LITERATURE IN RUSSIA

PETER SAWCZAK

In an article which appeared in the first 1993 edition of *Literaturnaia gazeta,* Chuprinin confidently asserts that 'at long last we have a normal literature'.[1] The suggestion here is that the disintegration of the Soviet Union, the end of bipolar confrontation and the decisive move towards democratic pluralism and a market economy have eliminated the narrow discursive boundaries of Soviet literary culture and signalled the assumption of Western 'universal' values. These developments have, in turn, permitted Russian literature to 'catch up' to and develop alongside 'normal' European/North American culture. For its part, the West, to which Chuprinin purports Russian literature now belongs, would baulk at the exclusivity implied in this observation. By invoking the universal of 'normality', Chuprinin's remark implies a hierarchy of evaluative norms which is considered immensely unfashionable, not to say meaningless, in the post-structuralist critical discourse of the West. Chuprinin's remark does, nonetheless, imply some interesting tendencies in post-Soviet Russian literature and criticism which could be productively examined from the perspective of postmodernity. Foremost among these is the provocation of the binary opposition Russia/Europe, along with its culturological synonyms populism/postmodernism, art for politics/art for art, incomplete culture/complete culture.[2]

Social and intellectual historians of Russia have fondly attributed a recurring dualism to this opposition, more often than not in terms of the recurring Slavophile/Westerniser debate. Most recently, this has been apparent in portrayals of parliamentary conflict between conservatives and reformers up to the dissolution of the Congress of People's Deputies in October 1993. The multifarious aspect of recent intellectual debate and literary production suggests, however, that the process of progressively dismantling and rejecting Marxist-Leninist teleologies has assumed a dynamic of its own which is addressing the paradoxes and contradictions of post-Soviet reality purposefully and comprehensively. The official culture of assent and the oppositional culture of dissent have both become fair game as the object of revision and parody.

The present paper is an attempt to outline some of the circumstances which have precipitated the very vocal literary debate in Russia, as well as to highlight creative and critical responses to ideological oppositions and the new creative pluralism ushered in by the post-Soviet order. While any examination of Russian literature profiting from the Western intellectual experience of postmodernity incites charges of cultural imperialism, no apology is offered for the paper's argumentative parameters. These comprise both an acceptance and a rejection of Chuprinin's remark: an acceptance of the possibility of applying non-hierarchical intellectual norms cross-culturally and a rejection of the validity of notions of cultural universality.

Russian narratorial authority

In light of the tumultuous social consequences of de-Sovietisation, it is hardly surprising that present-day literary polemics in Russia remain more emotive than scholarly, resembling in nature and exceeding in scope the literary debates of the 1920s. The polarisation of literary conservatives and reformers on an institutional level might be conveniently dated from the Eighth Soviet Writers' Congress in 1986, when expectations that far-reaching reform would be initiated were disappointed. The upshot of this was the establishment of a diverse number of alternative groups within the Union of Soviet Writers, the most important of which was the pro-reform protest movement 'Writers in Support of *Perestroika*', subsequently called *Aprel*. Up until the dissolution of the Soviet Union, literary groups had become highly politicised by the stop-start nature of reform under Gorbachev.[3] Indeed, in the mid to late 1980s there was little evidence to suggest that the 'thaw' paradigm, which gauged political liberalisation in terms of censorship relaxations, would be exceeded. However, with the emergence of an assertive Russian presidency and its unambiguously reformist agenda, much politicking could be dropped from the literary agenda. Worth noting is the fact that, in recognition of the pluralism of the new social order and attendant diversification of literary concerns, many alternative literary groups were set up specifically to represent minority interests, such as the women's group and the green group.[4]

The relaxation of controls over artistic expression and the resultant emergence of creative pluralism has come at the expense of harsh socioeconomic realities, the dramatic preface to which was the liberalisation of prices in early 1992. The prosaic flavour of the Yeltsin age, as opposed to the romantic lyricism of the Gorbachev era, with its increasingly distant hopes of renewal, has been strongly flavoured by the requirement that Russian society undergo a dramatic conceptual shift away from the Soviet notion of materialism to the materialism propagated by free market economy with its attendant consumer orientation, commercialism and strong emphasis on the individual. An indication of the difficulty in overcoming the collective notion of material prosperity and welcoming a 'dictatorship of the consumer' is implicit in Prime Minister Chernomyrdin's remark that Russia had turned into a 'nation of street vendors'.

One of the most obvious consequences of the new socioeconomic circumstances and the attendant shift in the critical boundaries of discussion on contemporary literature has been the complete subversion of the traditional place of the writer in Russian society. Indeed, 'official' Soviet writers have been discredited to the point of an ironic role reversal. Just as dissident writers were superfluous to the politicised culture of the Soviet regime, Soviet writers are becoming redundant in the increasingly pluralistic political culture of post-Soviet Russia. Some commentators make a point of demonstratively not shedding any tears over the *disjecti membra poetae*. In an open letter to Egor Isaev, for example, Pavel Basinskii answers his own question concerning the whereabouts of Soviet writers with the reply 'the "Soviet writer" has vanished. He picked up his hat and left'.[5]

Reflecting the shift in the political authority and status of the writer, recent Russian prose has demonstrated a marked predilection for ironic self-reflection on the part of narratorial personae, many of which are cast as writers. The narrator in Evgenii Laputin's *Priruchenie Arlekinov (Taming of the Harlequins)*, for example, continually shifts narrative point of view while drawing attention to the authorial prerogative behind these shifts with such unambiguous interjections as 'I shall write it trying not to notice my own bent over figure'.[6] Such shifts, blurring the identity between the narrator/author and the alternately first and third-person narrative subject ('I'—'Andrei'), are even compressed to the point of physical contact between the two in the actual act of writing: 'I shall write, trying not to wallow in my regret and pity, since I sympathised with him deeply. I could feel the beat of his heart to the point of pain in my own heart, my sadness tried with all of its strength not to fall out of time with his prosaic breathing. But, as before, he didn't notice me or my frigid fingers pressing hard into his impatient, sweaty palm'.[7] Strongly reminiscent of narrative relationships in the works of Andrei Belyi and Vladimir Nabokov, this sort of identification permits the actual author little more claim to reality than the character he constructs.

A similar case of such narratorial authoritarianism is evident in Liudmila Petrushevskaia's *Vremia noch* (*Time Night*) in which the narrator-mother of two rebellious grown-up children not only frequently interjects the cited text of her daughter's memoirs with commentaries and fancifully composed additions of her own from her daughter's point of view, but does so self-consciously: 'In this place, I unexpectedly wrote down a few words and, what is more, from my daughter's person, as if her recollections, *her point of view*, came tumbling down on me as I sat sleeplessly in the kitchen'.[8] The narrator herself, moreover, wastes no opportunity to point out the fact that she is a poet, with the none too subtle implication of being a cut above the rest, despite the fact that her literary efforts have yet to result in publishing success.

The subversion of narratorial authority features as an exercise in parodying the traditional authority of the Soviet writer who, by the mere fact of being published, could not but speak *ex cathedra*. By retaining this authority while destabilising the right to it with a playful, to the point of mentally unstable, narrator or a petty, almost senile one, the above writers deconstruct the Soviet narrator by means of the most noticeably absent quality of socialist realist literature, namely, irony.

Provoking a more implicit ideological hierarchy, *Vremia noch* also seeks to subvert the patriarchalism of Russian literature. By providing her female narrator with almost absolute control over the means of discourse, in which her daughter Alena features as a modern home-breaking Anna Karenina and her son Andrei as a rebellious, money-wheedling Dmitrii Karamazov, the narrator is alternately cast as the husband Karenin and father Karamazov. The curious epigram to the novella also evades the unambiguous fashion in which Russian pronouns and verbs delineate gender, leaving the sex of the first person undefined at the very outset of the work. It would, nonetheless, be premature to suggest that feminism has taken a firm hold in Russian literary culture. Petrushevskaia, for instance, is one of the very few female prose writers of any real note in Russia at the present time—a situation which is well poised to change rapidly in coming years. The demythicisation of the Soviet writer has been reinforced by a thoroughgoing process of decanonising Soviet genres. More than a faint echo of Vissarion Belinskii can be detected in the iconoclasm of the new literary generation. Just as the influential nineteenth-century critic dismissed medieval and pseudo-classical canons in favour of the late Romantics and early Realists of his day, a large number of contemporary writers and critics, some with unconcealed glee, are measuring the demise of traditional Soviet genres and canons. Lev Anninskii, for example, notes that such

Soviet genres as secretarial prose, socialist realism, the thick journal and the popular epopee are dying out.[9]

It is interesting to note that this same process of decanonisation applies to the works of dissident writers whose historical and artistic value are compromised by the sociopolitical circumstances in which they were written. Viktor Erofeev, for example, condemned to the scrap-heap of literary history not only the official canons of socialist realist literature and semi-official village prose works, but also oppositional dissident literature as early as spring of 1990.[10] One commentator remarks that the motivation for his condemnation was the need for a generational change establishing apolitical literary trends: 'Erofeev belongs to the group of critics who contrast the "over-politicised" literature, mainly produced by authors belonging to the 1960s' generation, with the "alternative" or "new" literature, written chiefly by younger authors'.[11] Scarcely concealed in Erofeev's remarks is the presupposition that all good literature is apolitical or at least cannot be engendered in unfavourable sociopolitical circumstances. While a highly contentious point, there is some truth to the fact that many dissident writers have had an inordinate amount of attention paid them by virtue of their moral courage in protesting against the Soviet regime.[12] The point implied by critics such as Erofeev is that any appreciation of dissident literature from a literary historical point of view should not be morally conditioned.

The fate of literature

The concerns of the ex-Soviet, now *déclassé*, intellectuals, on the other hand, are accurately, if a little melodramatically, paraphrased by Anninskii: 'People are no longer reading. Literature is perishing. "Our literature, our pride, the best thing created by us as a nation" is on the verge of bankruptcy. Some maintain this with derisive coolness, others howl with fear and inauspicious forebodings'.[13] Dispossessed of its critical monopoly over Russian literature and the creative norms of Soviet literature, the old guard's only defence against the intellectual and cultural pluralism ushered in by the new sociopolitical order is to continue invoking the historical purposefulness and moral obligation of art in accordance with the dialectical historicism and didacticism of Soviet literary culture. Mariia Rudenko's reduction of contemporary literature to the two very broad and ill-defined categories of neo-romanticism and the post-avant-garde is symptomatic of the reaction against the invasion of postmodernity in Russia.[14] The title of the article in which she presents these categories—'After Literature: Game or Prayer?'—is in itself a morally loaded one. It would therefore be only a slight exaggeration to say that the former apparatchiks of controlled literary production concur with the face-value of another of Belinskii's musings, namely, 'we have no literature'. Giving support to this opinion is a claim in a review of literature published in *Literaturnaia gazeta* to the effect that 1992 was a fallow year for literature of any note.

The broadly either/or situation, read into contemporary literary culture by critics, has found a strong response by writers who have used the interplay between the two to decanonise the pantheon of Soviet classics. One way in which this has been executed is through provoking arbitrary genre appellations. Mark Kharitonov's *Linii sudby, ili sunduchok Milashevicha* (*Lines of Fate, or Milashevich's Trunk*), for example, functions as a commentary on the text of the fictional provincial writer Milashevich. Milashevich's own oeuvre—a diverse collection of elusive aphorisms and philosophical musings written on sweet wrappers—is a fanciful one which parodies the obviousness of the sloganistic culture of Soviet Russia in the 1920s and 1930s. This it does in a very subtle and non-confrontationist way. One aphorism authored by Milashevich, for example, notes the alliterative quality between *lozungi* ('slogans') and *luzhi* ('puddles'),[15] while at the same time, like his entire sweet wrapper corpus, defying comprehension on a semantic level. The effect is an indirect suggestion of a more obvious alliteration as well as thematic association, namely, *lozhi* ('lies'). Most of Milashevich's musings, however, parody his era's culture by their quality of being slightly otherworldly and therefore not representative of their literary historical context: 'They were both ideas and a philosophy, a means of contemplating and imagining the world as an eternal accumulation of moments, broken down and extracted from time'.[16] Providing a further contrast to the canonisation of socialist realism as the official literary method in this humourless era of Russian literary history, Milashevich's commentator, the aspirant Lizavin, speculates about the possibility of designating a 'sweet wrapper genre'.[17] The Russian for sweet wrapper—*fantik*—forms the attributive *fantichnyi*—a pun on the word 'fantastic'.

The peculiar nature of Milashevich's genre also provokes the historical dimension of Soviet Russian literature. While there is only the barest demarcation of time and place in the work, it is implicit that Milashevich's medium and genre are conditioned by the Stalinist era. The paucity of paper supplies, for instance, might serve to explain the fact that Milashevich scrawled his musings on sweet wrappers, while the cryptic nature of his aphorisms and the employment of such bland themes as gardening and vegetarianism might well have been shaped by fear of persecution. Nonetheless, there is no overt indication that this is indeed the case. Milashevich's persona is a construct for the reader, as it is for Lizavin, to imagine and restore through the text which he left behind. His *fantiki* are the stage 'where reality interwove itself with fantasy, where unnamed persons were both themselves and Milashevich; here there seemed to be some sort of code of his life which appeared, at times unintentionally, at times deliberately, as though the author wished it and, at the same time, was afraid of being understood'.[18] A topical parallel have been the efforts of Russian literary journals and almanacs since the *glasnost'* years to reinstitute and publish persecuted writers whose works had not hitherto appeared in Russia. The unsatisfactory nature of such a process of recanonising as '(posthumously) rehabilitated' writers disgraced or persecuted under Stalinism is pointed towards by the need for Milashevich's *Deus ex machina* towards the very end of the novel, where he enters into conversation with Lizavin. But even this proves ultimately disappointing: in a fanciful, dream-like dialogue the subject of Lizavin's study instructs him that there is no reality independent of the perception of reality. His final remarks that 'We are created by our creations' and 'I am real if you are real'[19] provide no gratification for the aspirant in his efforts to shed light on the man behind the author Milashevich or his oeuvre. In a broader sense, Milashevich issues a warning against the efforts of literary historians who have set themselves the task of uncovering the truth about the black holes in Soviet culture under Stalin.

Russian criticism

Russian criticism has generally not responded to the new cultural pluralism in the same multifaceted and intelligent way which has underscored contemporary prose. It is perhaps not surprising that writers-turned-critics are the notable exceptions. Vladimir Makanin, for instance, makes decidedly postmodern observations about Russian culture in his essay 'Kvazi,' which appeared in *Literaturnaia gazeta* in March 1993. Drawing on Fukuyama's notion of the End of History, his analysis of the new historical and social circumstances facing Russia draws on a commonality of experience with Western civilisation: 'We are part of Europe and, along with it, we have also approached the end of history—admittedly, lagging behind, even quite perceptibly. But this makes no real difference, since three to four centuries are in fact but a short moment—not even a full second—in the march of history!'[20] In particular, his observation that the writer 'is no longer able to connect present-day realities with that which immediately precedes them, since the problem of disconnectedness has at once become reality itself'[21] provides a very postmodern distrust of the possibility of universalising conceptions of chronological time and historical progress. In Makanin, it is possible to identify a third force in current literary polemics in Russia which is neither iconoclast, nor traditionalist and, prior to the relaxation of controls over artistic freedom, was neither dissident, nor official. His lamentations over the loss of the spiritual profundity of Russian culture ('Oh, where is it, our depth!') are a Quixotic gesture at establishing an *Ersatz* opposition to Russia's embryonic commercialism. As a solution to the spiritual woes of Russian culture, Makanin proposes a process of 'mythological reflection' (*mifologicheskoe myslenie*), which he defines as 'the ability of humans or the human masses to create heroes and gods'.[22]

Worth noting by means of comparison is the assessment of the Russian intelligentsia in response to the 1905 revolution contained in *Vekhi*, a collection of essays by the philosophical idealist and erstwhile 'legal Marxist' intelligentsia (Berdiaev, Bulgakov, Struve, Frank, Izgoev). In his essay 'Heroism and Asceticism: From Reflections on the Religious Nature of the Russian Intelligentsia,' Sergei Bulgakov makes observations about post-revolutionary Tsarist Russia which are very similar to ones being made now about post-Soviet Russia: 'Russian society, exhausted by previous exertions and failures, finds itself in some sort of torpid state, apathy, spiritual stupor, despondency. The Russian state has yet to demonstrate signs of rejuvenation and strengthening which are so vital for it, but rather, just as in the land of the sleeping, everything has frozen once again, fettered to an invincible drowsiness. Russian citizenry, blinded by multiple mortal punishments and the extraordinary rise in crime and the general decline in manners, has steadily regressed. Russian literature has been overwhelmed by a powerful wave of pornography and sensation-mongering'.[23] Despite or perhaps because of unrelenting vilification of *Vekhi* by the Soviet authorities, taking their cue from particularly vitriolic attacks by Lenin, there has been a considerable revival of interest in *Vekhi* and similar texts expounding the religious or philosophical idealist nature of the Russian intelligentsia in reaction to political and social upheavals.

A more reactionary viewpoint and pining for *le bon vieux temps* is evident in the works of village prose exponents such as Valentin Rasputin and Viktor Astafiev. In Astafiev's short story *The Blind Fishermen*, there are several unmistakable references to the regrettable decay of Russia's country idyll and the increasing cultural imperialism of the West as the source of blame for this, such as the contrastive use of archaisms and of profane language and English. The gentle Neo-Slavophilism and Russian Messianism of the *derevenshchiki* is neatly summed up at the end of Astafiev's *Blind Fishermen* with the stylistically anachronistic exclamation: 'Oh, Russian land! Where is the end to your majesty and suffering!'[24] There is none of the earlier identified narrative irony in this all too obvious transgression by the implied author.

One way in which Russia or, more precisely in this case, the former Soviet Union, enters the fray of topical culturological discourse is under the rubric of post-colonialism. The widespread use of Russian by writers representing any of the diverse non-Russian ethnic groups contained within the former Soviet Union has been and continues to be conditioned by the promise of a wider readership and, potentially therefore, literary recognition and acclaim. Few people have heard of the national bards of Abkhazia or Kyrgyzstan, for instance, but anyone who knows Russian literature will have heard of Fazil Iskander and Chingiz Aitmatov. Notably, this situation is not comparable to, say, that of Black or Native American writing in the United States, since a linguistic and cultural choice must be made by the writer, namely, to write in his or her own native tongue and thereby contribute to the development of that tongue's literary culture or to bring about a second-hand awareness of his or her culture by writing about it in an alien tongue. The *prima facie* professional-patriotic conflict involved in such a choice has strong ethical overtones which may determine the entire spectrum of writing from expression to reception. Although this situation will slowly change as the experience of statehood is consolidated and national languages usurp the place of Russian as the official language and assume more prestige, problems of literary heritage will still have to be addressed in an intelligible discourse which will take its cue from the post-colonial condition.[25]

By the same token, Russian literature will have to redress the myth of the 'friendship of nations' by refining the formerly Soviet and extra-national as the periphery assuming its place in the metropole. The works of Iskander and Aitmatov are excellent examples of this, as attested to by their popularity among Russian Soviet audiences in past years. Military and political adventurism in the 'near abroad' and the *de facto* economic union linking the fates of the former Soviet republics to Russia would seem to indicate, however, that the 'inviolable union of free republics' is not an empty metaphor in the minds of many in the Russian administration and that it will take some time before a post-colonial mental leap can be executed.

It would, of course, be difficult to deny the recent influence of the West, both as model for and consumer of Russian literature. An ironic development has been the popularisation of Russian writers who have made a significant contribution to Anglophone literature, by far the most prominent among which is Vladimir Nabokov. Indeed, he has been labelled the 'writer of *glasnost"*, while his influence in the Russian short story of the 1980s is unmistakable. In other instances, works which were never published in the Soviet Union are appearing in Russia on the basis of Western editions, notably those prepared by Ardis in the United States. Conversely, Russian intellectuals are taking a strong interest in the fate of emigre colleagues in the West. Feliks Medvedev's collection of interviews with noted Russian writers and artists residing in Europe and North America, entitled *After Russia (Posle Rossii)*,[26] is a case in point. On the literary production front, the introduction of market economics into the publishing industry is forcing *gosizdat* to become a self-justificatory *samizdat*. High inflation and a readership adjusting itself to its newly acquired freedom and influence as a consumer have introduced further uncertainties into Russia's literary situation. Russians have been traditionally regarded in the West as being culturally high-browed—reading the great novel classics, going to the opera, ballet and theatre and filling football stadiums in order to hear poets recite their works. Greater diversity and intellectual liberty is, however, rapidly changing cultural tastes. It is not inconceivable that Jackie Collins might replace Dostoevskii in the popularity stakes in years to come. Until privatisation of publishing houses has occurred and efficient production has been ensured, increasing demand for pulp fiction might eliminate publishing opportunities for up-and-coming writers.

The award of a Russian Booker Prize since October 1992 on the basis of criteria similar to those established for the Anglophone prize, such as universality and timelessness of appeal, has already prompted fierce controversy and competition among nominees. The popularisation of Russian literature in the West, on the other hand, has proceeded more slowly. Western audiences have been long held captive by dissident and early Gorbachev era-writers, more because of the political hype generated by them than the artistic merit of their works. Worth noting in this respect is the fact that Anatolii Rybakov's very marginally post-socialist realist *Children of the Arbat* was translated shortly after its appearance, while Bitov's *Pushkin House* had to wait almost ten years before being introduced to an English-speaking readership. The stigma of dissident writing will also prove a difficult one to overcome in the West. Aleksandr Solzhenitsyn's long-awaited return to Russia, for example, is continuing to capture considerable media attention in the West. Chukhontsev's English-language edition of recent Russian short stories, on the other hand, came out in 1991 with the title *Dissonant Voices*. In his preface, Chukhontsev notes that the writers whose works are contained in the volume are 'not choirboys but soloists'.[27]

Despite the rejection of hierarchies in its intellectual discourse, the West is hardly innocent of betraying relativistic prejudices similar to the one implied in Chuprinin's deliberations on contemporary Russian literature and its integration into 'universal' culture. Many thinkers continue to fondly invoke the Slavophile/Westerniser dimension in commenting on tendentious divergences of opinion in Russian politics, culture and society, with the legacy of progress being associated, often unqualifiedly, with Westernising monarchs or *Kulturtraeger*. The 'Gorbymania' phenomenon of the mid-to-late 1980s, for example, was engendered largely by the identification by Western leaders of their own humanistic traditions in Gorbachev's endeavours to introduce social and economic reform in the Soviet Union. Former British Prime Minister Thatcher put it most succinctly when she remarked that Gorbachev was 'a man one could do business with,' with the strong implication that this was hardly possible with the traditional Soviet leader. Most recently, the dowdy pre-Yeltsinites have hardly been able to compete in the Western popularity stakes with the fresh-faced technocrats operating with the imprimatur of the International Monetary Fund.

Admittedly, the opposition Russia-Europe is not as balanced as it might have been in the nineteenth century and most of the present one. Things Soviet have been too thoroughly discredited, the most persuasive metaphor for which has been the bloody routing of conservative forces at the White House in October 1993. Nonetheless, the post-Soviet order, as we have seen, has revealed myriad cultural problemata which are invoking diverse and talented responses in the literary community. As Russia assumes, however superficially, Western forms of government, economy and social structure, there is bound to be ever increasing similarity of intellectual experience with the West. It is therefore perhaps too irresistible a literary critical pun to suggest that, while *perestroika* (reconstruction) facilitated something of a literary renaissance in Russia, *rasstroika* (deconstruction)—the hallmark of postmodernity and of de-Sovietisation—is providing very attractive Baroque embellishments.

Notes

1 *Literaturnaia gazeta*, 13 January 1993, p.4.
2 These are among some of the oppositions Marko Pavlyshyn attributes to contemporary Ukrainian literature. See Marko Pavlyshyn, 'Ukrainska kultura z kutu zoru postmodernizmu', in Marko Pavlyshyn and J.E.M. Clarke (eds.), *Ukraine in the 1990s: Proceedings of the First Conference*

of the Ukrainian Studies Association of Australia. Monash University, 24-26 January 1992 (Melbourne: Slavic Section, Monash University, 1992) pp.38-49 at p.39.

3 For further discussion, see Riita H. Pittman, 'Writers and Politics in the Gorbachev Era', *Soviet Studies*, vol.44, no.4, 1992, pp.665-685.

4 Pittman, 'Writers and Politics in the Gorbachev Era', p.677.

5 Pavel Basinskii, 'Pismo Egoru Isaevu. O staroi i novoi literature', *Literaturnaia gazeta*, 31 March 1993, p.4.

6 Evgenii Laputin, 'Priruchenie Arlekinov', *Novyi mir*, no.7, 1993, pp.3-91 at p.20.

7 Laputin, 'Priruchenie Arlekinov', p.21.

8 Liudmila Petrushevskaia, 'Vremia noch', *Novyi mir*, no.2, 1992, pp.65-110 at p.92.

9 Lev Anninskii, 'Konets literatury?', *Druzhba narodov*, no.8, 1992, pp.244-46 at p.246.

10 Cited in Pittman, 'Writers and Politics in the Gorbachev Era', p.665.

11 Cited in Pittman, 'Writers and Politics in the Gorbachev Era', p.665.

12 For a comprehensive discussion of the literary legacy of dissident writers in Ukraine and the former USSR, see Peter Sawczak, 'Poetyka vidpovidalnosty i vidpovidalnist krytyky: dekanonizatsiia tvorchoi osobystosty i tvorchosty Vasylia Stusa', in Marko Pavlyshyn (ed.), *Stus iak tekst* (Melbourne: Monash University, 1992) pp.79-91; Marko Pavlyshyn, 'Aspects of the Literary Process in the USSR: The Politics of Re-Canonisation in Ukraine After 1985', *Southern Review*, no.1, 1991, pp.12-25.

13 Anninskii, 'Konets literatury?', p.244.

14 Mariia Rudenko, 'Posle literatury: igra ili molitva?', *Znamia*, no.6, 1993, pp.186-192.

15 Mark Kharitonov, 'Linii sudby, ili sunduchok Milashevicha', *Druzhba narodov*, no.1, 1992, pp.38-117 at p. 65; no.2, 1992, pp.94-178.

16 Kharitonov, 'Linii sudby, ili sunduchok Milashevicha', no.1, p.113.

17 Kharitonov, 'Linii sudby, ili sunduchok Milashevicha', no.1, p.65.

18 Kharitonov, 'Linii sudby, ili sunduchok Milashevicha', no.2, pp.160-61.

19 Kharitonov, 'Linii sudby, ili sunduchok Milashevicha', no.2, pp.160-61.

20 Vladimir Makanin, 'Kvazi', *Literaturnaia gazeta*, 31 March 1993, pp.3, 5.

21 Makanin, 'Kvazi'.

22 Makanin, 'Kvazi'.

23 S.N. Bulgakov, 'Geroizm i podvizhnichestvo: iz razmyshlenii o religioznoi prirode russkoi intelligentsii,' in *Vekhi. Intelligentsiia v Rossii: Sborniki statei, 1909-1910* (Moscow: Molodaia gvardiia, 1991) pp.43-84 at p.43.

24 Viktor Astafiev, 'The Blind Fisherman', in Oleg Chukhontsev (ed.), *Dissonant Voices: The New Russian Fiction* (London: Harvill, 1991) pp.351-370 at p.370.

25 I have addressed this problematic in the context of Ukrainian literature in my article 'H/G chy 'H'?: Do modeliu synkretychnosty ukrainskoi kultury', *Suchasnist*, 12 December 1993, pp.96-100.

26 Feliks Medvedev, *Posle Rossii* (Moscow: Respublika, 1992).

27 Chukhontsev (ed.), *Dissonant Voices: The New Russian Fiction*.

12 ALTERNATIVE VISIONS OF THE RUSSIAN FUTURE

JOHN MILLER

For as long as any of us can remember the juxtaposition of a 'strong state' and a 'weak society' has been a key concept in the analysis of Russian and Soviet history and politics. Articulated, this concept stood for: an authoritarian, bureaucratic and centralised administration; state control of public association, interest group activity and local government; a major degree of state control over the media, education and culture (for example through a 'state ideology'); a major degree of state ownership and control of the economy and disposal of its surplus; the downgrading of law and constitutionalism as impediments to state power; and in general the inhibition of 'civil society' and its replacement by state programmes of 'mobilisation' and 'state-building' from above, such that society seemed to have lost much of its capacity for spontaneous evolution and the state appeared to manage such social change as there was.

Clearly the forces unleashed by Gorbachev's *perestroika*, the collapse of the Soviet communist system and of the Soviet Union itself have dealt a massive blow to the 'strong state' in this familiar sense. Witness the two successive elected parliaments that have gone out of their way to defy the executive; the regions of Russia that have declared their autonomy or 'sovereignty', and (more serious) the refusal of many to pay their taxes; the President's inability to control the printing of money; the surge in crime and sporadic public violence; or the activities of warlords and private armies, not (so far) within Russia itself, but sometimes organised from inside Russia.

But 'society' has not exactly leapt into the breach opened by this collapse of state power. The professional middle classes or the spontaneous public organisations in which Gorbachev placed such faith have proved a disappointment, then and since; organised labour has been conspicuous in its passivity; peasants are reluctant to leave collective and state farms; privatisation has proved far more difficult than was envisaged; political parties are still largely the personal followings of would-be charismatic leaders; the August coup collapsed through the efforts of the capital cities alone, and the provinces were similarly silent in October 1993; and the former *nomenklatura* has shown remarkable tenacity in hanging on to resources, power and privileges. What exactly did we expect when we talked about the return of 'civil society'? Its simple reemergence, as in the Czech Republic or Poland? Some kind of upsurge of 'purified' national consciousness, perhaps, like that in Turkey in the early 1920s? Better models would have been the confusion and exhaustion of Germany after 1918, or of Russia itself after 1917; and better still—to capture the impact both of national humiliation and of the deskilling, politically juvenilising effects of one-party dictatorship—Germany after 1945. In post-war Germany it took a good twenty years before meaningful political participation reemerged—and, unlike Russia, Germany had considerable prior experience of law, market and democracy.

Yet this too is an unsatisfactory portrayal of Russian society in the early 1990s. Society is wielding an inarticulate and unorganised power over the state and state policy, just as it did in the NEP period in the 1920s. Scornful crowds can jeer a Head of State from a public ceremony, as happened to Gorbachev on 1 May 1990. The collapse of the Soviet trade and distribution system allowed regions to decide how they would dispose of their products, and this sometimes led to the boycotting of unpopular customers (like the 'Great Wen', Moscow). Private land ownership and the privatisation of much industry is being frustrated, not just by the former management, but by widespread popular reluctance and objections. Above all, management in thousands of localities has taken fright at the prospect of mass unemployment, has kept people on the pay-roll and passed popular pressure on to the authorities—pushing the ministries into bailing management out financially and the Central Banks into printing money to back ministerial credits. In all this society is setting limits on state policy, making exorbitant some policies dear to reformers, and narrowing the options within which Russia can develop. Such implicit pressure is surely more potent than that of a hostile parliament; the President, after all, cannot dissolve society! My objective in this chapter is to explore the range of perceptions ordinary people may have about Russia's triple crisis—political, socioeconomic, and national—the kind of perceptions that inform their pressure on the state.[1]

Now in part this pressure is an updated form of Russian society's age-old strategies for keeping the interventionist state at bay (and in that sense the state was never quite as strong as foreign Russophobes and Soviet leaders may have fancied). But in two respects this is not simply the old political culture resurgent, and its evolution during the twentieth century is instructive.

First there is very little sign hitherto of the kind of mass, neighbour-to-neighbour social breakdown and violence that has afflicted Bosnia, Georgia or Tajikistan. For centuries fear of *Russkii bunt, bessmyslennyi, besposhchadnyi*—'Russian revolt, senseless, merciless'[2]—has haunted the elite, the towns and the intelligentsia, and provided the state with support and excuses for its repression of social 'spontaneity'. Over the last five years there has been some rioting over the supply of goods, or against unpopular local officials, and there has been a considerable increase in random criminal violence; but, in areas of Russian settlement, nothing to compare with the peasant revolts of old, or the rural aftermath of the 1905 or 1917 revolutions. The comparison gives the reason away: *Russkii bunt* was something agrarian and anti-urban: but by now only 26 per cent of the population is rural, and this rural sector is disproportionately old, unskilled, female,[3] and—anecdotal evidence suggests—demoralised. The 'average' citizen now lives in a town slightly under 100,000 in population, typically one which took off in the 1930s. And the evidence suggests provisionally that these small-town residents have acquired habits of social cooperation and discipline that were unfamiliar to their peasant grandfathers. Despite the turmoil of Stalinism and the deskilling effects of communism, urbanisation has promoted a measure of social cohesion and stability that is new in Russia's political culture.

The second change to Russian society flows on from this. This is by now a literate and highly educated society, a fifth of which has tertiary or 'secondary specialist' qualifications. One may (with Aleksandr Solzhenitsyn) have one's doubts about the standard of some of these qualifications and the culture they generate,[4] but we should be in no doubt that this is now a society thoroughly familiar with modern technology and mass communications, as well as knowledgeable and inquisitive about the outside world.

When the Soviet order collapsed one of the most noticeable differences for this educated small-town world will have been the collapse of attempts to mould and coordinate popular perceptions from the capital. This came about in two ways. First the state's role in the control of the print media[5] suffered a major blow with the August 1990 Law on the Press which permitted the foundation of new media organs and allowed existing organs a certain measure of freedom to choose their own 'proprietors'. By itself, however, this might simply have strengthened the authority of the city intelligentsia, through their 'fat journals' and the excellent new newspapers founded under the terms of the new law. But commercial realities in an economic depression soon put paid to this. Sales of quality media, concerning both cultural and current affairs, have plummeted: if *Nezavisimaia gazeta* prints 100,000 copies, it seems unlikely that many of these are read outside Moscow and St Petersburg.[6] Ordinary people have less leisure for thinking about society and politics than they did in the 1970s—but systematic and coordinated intellectual packages are no longer being handed down to them to anything like their former extent. The outcome must be that ordinary people are fending intellectually for themselves far more, and that their perceptions are being moulded by a more varied and (I should guess) more 'low-brow' array of opinion-makers than formerly. To borrow from Benedict Anderson,[7] it seems appropriate to speak of such people 'imagining' the sort of Russia they would prefer, and of such images being accepted or rejected for quite personal, sometimes idiosyncratic, parochial or incoherent reasons.

On what kind of resources may ordinary people and 'petty opinion-makers' draw in this imaginative process? Two would seem to have gained in importance: personal experience of life in the Soviet period, of course; but, second and more significantly, people's perceptions of Russian history. The latter, however, will not be simply the platitudes of Soviet textbooks (though these books must still be around by the million): as T.H. Rigby points out this volume's concluding chapter, disillusion with received wisdom involves an attempt to recover the past. This is bound to include a great deal of autodidactic, 'do-it-yourself' revisionism, often uncritical and romantic—like the notorious letter of Nina Andreeva 'I Cannot Renounce Principles'[8]—and sometimes determinedly 'alternative', as a variety of subterranean countercultures come into the open.[9] Above all, elements of the traditional political culture—that 'subjective perception of history and politics'[10]—will have reasserted themselves, in reaction to seventy five years of politicians telling people what their values and symbols ought to be. The influence of such popular perceptions—and, because of Soviet isolationism, these are above all perceptions of Russia—can rarely have been so strong. I suggest that, in imagining their preferred future Russia, people are drawing on a number of distinct visions, models or traditions of its polity, each with exemplars in the past, and each linked to characteristic perceptions of the problem and attempted solutions. I propose to survey four of these visions, and then to examine the strengths and weaknesses of each vision's appeal. This will be attempted in the abstract, without use of empirical survey data:[11] it is an essay in thinking oneself into the perceptions of the ordinary Russian.

Four alternative visions

Statism

Let me start with the vision which corresponds most closely to what Russia was until very recently: a strong, authoritarian, bureaucratic, centralised state, presiding over society and social change, as outlined in the opening paragraph of this chapter. I call this 'statism'—the image of the traditional Russian state (or *gosudarstvo*).[12] Models of it in Russian history include both the 'revolutions from above' of Ivan the Terrible, Peter I and Stalin, and the conservative disciplinarianism of Nikolai I and II and Brezhnev.[13] Both are by origin military models of ordering society, and for this reason, perhaps, the traditional Russian state has been much admired and apparently never overthrown by the military. In its politics and economics it is a highly conservative vision: it seeks no coherent analysis of why the Soviet system failed, nor indeed (although its exponents may make tactical concessions to modernity) does it come to grips with the political implications of mass literacy, *Berufsethik*, or price-forming markets. Nor does it show much interest in modern nationalism: although the Empire and the Soviet Union were organised primarily by and for Russians, they nevertheless remained multinational states and always offered careers to non-Russians prepared to put state above nation.

Reformism

Next, what has always been the clearest alternative to statism: political and socioeconomic reform. The origins of the reformist tradition lie in the centuries-old perception that Russia is a laggard or late starter along a historical road general to European societies and thus has to learn from more advanced ones. Historical figures who sought to realise such lessons are M.M. Speranskii (1807-12), Aleksandr II (the Emancipation of 1861), P.A. Stolypin (1906-11)—and we are surely right to see Mikhail Gorbachev and Boris Yeltsin as working in the same tradition. By the nineteenth century reformism had come to mean the ability to emulate the high productivity, high growth economies of Western Europe, together with the West's social enterprise, inventiveness and resilience. The traditional strong state was readily identified as the obstacle to this, and the reformist vision was thus one of reducing and circumscribing state power, and liberating spontaneous, self-generating societal evolution. It is also not surprising that reformism and 'Westernism' became virtually interchangeable terms.[14] By the 1980s reformism's objectives had become more precise: democracy and political pluralism, a free market and private property, and law and constitutionalism.

Where Russian statism is conservative, reformism is derivative and some of its important characteristics stem from this. It has always depended, first, on a cadre of analysts and interpreters of foreign society—something not easily achieved given Russia's huge size and poor communications with the outside world. Reformists have thus tended to be tiny elites and to approach their own society with evangelical zeal, if not motives of social engineering: all too easily this could prompt them—the Bolsheviks are an example—to cross the fine boundary between reform and revolution from above. They were, second, rather selective in what they borrowed, preferring rational and theoretical neatness to hard-nosed analysis of the Russian condition; in particular the links of the literacy and communications revolutions with nationalism seem to have passed them by.[15] Third, of course, Westernist recipes suggested that Russia could never take the initiative and this was humiliating to a populous and energetic society and readily provoked xenophobia.

Hence the paradox of reformism: its vision was one of emancipation from the state, but no one except a high official of the state was ever in a position to try to realise it! In practice reformism never got much beyond notions of the state's voluntary withdrawal from power, and its invitation of society into partnership.[16] And the opportunities to try even that presented themselves rarely: they depended on a conjuncture of leadership intelligence, benevolence and persistence, societal patience, and circumstances of relative security and prosperity. Strike out any of these variables and leaders would retreat with relief to the traditional *gosudarstvo*.

Russian nationalism

The third vision is what was called Slavophilism in the nineteenth century, and nowadays Russian nationalism. It draws on the vocabulary of Central European nationalism[17] to articulate the reaction against both Westernism and the restriction of initiative to the state. Its accent is on the nation rather than the state, and on organic consensus rather than organisation. Society is pictured as cohering naturally and governing itself from below on the basis of common primordial Russian or Slav values and discipline—but what results is a united, resolute and internationally imposing Russia. It is an image that leaves institutions deliberately vague, or tends to blur the distinctions among political, social, legal and economic institutions—and one cannot but suspect that in practice its politics are destined to be authoritarian, and probably an authoritarianism of the charismatic or clerical, rather than bureaucratic kind. In *Rebuilding Russia*, Aleksandr Solzhenitsyn goes to considerable lengths to counter this charge of political vagueness, but at critical points—for instance, in the proposal to stop elected representatives organising amongst themselves—even he insists on leaving matters informal.[18] Such political innocence is perhaps why no historical regime has relied on Russian nationalism alone, although both Tsars and Soviet leaders made much use of it.

Nationalist thinking developed in two distinct ways in the twentieth century.[19] One tendency, that of the *pochvenniki* (or 'Back to the Soil' movement), clung to the moral, spiritual and consensual virtues of Russianness and, in their name, came increasingly to challenge the Soviet state's social engineering: Solzhenitsyn is the outstanding representative of this movement, and it has had considerable influence on the Russian Orthodox clergy. The other stressed the political and international effectiveness of mobilised nationalism, and under the label 'national Bolshevism' was largely coopted by the state: it is from this source that the nationalism of V.V. Zhirinovskii and his 'Liberal-Democratic Party of Russia' springs. There is an impressive coherence to *pochvennik* thinking, but it is in the domain of personal morality rather than of politics; 'political' nationalism, by contrast, is an eclectic hotch-potch, but its exponents, like Zhirinovskii or Colonel V.I. Alksnis, show considerable stylistic and rhetorical talents. It is hardly surprising, therefore, that in today's hectic times, and in the intellectual vacuum left after the collapse of Soviet state *agitprop*, slick and emotional sloganeering should drown out the modest and spiritual efforts of the *pochvenniki*.

Communitarianism

These three models have dominated thinking about political arrangements in Russia—as it has been presented to the outside world. But there is ample evidence that a fourth model is influential beneath the surface and reasserts itself in times of crisis of the state and nation: the Time of Troubles (*smutnoe vremia*) of 1598-1613, for instance, or the five years after the 1917 Revolution[20]—or the current period beginning in 1991.[21] This is the vision of a stateless society, of 'getting the state off our backs', and of a return to the pre-Tatar world of autonomous and preferably autarkic city states, or Herzen's federation of free peasant communes. Like nationalism, such 'communitarianism' is vague about formal political arrangements. Unlike nationalism, the stress is not on Russian unity or collective action, but on the self-management of a community whose members know one another personally, a pre-modern *Gemeinschaft*—and one of the motives for this vision nowadays must surely be simple rejection of state-imposed modernity. This difference between communitarianism and nationalism is well illustrated by the early stages of the breakdown of the Soviet order in Russia proper, which were opposed by communists and nationalists alike: the erection of 'trade barriers' and emergence of scores of would-be autarkic mini-economies based on large provincial towns and their hinterlands.[22]

Contemporary versions of each of these four visions have their adherents in post-Soviet Russia. Indeed the general elections of December 1993 reveal that support for them is distributed with surprising evenness.[23] Of the 444 deputies elected to the State Duma, 80% can be apportioned as follows. Parties favouring some measure of return to statism (the Communist Party of the Russian Federation, the Agrarian Party of Russia) won 100 seats. The three main reformist groups (Russia's Choice, the Party of Russian Unity and Consensus, and 'Bloc Iavlinskii-Boldyrev-Lukin') gained 133. Zhirinovskii's nationalist Liberal-Democratic Party of Russia (together with the small 'Russian Way' group) won 68. Finally 67 of the 131 deputies who were elected as independents (that is, who defeated the candidates of the 'national' parties) later united to form the 'New Regional Policy' bloc—whilst some 60 other independents, once they got into the Duma, joined the parliamentary organisations of the 'national' parties or blocs. That the former refused to combine with Moscow-based movements, both before and after the election, suggests, at least prima facie, an element of communitarianism.[24]

Strengths and weaknesses

In these elections and elsewhere we witness Russians comparing and contrasting four possible models of their future. What considerations might they invoke in doing this? Let us look again at each model in turn:

Statism

The main factor working against the traditional statist model in early 1994 was of course that it had failed only two years earlier, and that—in many people's opinion still—it had deserved to fail. By the late 1980s millions of people had become consciously hostile to the basic principles of the Soviet order, and in particular to four of them: its intrusiveness and dogmatism in ideological, cultural, spiritual and lifestyle matters; its contempt for social interests and opinion, and especially of urban professional *Berufsethik*; its neglect of the small-scale retail and services economy, whilst refusing to let anyone else develop it better; and the use of the secret police, rather than 'political methods', to get its way in all these matters. This discredited the image of statism and challenged the conventional balance of power between state and society. People who may otherwise be clamouring for a 'firm hand' do not wish to see a state as centralised or unconstrained as the Soviet one, and the parties like the Communists that are nostalgic for statism have toned down their policies with this in mind.[25] Indeed industrialisation and urbanisation may have made it impossible to construct again a stable state as powerful as the Soviet one.

Nevertheless the statist model has things going for it. As inflation, unemployment and crime increase, and as Yeltsin tries and fails at tasks that defeated Gorbachev, it has become easy to forget that reform was introduced because the Brezhnevite system was not working; the allegedly 'destabilising' decision to embark on reform comes to be blamed instead. A return to a statist model holds out the prospect of public order and a reasonably stable economy; in particular there would seem to be strong public support for state ownership of heavy industry, and strong objections to private trading in land. And when the collapse of the Soviet Union went so far as to cut off Ukraine and Belarus from Russia, this was interpreted as a body blow, not just to the Russian nation, but to the territorial integrity of the historic Russian state; the result was a surge of support both for nationalism and statism. Such a revival of support is facilitated by two further factors: the recurrent temptation (noted above) for both reformists and nationalists to adopt policies or methods from the statist package; and the fact that the bureaucracy of the old regime is still largely intact, capable of resuming its old role and of frustrating policies which it distrusts.

Reformism

The strengths of the reformist vision are perhaps two. First the appeal to many people of what they see as progress, the appeal, as Gorbachev put it, of 'rejoining civilisation'.[26] Nor should these be seen just as slogans: the emergence of the 'Memorial' Society of victims of Stalinism, for instance, suggests that a considerable number of people (if only we could put a rough figure on it!) see law, pluralism and the market, not just as foreign concepts, but as institutions that can matter for the fate of the ordinary person. Reformism's second and distinct appeal is that it holds out the prospect of living and consumption standards on the way to those of Western suburbia. This is a powerful attraction, but in the long term it may be double-edged. Sir Karl Popper has said that 'the capitalism of the supermarkets ... will remain beyond their reach'.[27] If he turns out to be correct on this, then the realisation among ordinary Russians will serve to disillusion them mightily from the reformist vision, and incline them to others. This is after all not so very different from how Slavophilism emerged.

This is to anticipate discussion of the reform model's weaknesses. Above all, as everyday misery and uncertainty persist, and ever more difficulties are encountered with privatisation and marketisation, support for reform is bound to be eroded. Reformism and Westernism, it was noted above, are close to interchangeable, and Westernism is all too easily associated with the 'come-and-rule-over-us style'[28]—hence with the threat of humiliation to both state and nation. Not only the Yeltsin administration, but those of the United States and the European Union, the IMF, G7, and thousands of ordinary western businesspersons, advisers and pollsters must walk delicately if they are not to seem 'carpetbaggers'. Reformism is weak in a further sense: law, pluralism and the market may be beginning to be valued, but they are probably understood in detail only by a small elite, concentrated in the big cities, people whom it will be easy to portray as semi-foreignised and socially greedy and exploitative. One could imagine a reformist regime like Yeltsin's being tempted to try overcoming such resistance by state-sponsored 'mobilisation' or 'education campaigns'. We've been here before: whether such programmes worked or not, such a regime would have lost the defining element in the reformist vision.

Nationalism

Initial analyses of the electoral support for the Liberal-Democratic Party of Russia in December 1993 portray the typical Zhirinovskii voter not as poor and downtrodden—such support is more likely to have gone to the Communists or Agrarians—but as a young, skilled, urban male, employed, earning something above the average, ambitious and anti-establishment.[29] If this is correct, the parallels with support for Hitler are striking.[30] More broadly we can place Russian nationalism in a pattern familiar from other parts of the world, one which associates nationalism in particular with moderately educated and moderately prosperous, *deraciné*, lower middle class outgroups[31]—not a bad description (it was suggested above) of the 'average' contemporary Russian. Such people have the education, leisure and widened horizons to care about an imagined community—about its crime statistics or foreign policy posture, for example, or the twenty five million Russians who now live outside the Russian Federation—but a combination of pressures makes them see politics in terms of ideas and symbols, rather than of problem-solving, 'pork-barrelling' or adjudication of competing interests. I have argued elsewhere that the Soviet regime fostered exactly such a symbolic conception of politics: it depoliticised and sentimentalised culture and it inhibited (except

among the tiniest of elites) the acquisition of political experience—
the articulation, expression and negotiation of interests and
participation in decisionmaking.[32] This is the social environment
in which Zhirinovskii's kind of nationalism has flourished, and it is
one that is likely to persist even if Zhirinovskii and his Liberal-
Democratic Party of Russia do not.

This conveys something of the strengths of nationalism and the
mechanisms of its maintenance. Nationalism's main weakness (in
its currently dominant form) is its intellectual parasitism and
incoherence. It is poorly organised and lacks discipline.[33] Unlike
statism and reformism it lacks clear policies, and in particular has
no economic policy worthy of the name. This helps explain, to my
mind, the fact that most of the Liberal-Democratic Party of
Russia's success in the December 1993 elections came in the Party
List vote: voters supported nationalism in the abstract—but when
faced with a concrete choice of options concerning their local
situation they preferred other candidates.[34] And—so far at least—
nationalist politicians lack experience, leadership and plain
dignity: Zhirinovskii's half-baked interventions in West European
politics soon after his election must have reminded Russians of
Khrushchev at the United Nations in 1960, and they learn about
these things more readily nowadays. These are weaknesses that
nationalism can remedy by drawing on the policies, methods or
personnel of other traditions, especially the statist one: Hitler's
borrowings from German conservatism are probably a better
guide than the self-sufficiency of Argentinian Peronism. Unless
nationalism adapts in this way, its contribution to policy will
remain one of signalling popular dissatisfaction and setting limits
to what politicians of other traditions can do.[35]

Communitarianism

Communitarianism was portrayed above as an aspiration that
has usually been smothered in Russian history, but which comes
to the surface at times like the present when state controls break
down. What has lent communitarianism particular strength in the
present juncture is that autarkic local self-government reflects the
skills and experience of the local elites left in power when the
Soviet order collapsed. The tendency towards a feudalisation of
relationships between provincial officials and Moscow under
Brezhnev has often been noted.[36] In the command economy this
led local elites to assume a supervisory role in the local economy
that to them must have been hardly distinguishable from
ownership. When the 'Centre's' orders petered out, or (more
commonly) became impossibly confusing, these elites moved
easily into a patrimonial role over 'their' territories,[37] and began

to turn them into what Weber called an *oikos*, a household economy writ large.[38] Not for them the inanities of nationalist rhetoric: communitarianism offered them personal advantage and an outlet for their talents—and widespread support from ordinary people whose vital concern was to keep their communities in employment. The outcome has been an alliance between provincial agents of the statist tradition, dislodged from power at the Centre, and local communitarian pressures.[39]

Working against communitarianism is the fact that it represents only a partial rejection of Russian statehood and unity. There are no signs so far that it extends to rejection of common defence, nor that local military commanders have allied with local political elites against Moscow.[40] Such a development would represent for Russians (far more, for instance, than it would for Ukrainians) a quite shocking departure from a statehood tradition half a millenium old; even in the original *smutnoe vremia* almost four hundred years ago the contending warlords aimed to capture Moscow and the dynasty, not to set up separate states. We should expect the same nowadays: military intervention in Russian politics is much more likely to take the form of maintaining or challenging Central administrations than that of Chinese-style 'warring states'.

Processes

How might these four visions fare in competition among themselves? What stands out from the above analysis is the strength of the traditional political culture, the difficulties of changing it on a permanent basis—and especially in hard and troubled times. Reformism, nationalism and communitarianism are all under pressure to adopt policies or methods from the statist tradition.

Support for reformism is being eroded as mere untested idealism and market fetishism are weeded out, as the reformists sense society's lack of understanding for and commitment to their ideas, and as they are pushed increasingly into dependence on existing state servants. Communitarians must modify their priorities as the realities of international defence (the Gulf War and those in Bosnia, Transcaucasia and Tajikistan) strike home; as they learn about economies of scale; above all as the implications of Ukrainian and Belarussian secession sink in. Nationalism by contrast has made impressive gains in public support—but can hardly retain them on the basis of nationalism alone.

In some form or other the statist tradition thus seems likely to prevail. What we may increasingly come to see is a struggle over the precise form of this restored statism, in an attempt to push its detailed emphases and nuances in the direction of one of the other models. If the reformists can maintain some influence the outcome could be a Russian *gosudarstvo* which has learnt from the Soviet experience and its collapse, and is closer now to eighteenth century Prussia, Meiji Japan, Bismarck's Germany or Gaullist France, than it is to Stalin's or Brezhnev's Soviet Union. Or, in an alternative scenario, popular pressures might push the administration into halting or reversing privatisation, and then, to defend the currency, into increasing controls on foreign trade and prices, increasing isolation of the Russian from the international economy, and increasing regulation of information and lobbying activity. With Siberian resources Russia could probably sustain such a return to autarky for quite some time—it is one of the few countries in the world that could—but the process would almost certainly depend on the cooptation of nationalist support. The outcome would be a statism moulded by both communitarian isolationism and nationalism, and in this bearing some resemblance to the course of developments in Iran in the 1980s.

Notes

1 I wish to acknowledge the particular influence of three recent papers by colleagues or former colleagues: David Dyker's 'Nomenklatura Nationalism—the Key to an Understanding of the New East European Politics?', presented to the conference on Europe at La Trobe University, 5-9 July 1993; Adrian Jones's 'Competing Ideas of the "Self" in Russian Self-Determination, Past and Present', presented to the conference on Self-Determination, Centre for Slavonic and Eastern European Studies, Macquarie University, November 1993; and T.H. Rigby's concluding chapter in the present volume. The Chapter also develops themes from my paper 'Why was the Post-Communist Ethnic Revival so Vigorous?', submitted to *Ethnic and Racial Studies*.

2 A.S. Pushkin, 'The Captain's Daughter', in A.S. Pushkin, *The Queen of Spades and other Stories* (New York: Signet, 1961).

3 The following percentage distributions come from the 1979 census: see *Itogi vsesoiuznoi perepisi naseleniia 1979 goda* (Moscow: Goskomstat, 1989) vol.II, part 1, pp.7, 41-43; vol.III, part 1, pp.25-27:

	Urban		Rural	
	Male	Female	Male	Female
Total population:	46.1	53.9	45.8	54.2
In given group, of pensionable age:	7.8	20.6	10.1	28.3
In given group, having no more than primary education or less:	24.3	31.0	45.7	58.1

4 See Alexander Solzhenitsyn, *From Under the Rubble* (London: Fontana/Collins, 1976) pp.229-78.

5 However, Presidents Gorbachev and Yeltsin both maintained a shaky executive control over Central Television.

6 And notice that whole regions in the December 1993 elections went without nominating candidates for any of the 'national' political parties: see the list of constituency candidates for the State Duma in *Rossiiskaia gazeta*, 30 November 1993.

7 Benedict Anderson, *Imagined Communities: Reflections on the Origin and Spread of Nationalism* (London: Verso, 1983).

8 See *Sovetskaia Rossiia*, 13 March 1988.

9 See also 'Why was the Post-Communist Ethnic Revival so Vigorous?'.

10 In full, the 'subjective perception of history and politics, the fundamental beliefs and values, the foci of identification and loyalty, and the political knowledge and expectations which are the product of the specific historical experience of nations and groups': Archie Brown, 'Introduction', in Archie Brown and Jack Gray (eds.), *Political Culture and Political Change in Communist States* (London: Macmillan, 1977) pp.1-24 at p.1.

11 To which, by reason of my location and the eccentricities of Australian research funding, I have very little access. The four abstract models are no more than the working out, in the Russian environment and political culture, of the possible permutations generated by combining two variables, the state (strong or weak) and society (assertive or passive). And let me stress: these are models and archetypes of political perceptions, and the proclaimed beliefs of politicians may be intermediate between them, or just plain confused.

12 The reader may react that this is to underrate the distinctively communist features of the Soviet Union. I have argued elsewhere (John Miller, '"The Decline and Fall of the Soviet Empire" ... Making a Start', *Quadrant*, vol.37, no.4, April 1993, pp.18-24) that the accession of Brezhnev marked a crucial turning-point of the Soviet system to a state of traditional Russian type.

13 There was a natural cyclical oscillation between these two modes of the state, but neither (despite what some of the authoritarian modernisers may have thought) succeeded in altering the balance of power between state and society: see T.H. Rigby, *The Changing Soviet System: Mono-organisational Socialism from its Origins to Gorbachev's Restructuring* (Aldershot: Edward Elgar, 1990) pp.183-206.

14 'Reformist' or 'Westernist' are, to my mind, clearer labels for this tendency than 'democrat', 'liberal' or 'radical'. But note that 'Westernism' here represents the Russian label for a specific, native Russian tradition of interpreting the West; it should not be equated with our colloquial or post-modernist notions of 'westernisation'.

15 But, to be fair, the English-speaking tradition has also been obtuse about this.

16 Even so this is a process very foreign to English-speaking experience; analogies from elsewhere in the world might be the evolution of Prussia from the time of the Great Elector, the Meiji Restoration in Japan, or, more recently, the industrialisation of Singapore and South Korea.

17 And in this sense, like Westernism, Russian nationalism is by origin imported, but it took native root more readily than Westernism—though not as readily as in the South Slav lands that lacked Russia's statist tradition; see Jones, 'Competing Ideas of the "Self" in Russian Self-Determination, Past and Present', pp.4-5.

18 See Alexander Solzhenitsyn, *Rebuilding Russia* (London: Harvill, 1991) pp.70-71.

[19] See, for instance, John B. Dunlop, *The Faces of Contemporary Russian Nationalism* (Princeton University Press, 1983) pp.242-273, and Dimitry Pospielovsky, 'The Neo-Slavophile Trend and its Relation to the Contemporary Religious Revival in the USSR' in Pedro Ramet (ed.), *Religion and Nationalism in Soviet and East European Politics* (Durham: Duke University Press, 1984) pp.41-58, both against the background of Alexander Yanov, *The Russian New Right* (Berkeley: Institute of International Studies, University of California, 1978).

[20] Ending for Russia with the re-incorporation of the 'Far Eastern Republic' in November 1922. The anarchic strand in Lenin's *State and Revolution* and his willingness to trust mass 'revolutionary conscience' would seem to owe something to such communitarian influences, as would Stalin's economic isolationism.

[21] For details see Vera Tolz, 'Regionalism in Russia: the Case of Siberia', *RFE/RL Research Report*, vol.2, no.9, 26 February 1993, pp.1-9; Vera Tolz, 'The Role of the Republics and Regions', *RFE/RL Research Report*, vol.2, no.15, 9 April 1993, pp.8-13; and especially Elizabeth Teague, 'North-South Divide: Yeltsin and Russia's Provincial Leaders', *RFE/RL Research Report*, vol.2, no.47, 26 November 1993 pp.7-23. The state may seek to play on such aspirations even in times of stability: think of Khrushchev's 'comradely courts', neighbourhood or shop-floor meetings that were given minor judicial powers.

[22] The earliest clear case would seem to be the demands of the Kuzbass miners in July 1989; see Elizabeth Teague, '"Embryos of People's Power"', *Report on the USSR*, vol.1, no.32, 11 August 1989, pp.1-4.

[23] Figures based on *Argumenty i fakty*, no.4, 1994, p.2 and *Rossiiskaia gazeta*, 28 December 1993. Not apportioned are 'Women of Russia' (23 deputies) and the Democratic Party of Russia (15)—who would seem to be mainly centrist in preference; 'Union of 12 December' (23, probably pro-reformist); and 15 deputies whose alignments have not been identified. A slightly different distribution in Wendy Slater, 'Russian Duma Sidelines Extremist Politicians', *RFE/RL Research Report*, vol.3, no.7, 18 February 1994 pp.5-9 at p.6 seems to apportion the missing fifteen to the nationalist 'Russian Way'.

[24] In 'Gosudarstvennaia duma: dve sensatsii v techenie poluchasa', *Izvestiia*, 14 January 1994, p.2, Sergei Chugaev refers to this tendency, but gives it less weight than the managerial interests in 'New Regional Policy', making it, in his opinion, a successor to the centrist 'Civic Union'. See further below.

[25] See, for example, *Argumenty i fakty*, no.47, 1993, p.2.

[26] Mikhail Gorbachev, 'Sotsialisticheskaia ideia i revoliutsionnaia perestroika', *Pravda*, 26 November 1989.

[27] See '"The Best World We Have Yet Had": George Urban Interviews Sir Karl Popper', *Report on the USSR*, vol.3, no.22, 31 May 1991, pp.20-22 at p.22.

[28] Solzhenitsyn, *Rebuilding Russia*, p.35.

[29] See Elizabeth Teague, 'Who Voted for Zhirinovsky?', *RFE/RL Research Report*, vol.3, no.2, 14 January 1994, pp.4-5, quoting two sources from the respected sociologist, Iurii Levada; compare also Vera Tolz, 'Russia's Parliamentary Elections: What Happened and Why', *RFE/RL Research Report*, vol.3, no.2, 14 January 1994, pp.1-8 at p.3; and Victor Yasmann and Elizabeth Teague, 'Who is Vladimir Zhirinovsky', *RFE/RL Research Report*, vol.3, no.1, 7 January 1994, pp.34-5.

[30] See Thomas Childers, *The Nazi Voter: The Social Foundations of Fascism in Germany, 1919-1933* (Chapel Hill: University of North Carolina Press,

1983) especially pp.262-65; R. I. McKibbin, 'The Myth of the Unemployed: Who Did Vote for the Nazis?', *Australian Journal of Politics and History*, vol.15, no.2, August 1969, pp.25-40, especially pp.32-33. There are broader parallels with the German situation of the early 1920s: national and state humiliation, unemployment and inflation (dissipating middle-class savings), footloose 'public servants' of the old regime, and a precocious electorate more used to the politics of symbols than of interests.

31 The pioneer references are Miroslav Hroch, *Social Preconditions of National Revival in Europe* (Cambridge: Cambridge University Press, 1985) and Hugh Seton-Watson, *Nations and States: an inquiry into the origins of nations and the politics of nationalism* (Boulder: Westview Press, 1977). The theme has been developed in a variety of ways by, for example, Anderson, *Imagined Communities*; Ernest Gellner, *Nations and Nationalism* (Oxford: Blackwell, 1983); and Anthony D. Smith, *The Ethnic Revival* (Cambridge: Cambridge University Press, 1981).

32 See 'Why was the Post-Communist Ethnic Revival so Vigorous?'.

33 On 17 February 1994, Viktor Kobelev, Deputy Chairman of the Liberal-Democratic Party of Russia Duma fraction, resigned from that office. Voters, he stated, 'elected me to the Duma to carry out the program of the party, not to support its leader's crazy tricks' (*The Age*, 18 February 1994, p.8).

34 The Liberal-Democratic Party of Russia put up candidates in some sixty electoral districts, but was successful (by my count) only in five of them: Achinsk (district number 46), Kirov (number 93), Shchelkovo (number 114), Pskov (number 141) and Balashov (number 156). In three of these it defeated Communist or Agrarian candidates—but there were at least nine districts where it lost to them, or other statist or nationalist candidates, and at least twelve where the Liberal-Democratic Party of Russia lost to reformists: *Rossiiskaia gazeta*, 30 November 1993; *Rossiiskaia gazeta*, 28 December 1993.

35 As Rigby suggests in the conclusion chapter of this book concerning Yeltsin's new domestic and foreign policy stances of early 1994.

36 See in particular Kenneth Jowitt, 'Soviet Neotraditionalism: The Political Corruption of a Leninist Regime', *Soviet Studies*, vol.35 no.3, July 1983, pp.275-297.

37 This is the central thrust of Dyker's 'Nomenklatura Nationalism ... '. For analysis of Russia, however, I think it is important to distinguish 'communitarianism' from 'nationalism', where Dyker's account tends to merge the two.

38 An economy in which 'the dominant motive' is not investment or development 'but the lord's organised want satisfaction in kind.' Characteristics are the promotion of autarky and monopoly rather than trade and competition, and of 'public service' in kind (Weberian 'liturgies') rather than monetary exchange. 'Exchange takes place only if surplus is to be dumped or if goods simply cannot be procured in any other way': see Max Weber, *Economy and Society: An Outline of Interpretive Sociology* (New York: Bedminster Press, 1968) p.381, also pp.379-83, 1010-1014, 1022-25. Weber does not of course present this as a static situation; if other factors (see below) did not make for Russia's military unity, one could conceive of the emergence of independent trading republics in places like Saint Petersburg or Nizhnii Novgorod—updated versions of Novgorod Velikii before 1478!

39 See, for instance, Elizabeth Teague, 'Russia's Local Elections Begin', *RFE/RL Research Report*, vol.3, no.7, 18 February 1994, pp.1-4 at pp.1-2.

40 There are Russian warlords involved in the politics of Moldova, Georgia and Tajikistan, but apparently none so far in the regional politics of Russia.

13 CONCLUSION: RUSSIA IN SEARCH OF ITS FUTURE

T.H. RIGBY

Question: *What is Socialism?*
Answer: *Socialism is the longest and most painful path to capitalism*

Six or eight years ago variants of this joke were current throughout the Comecon countries, but few could have guessed the full tragic irony of what they were saying. For it carried the unspoken and often unrecognised assumption that the hardest part of this 'path' was the step-by-step roll-back of the dictatorship of the Communist Party, its *nomenklatura* and its ideology, after which it would be plain sailing all the way to 'normality'. Few of those who aspired to a democratic free-market society were prepared for the arguably Sisyphean task of entrenching the institutional and legal foundations of such a society through a population unprepared and unskilled (or deskilled) for it. Few grasped the full extent of environmental and health damage bequeathed by 'real socialism', the legacy of infrastructure neglect, or the uselessness of much of the 'real economy' in a post-Cold War world. Few foresaw the impact of ethnonationalism, of cultural and moral disorientation, or of common criminality unleashed by the collapse of communist quasi-totalitarianism. Not surprisingly, the actual progress of the twenty-odd countries concerned along the path from 'socialism' to 'capitalism' has varied from the disappointing to the disastrous, and not one of them has yet demonstrated conclusively that the desired goal can in fact be attained.

Turning to Russia, there are some obvious reasons why the path might prove particularly long and difficult. It experienced a generation more of 'socialism' in which to disable itself for the task of building a democratic free-market society, and insofar as the search for its future involves for each of these countries a recovery of its past, this was a more remote past in the Russian case, one less obviously adapted to the needs of the turn of the 21st century. Its cultural heritage has less affinity than at least the 'northern tier' of ex-communist countries with the Western market democracies. Its size and geographical location also greatly accentuate many shared problems. And the combination of its ethnonational diversity with the loss of its imperial role imbue the issue of national identity with a particular intensity, exceeded only in the former Yugoslavia. In this volume we have seen ample evidence of the force of these factors in hampering an effective transformation in many areas of Russia's political, social, economic and cultural life and its international relations. Yet when one considers the combined weight of these factors, one cannot fail to be impressed with the actual extent of change nevertheless achieved, and achieved, up to now, without disastrous side effects. I shall come back to this point later, but first let us review how far and by what routes Russia has gone in search of its post-Soviet future.

Paths to the future

As in all other countries which have thrown off communist rule, this search involves the quest for both a new political system and a new socioeconomic order, and as in most of them, for a new—or renewed—national identity as well. The fundamental and multidimensional character of these transformations distinguishes them from other 'transitions from authoritarianism' (as in Spain, Portugal, Chile) and warns us against simply assimilating them theoretically.[1] In contrast with those cases where authoritarian rule finds itself undermined and ultimately brought down by a bourgeois socioeconomic order developing under its aegis, thus making way for a democratic polity, in post-communist countries a socioeconomic order congenial to democracy has to be created at the same time as democracy itself, and that in a context where not even the national basis of the state can be taken for granted.

How, then, could a process of revolutionary change have possibly emerged and gathered force in such a country in the first place? This question lies outside the main focus of this volume, but it is obviously relevant for judging the current trajectory of change. The answer, surely, lies somewhere in the cumulative effects of all those decades of industrialisation, urbanisation and educational advance, inspired initially by the goal of 'building communism', sustained by the imperatives of the Cold War, and coloured by influences inevitably permeating from the 'imperialist' enemy. The cultural and attitudinal changes which these processes engendered were given rein by the incompleteness of Soviet 'totalitarianism'. Even Stalin's monstrous regime, in contrast with China under Mao's 'Cultural Revolution', continued to allow substantial access to the Russian and Western classics, which provided the millions graduating from Soviet schools and universities with values and models often more influential than 'communist' ones. After Stalin, the curbing of political police powers, evidently motivated in part by the new leaders' perceptions of the dangers these powers held for themselves and partly by their realisation of the costs they entailed for technological and economic progress, engendered a totalitarianism more of intention than of fact, or at most, as I have suggested elsewhere, 'a crippled totalitarianism'.[2] Hence the emergence of a many-sided 'shadow culture', denied outlets in the public sphere, but flourishing within the private realm. As John Miller has argued,[3] the key bearers of this 'shadow culture' were the burgeoning and increasingly sophisticated urban professional classes. This shadow culture permeated into the overlapping political and intellectual elites of the USSR, and especially into the influential Moscow 'think-tanks' and Communist Party ideological departments, with their privileged access to sensitive information and to Western ideas.

Thus the success of economic development engendered the sociocultural preconditions for the rejection of mono-organisational socialism. It was, however, the failures of economic development that engendered the political conditions for its demise. For decades the Soviet leadership could remain confident that their socialist system was catching up with the most advanced capitalism and would soon surpass it, but by the 1970s the evidence to the contrary was becoming overwhelming. The USSR was lagging ever further behind in the computer-based 'Third Industrial Revolution'. The inefficiencies of the centralised command economy multiplied along with its size, complexity, and technological level. The Politburo found itself no longer capable of simultaneously matching the Western alliance militarily, investing to ensure significant growth, and maintaining some improvement in mass living standards. They also faced alarming evidence of environmental pollution, of worsening mortality and morbidity levels, of alcoholism, corruption and violent crime, and of ethnic and social antagonisms and 'alien' political ideas.

By 1982, when Iurii Andropov succeeded Leonid Brezhnev as General Secretary, it was obvious that these maladies would go on worsening unless some drastic institutional or policy changes were undertaken. This did not necessarily mean, however, that the collapse of the system was imminent, that the 'Soviet sickness', as I put it at the time, was already 'terminal'.[4] It possessed such formidable defences—external defences crowned by a massive nuclear deterrent, and internal defences based on close and comprehensive police-backed controls over all public expression and association—that for the foreseeable future it could live with its disorders, provided only that its masters hung together, acted with reasonable prudence, and maintained those defences at an adequate level.

Ah, there's the rub—they didn't. The experience of Gorbachev's 'new political thinking', his *glasnost'* and his *perestroika*, is too recent to need retelling here. It started with an attempt at serious within-system reform, and only when the system's inertia threatened him with defeat did Gorbachev move to a progressive dismantling of its internal defences, by licensing ever greater freedom of information, expression, association, and assembly, and ultimately depriving the Communist Party of its political monopoly. Only a quite exceptional individual could have accomplished this, and his combination of imagination, commitment, energy and political skill was unique among Soviet leaders. Yet, paradoxically, his very limitations bred of decades of operating within the system were also, perhaps, indispensable to what he achieved. For not only did they blunt *nomenklatura* resistance to his innovations, they also blinded him to the dangers these entailed. There is still insufficient evidence to be certain what Gorbachev's developing vision of Russia's future really comprised before and during the *perestroika* years, but they certainly did not include a total discarding of the socialist ideal or the dismemberment of the Soviet Union. His resulting failure in 1990-1991 to commit himself to a radical market-reform program and to come to terms with the national aspirations of the non-Russian republics hastened his own political demise and with it the total collapse of the system and the state he had sought to reform.

There is a further aspect of Gorbachev's role as a catalyst of Russia's future which deserves attention here. It was he who brought together the cultural and the political preconditions for the rejection of mono-organisational socialism. He did so by listening to radically reform-minded 'establishment' intellectuals and giving them key roles in policy-making and implementation. The origins of this nexus go back before he took over the party leadership and owe something to his predecessor-but-one Andropov.[5] Of central importance in this connection was 'the father of *glasnost*', Aleksandr Nikolaevich Iakovlev.

There are several observations we may draw from this brief excursus into the origins of the transformation process in Russia. Firstly, its essentially negative character: it was focussed on overcoming the obstacles to change rather than on a clear and consistent vision of where change should lead. Secondly, to the extent that such a vision did emerge, it was an essentially derivative one: a 'normal', 'civilised', 'democratic' country, a Rechtsstaat (*pravovoe gosudarstvo*), a mixed (*mnogoukladnaia*) economy. Thirdly, it was a classical revolution from above, for although Gorbachev was responding to changes in the real world and was influenced by advisers' views on the implications of those changes, his actions were hardly those of just an 'agent', witting or unwitting, of powerful social interests or forces generated by them. And finally, the immediate consequence of this negative revolution from above was to trigger a chaotic revolution from below of competing visions of Russia's socioeconomic future, of its political future, and of its future as a nation. For the 'capitalism' of the old joke is hardly a universal ideal in post-communist Russia, any more than is Gorbachev's democratic Rechtsstaat or Yeltsin's rump federation.

The politics of the last four years have embodied the complex interplay of competing visions on these three levels, as mediated through the personal ambitions and group interests of those articulating them. True, they are not wholly reducible to this, since the varied concrete issues demanding resolution often generate their own specific alignments and cleavages. But it is these visions which have for the most part structured Russian political life during this transition period, as I will outline in the pages that follow.

The 1990-1993 transition period

Up to September 1993, the main arenas within which political conflict was pursued consisted of the half-reformed Soviet-era structures bequeathed by Gorbachev's *perestroika*. There is therefore something in the view that Russia's 'Soviet era' did not really come to an end with the collapse of the USSR at the end of 1991, but only two years later with the adoption of a totally non Soviet constitution and the election of new parliamentary bodies envisaged by that constitution. Nevertheless, I suggest that it may be more useful to see the years 1990 to 1993 as a transition period between Russia's 'Soviet' and 'post-Soviet' eras. It would obviously be foolish to minimise the significance for Russia of the collapse of the USSR and the emergence of the Russian Federation on 1 January 1992 as merely one (albeit easily the largest) of the fifteen resultant successor states. The continuities, however, were numerous and powerful. The Russian government simply took over most of the USSR's central administrative structures, their buildings and staff, including the Ministries of Foreign Affairs, Defence, Interior and Security; and most Soviet scientific, cultural and social organisations and associations were likewise transformed into Russian ones. Moreover, they were brought under Russian political structures set up in 1990-1991 in imitation of the structures created at the USSR level by Gorbachev, and these, in turn consisted of the decades-old Soviet structures, as partly reformed to meet the General Secretary's political needs and purposes in the period 1988-90. The year 1990 marks the beginning of the transition period, because it was in February-March of that year that the cornerstone of the Soviet system was removed, namely the Communist Party's political monopoly and administrative authority over all official and legally permitted unofficial organisations. Simultaneously—and logically—the apex of political authority shifted from the Politburo to a newly created state Presidency. Two further corollaries were the emergence and legalisation of non-communist political parties, and the removal of the last major impediments to the growing freedom of public expression, association and assembly.

A Congress of People's Deputies of the Russian Soviet Federated Socialist Republic was elected in March 1990, in imitation of Gorbachev's Congress of People's Deputies of the USSR elected a year earlier, which like the latter then elected from its number a full-time 'inner parliament', the Supreme Soviet. Although the majority of seats for the Russian Congress were contested, the election was held ten days before the Communist Party's monopoly of power was formally abrogated and alternative parties were only beginning to be organised. The communists still ran all the local authorities and dominated the media, so the cards were stacked against candidates openly advocating a totally non-communist future for Russia. However, the Communist Party itself was already deeply divided between those who hankered after restoring the party's monopoly and those willing to go along with Gorbachev's reforms, and the latter included quite a few ready to go further and desert the CPSU altogether for one or other of the emerging 'democratic' parties. Thus while these elections fell well short of being fully free and fair, they produced a Congress and a Supreme Soviet in which the combined forces of the 'democrats' and the 'reform communists' (whose leading figure was General Aleksandr Rutskoi) were sufficient to get the radical reformer Boris Yeltsin elected as Chairman ('Speaker') of the Supreme Soviet—a position which Gorbachev's example in the USSR Supreme Soviet imbued with considerable power and authority.

In the following months, as the new political freedoms unleashed a tumultuous drive for autonomy and later independence in many of the non-Russian republics, Yeltsin's reaction was to make common cause with them against 'the Centre', at the same time seeking to make his Russian Federation a new focus of Russian national identity in place of Gorbachev's USSR. And meanwhile, he persuaded his Supreme Soviet and Congress to again emulate the USSR pattern by creating a new post of President, and then in June 1991 succeeded in being elected to this post in the first free and fair national elections ever held in Russia, winning a clear majority over all the other candidates combined. He now enjoyed unique political legitimacy, which was further reinforced by his firm and courageous role in the defeat of the conservative coup two months later.

Although Russia's parliamentary and presidential institutions emerged in 1990-1991 as arenas of national politics separate from and competing with those of the USSR, they were not only modelled on the latter but also part of the one political process. Indeed several leading figures of various orientations were members of both the Soviet and the Russian parliaments. This process, as suggested earlier, was driven by the three underlying issues of Russia's political future, her socioeconomic future, and her national future. This was reflected in the complex pattern of parties and blocs which came to characterise parliamentary and extra-parliamentary politics in this period, in their rhetoric, alignments and conflicts. The defeat of the August 1991 coup and the consequent collapse of the Communist Party of the Soviet Union (CPSU) drastically weakened conservative positions on all three of these issue areas, albeit temporarily, while at the same time shifting the main focus of political life from the USSR parliament and presidency to those of Russia and the other republics.

The years 1990-93 were also a transitional period for legislative-executive relations. The key factor here was of course the creation of the presidency, but it is important to note the broader context, which can be described as a shift from a pseudo-parliamentary to a presidential republic. The constitutional fiction under the old Soviet system was that the government (the Council of Ministers) was fully responsible to the parliament (the Supreme Soviet). In fact, of course, the true executive, in the sense of the country's supreme policymaking and administrative body, was the CPSU Politburo, while the Council of Ministers (or rather its inner Presidium) functioned as an administrative sub-committee on second-order business, and the Supreme Soviet had no independent role whatsoever. This began to change in 1989 as the new political freedoms made themselves felt in the new-style Supreme Soviet chosen by Gorbachev's new Congress People's Deputies, bringing the first real policy debate and the first cases of parliamentary refusal of the Prime Minister's ministerial nominations. Gorbachev's power at his point still resided essentially in his role as General Secretary of the ruling CPSU in what was still a single-party system, and once he decided the CPSU's monopoly was no longer viable he had two options. He could have sought election by the Supreme Soviet as Prime Minister, and pushed on towards a genuine parliamentary democracy. Instead, to chose to create (and to assume) a presidency with considerable executive powers, including the power to nominate and remove members of the government (now renamed the Cabinet of Ministers). Thus as Eugene Huskey has put it, 'a hybrid presidential-parliamentary system, born in France of the frustrations with the overbearing parliaments of the Third and Fourth Republics, was now transplanted to a country with virtually no legislative tradition ... '.[6] With the simultaneous displacement of the CPSU Politburo from its supreme executive role, the scene was set for an inchoate and conflictive division of power between President, Government and Parliament, which was to be replicated in Yeltsin's Russian Federation when the presidency was created there in mid-1991.

Thus, by the time Russia emerged as the chief successor state to the USSR, it had absorbed all the main transitional characteristics of its predecessor. The circumstances of its emergence, however, were themselves to make a lasting impact on the politics of the transition period. This had two aspects, the first bearing on Russia's future as a nation. Most conservatives naturally saw the dissolution of the USSR as a betrayal of their country's hard-won superpower role and of Russia's imperial past. Others, including many democrats, while welcoming Russia's loss of the burdens of empire and quite happy to see the Transcaucasian, Central Asian and even perhaps the Baltic states go their own way, were saddened or appalled by the splitting off of their Ukrainian and Belorussian 'brothers'. What at the time of the initial agreement of Yeltsin, Shushkevich and Kravchuk to join together in a new 'Commonwealth of Independent States' had seemed like a reconstitution of the lands of ancient Rus, quickly turned out to be, in the words of the leading Russian-Ukrainian reformer Aleksandr Tsipko, merely a 'velvet disintegration'. Kiev, which every Russian schoolchild knows as the 'cradle of Russian statehood', was to become the capital of a foreign country! Small wonder, then, that the beginning of 1992 saw a resurgence of conservative support and resolve against Yeltsin's leadership, and simultaneously an alienation of part of his democratic following. Meanwhile the issue of socioeconomic change was generating a parallel effect. Yeltsin, determined to succeed where Gorbachev had failed in achieving a radical shift to a market economy, and now free to attempt this within the borders of the new Russia, launched his 'shock therapy' reforms on the Jeffrey Sachs monetarist model, starting with a freeing up of prices. The early effects, and even more the anticipated effects, also hardened conservative resistance and caused some of his reformist supporters to drift into opposition. Thus, while the defeat of the August 1991 coup discredited and disarmed the opposition to Yeltsin's radical reform drive, the disintegration of the USSR four months later triggered a sharp reversal of conservative fortunes, as democrats deserted to the 'patriotic' cause or aligned themselves with moderate reformers in opposition to Yeltsin's 'shock therapy'-oriented government led by Egor Gaidar.

Political divisions in Russia

It is time now to consider the political process in the first two years of Russia's independence, insofar as it bears on our central theme. The party spectrum, as described in the Spring of 1992, consisted of five main categories.[7] First came the three communist parties and the somewhat more moderate Socialist Party of Toilers. Then came the 'radical' parties, the former spearhead of the anti-communist front, who were the most consistent supporters of Yeltsin's government and the idea of a strong presidential republic: they comprised Democratic Russia (several parties of radical westernisers, by now down to a core group after numerous splits), the Republican Party (evolved from the pro-reform wing of the Communist Party), the Constitutional Democrats, the Party of Free Labour, and the Free Democrats. Third there was a group of moderate progressive parties, generally supporting Yeltsin and his government, but also standing for a strong parliament: the Social Democrats, the Movement for Democratic Reforms, Nikolai Travkin's Democratic Party of Russia, the People's Party of Russia, and the somewhat more conservative People's Party of Free Russia led by Vice-President Rutskoi. Fourth came a cluster of 'New Left' parties, mostly young people oriented towards West European socialist ideas and opposed to strong authority: the Democratic Union (which originated as an illegal organisation in the early *perestroika* period), the Socialist (or Labour) Party, the Green Party, and the Anarcho-syndicalists. And finally there was an array of 'New Right' parties. These ranged from such 'democrat-patriots' as the Christian Democratic Movement and the Constitutional-Democratic Party of People's Freedom, through the 'statist' conservative parties the Russian People's Union and Colonel Viktor Alksnis's *Soiuz* (Union) group (which had been a major opponent of Gorbachev in the USSR parliament), to such maverick right-wingers as the Russian National Front and Vladimir Zhirinovskii's mendaciously named Liberal Democratic Party of Russia, and to the quasi-fascist *Pamiat'* ('Memory') organisation and National-Republican Party.

All these parties were represented in the Supreme Soviet and Congress of People's Deputies, whose extreme and obviously dysfunctional fragmentation was due to two main factors. One was the circumstances of the revival of democratic politics in the later Gorbachev period, in which the 'informal groups' (*neformaly*) which emerged from the Soviet 'shadow culture' played a vital part. Most of these groups and the parties that grew out of them were coteries of like-minded intellectuals, often formed around a particular individual and rarely grounded in any definite socioeconomic or local interest. The other cause of fragmentation is of greater interest for our present theme: it was the multidimensional character of political cleavages, such that those taking a particular position on say, the issue of Russia's socioeconomic future, might well take diverse positions on her political future or her national identity. This factor renders the conventional term 'party spectrum' used above rather misleading, and it also helps to account for the profusion and confusion of similar party titles.

This non-congruence of cleavage patterns also often extended to cleavages on different sub-issues within the same major issue area. Thus for example on the issue of Russia's nationhood there were (and are) four main sub-issues which have generated only partly congruent patterns of alignment. First came the centuries-old question of Russia and the West: is Russia essentially a European nation, following, albeit a step or two behind, the nations of the West, or does Russia have its own quite different (and implicitly superior) historical path? If the former, then pride is taken in Russia's special contributions to European (or indeed world) civilisation in such areas as high culture, science, technology and so on. If the latter, then what characterises Russia's special path is a further source of disagreement. Does it reside, as the 'neo-slavophiles' suggest, in Russia's leadership of the Slavic nations against the intrusive Romano-Germanic nations of the West? Or does it reside in the distinct interests, mechanisms and political traditions of the historic Russian state, as the 'statists' (*gosudarstvenniki*) contend? Or again, does it rest on the unique traditions and values of the Russian *narod* (the *pochvenniki*)? Or is Russia neither Western nor oriental but the core of a distinct 'Eurasian' culture area (which happens to include most of the other former inhabitants of the USSR)?

The second nationhood sub-issue concerns the 'non-Russian Russians' (a phrase which is not paradoxical in Russian since there are separate words for ethnic Russians and for Russian subjects— *russkie* and *rossiiane*) who make up some 20 per cent of the country's population. Should they be largely autonomous within their own historic territories or should the emphasis be on assimilation? The third sub-issue is the converse: the fate of the some 25 million Russians marooned in the other successor states to the USSR. And finally there is the Commonwealth of Independent States, which has turned out to be somewhat more than the pessimists anticipated. Should it confine its role to that of an economic clearing-house, should it go the direction of the European Union, or should the aim be a new Russia-dominated confederation?

All four of these sub-issues have injected their own complexities and heat into a stream of domestic and foreign policy disputes, not only such obviously pertinent ones as control of the media, public order, the use of Russian troops in other CIS states, or the Bosnian conflict, but also into disputes on questions lying within the other two main issue areas of Russia's political and her socioeconomic future. And each of the latter also embraces a group of sub-issues on which cleavages are not necessarily congruent. Does Russia need a period of conservative or transformative authoritarianism? If not, should it be a presidential or a parliamentary democracy? Should it be essentially a unitary state, a federation, or a confederation? How much freedom is consonant with social and political peace? Should as much 'socialism' as possible be retained? If marketisation is desirable and/or inevitable, what should be the role and extent of state involvement? Should market reforms go the 'shock therapy' Polish road, the authoritarian Chinese road, or some other? And so on, and so forth.

This sketch of the multidimensional cleavages over Russia's future is necessarily very schematic, but it should suffice to help to explain the extreme fragmentation and volatility of political life. The reality, however, is even more complicated than suggested so far. For these cleavages are found not only in the parliament, but in such other arenas as the media, the government, and even the President's staff. Further, the political groupings they embody themselves come to constitute interests which are in constant interplay with other institutional and socioeconomic interests, and the whole is permeated with the juice of personal ambition and rivalry.

All this suggests a near-chaos defying analysis, but as always in such contexts the politicians and others closely involved have been obliged to form a simplified but broadly realistic picture of it in order to act with reasonable despatch and effectiveness, and I shall employ this picture in the following narrative. It views the political process in the transitional period in terms of four broad contending 'orientations', as I shall call them, while using the conventional Russian labels for them, inappropriate as these may seem at times. First are the 'democrats', dedicated to the quickest possible transformation of Russia into a Western-type free-market democracy, while differing over reform strategies. Next are the 'centrists', regarding market reforms as desirable or at least inevitable, but urging a pragmatic step-by-step approach, minimising costs to existing managerial and administrative elites and their workforces. Third are the 'communists', keen to preserve as much of state socialism as possible, some longing to restore the old single-party dictatorship and the USSR and others reconciled to a democratic 'market socialism' or even a mixed economy (*mnogoukladnaia ekonomika*) in a multiparty Russia. And finally there are the 'patriots', viewing Western capitalist democracy and freedoms as alien, dedicated to restoring a powerful Russian state and a society based on authentic Russian values, though differing over precisely what these are.

The slide to crisis

The political struggles of 1992-1993 were at the same time a contest among these four orientations and an institutional conflict between parliament and president. As already noted, Yeltsin's commitment to a 'shock therapy' program at the end of 1991 and his simultaneous connivance at the 'velvet disintegration' of the USSR had the effect of alienating those democrats with little stomach for one or other of these measures, who now gravitated to centrist or patriotic positions. This left a radical democratic camp committed both to forced-pace market reform and a strong presidency, facing a clear parliamentary majority opposed to Yeltsin's policies, his 'shock therapy' government and increasingly to his presidency. Ruslan Khasbulatov, Chairman ('Speaker') of the Supreme Soviet and formerly a close supporter of Yeltsin, now made energetic and effective use of the organisational and patronage powers at his disposal to consolidate the conservative anti-presidential majority and to curtail the President's authority.

In the spring and summer of 1992 the centrists were the chief challengers to the democrats' dominance of the executive. In April the first centrists were appointed to Gaidar's government. In June the centrist Civic Union bloc was formed by Vice-President Rutskoi's People's Party of Free Russia, Travkin's Democratic Party of Russia, and the Renewal Union based on Arkadii Volskii's Union of Industrialists and Entrepreneurs, which represented mainly the embattled defence and heavy industry bureaucracies. The formation of the centrist Civic Union spurred closer cooperation among the democrats and some smaller anti-authoritarian groups on the one side, and between the communists and patriots on the other. Few Russians were surprised by this latter alliance: Russian nationalism had been a factor in legitimating the communist regime since the 1930s, 'national communism' had been a major intellectual current in the Brezhnev era, and communists and patriots were equally incensed at the disintegration of the USSR and the flood of Westernisation. This 'red-brown alliance' was present in embryo in Gorbachev's USSR parliament, and in the Russian parliament it took organisational shape as the Russian Unity bloc. Members of the latter also gave a lead to the extra-parliamentary National Salvation Front which claimed at its inaugural Congress in October 1992 to have established local branches in 262 cities.[8]

By late 1992 President Yeltsin found himself up against an unbeatable *de facto* parliamentary combination of patriots, communists, and centrists, and in December he was constrained to further dilute his reformist government, replacing Acting Premier Gaidar by the centrist Viktor Chernomyrdin. The Supreme Soviet centrists, however, remained implacable, persisting in their unholy alliance with the communists and patriots. The early months of 1993 saw a deepening paralysis of government stemming from this seemingly irreconcilable confrontation between a President enjoying far greater political legitimacy and a parliamentary majority enjoying far greater legal powers, including a free hand to enact or block changes to the existing constitution and to obstruct Yeltsin's efforts to accelerate the adoption of a new, post-Soviet constitution. Under pressure to resort to the unconstitutional step of decreeing the dissolution of parliament and holding new elections, Yeltsin in a characteristically 'populist' move sought instead to test the public support of each side in a national referendum, even making risky concessions to his opponents over the questions to be asked. The results of the April 25 referendum, with a voter turnout of 64.5%, of whom 58.7% expressed confidence in the president and 53% approved his reform policies, despite the widespread economic and social distress, 67.2% favoured early election of a new parliament but only 49.5% wanted an early presidential election, were widely seen as confirmation of the President's continued political legitimacy and a rejection of that of his opponents. However, lacking a formal mandate to immediately impose new parliamentary elections, which would have required the support of over 50% of the whole electorate, Yeltsin sought instead to go the constitutional road.[9] He published a new draft constitution, invited proposals for amendments, and on 5 June convened a 700-strong Constitutional Assembly, representing a wide array of political groupings plus the regions and republics. The opposition initially refused to participate, but most of the centrists were gradually drawn into the constitution-making process, including key members of Khasbulatov's Supreme Soviet Presidium. By 12 July the Assembly had a substantially revised draft ready, which incorporated *inter alia* elements of the Parliamentary Constitutional Commission's own draft—although not enough to satisfy the latter's secretary Oleg Rumiantsev. This revised draft envisaged a strong presidency and a bicameral Federal Assembly comprising a directly-elected State Duma and a Federation Council of *ex officio* representatives of the 89 republics and regions.

By this time, however, a highly divisive issue had come to the fore: the republics demanded additional powers, but the Russian regions objected that this placed them at a serious disadvantage, while behind this there still lurked the far more menacing spectre of the Congress of Peoples' Deputies' formal veto power over whatever final constitutional text might emerge. It was becoming clear that the breakthrough to speedy constitutional change which Yeltsin expected from his referendum victory was illusory, leaving the paralysing conflict with the conservative-dominated Soviet-era parliament unresolved. By early August Yeltsin was calling for parliamentary elections in the current autumn, and now threatening the parliament with forced dissolution if they did not comply, while the latter responded by approving in principle legislation that would slash the president's powers and virtually reduce him to a figurehead. There followed six more weeks of policy stalemate every bit as intractable as it had been in the early months of the year. Then, on September 21 Yeltsin finally carried out his threat, declaring the parliament dissolved and announcing elections to the new Federal Assembly in seven weeks time.

The deputies now had to decide whether to accept *force majeure* and either take their chance in the upcoming elections or accept the generous retirement arrangements offered them—and a substantial number did so decide—or to assume the risks to their personal safety and to civil peace entailed in direct confrontation. Khasbulatov and Rutskoi, reportedly euphoric that Yeltsin had finally overreached himself and signed his political death warrant,[10] found a credible number of deputies willing to sit it out with them in the 'White House', and to vote to strip Yeltsin of his powers and to appoint Vice-President Rutskoi as Acting President, in accordance with legislation placed on the statute book against any such contingency some months earlier. Here, then, was one of those perilous situations of rival claims to sovereign power, in which the question of which side can command the obedience of the coercive resources of the state, and/or the most active support of the population, becomes crucial. In this case, by contrast to August 1991, it was the obedience of the police and military that counted more than 'people's power'—and at the crucial juncture President Yeltsin proved to be the one who commanded that obedience.

Yeltsin evidently wanted a bloodless solution, but whether he pursued the best tactics to attain it will long be debated. It has been argued that it was his 'siege' of the 'White House' that drove the opposition leaders to that point of desperation where on 3 October Aleksandr Rutskoi was to give his blessing to the armed attack on the Moscow mayoralty and the Ostankino TV station, preparatory to a planned takeover of the Kremlin by the hard men of the 'red-brown alliance' led by the unreconstructed communist and leading figure in the National Salvation Front, retired Colonel-General Al'bert Makashov. Others, however, regard it as naive to believe that Yeltsin's opponents would have been less willing to employ force if he had not sought to constrain them. In any case, their putsch was stopped, but at the cost of scores of lives. Immediate decisive action was now required if this bloodletting was not to become the signal for civil war, and Yeltsin took it in the form of the controversial shelling and storming of the 'White House', with the arrest of Khasbulatov, Rutskoi and other core leaders. A short-lived state of emergency was declared, and a number of opposition newspapers—which had operated freely during the two weeks of 'dual power'—were suspended, most of them only temporarily.

One possible conclusion from this violent showdown was that Russia was not yet ready for democracy and would require a substantial period of enlightened authoritarian rule to create the socioeconomic, legal and institutional foundations of a true democratic order. Yeltsin, however, rather than putting the constitution-building process on hold, now reconvened the Constitutional Assembly, persuaded it to further amend the draft in the direction of strengthening presidential powers, though not egregiously, at the expense of the parliament and the regions, and then risked all by submitting it to a plebiscite, coinciding with the parliamentary elections set for December 12. Since the parliamentary bodies to be chosen were now the new State Duma and Federation Council envisaged in the draft constitution, which might or might not be legitimated by the plebiscite, they were to serve for only a two-year 'transitional' period pending fresh parliamentary and presidential elections in 1996. This would entail Yeltsin's serving out his full five-year term, instead of standing for reelection in mid 1994 as he had proposed under pressure, prior to the violence launched by parliamentary supporters on 3 October.

The election of half the 450 members of the State Duma on a national proportional representation basis, with a five per cent hurdle (as in Germany) and of half in single-member electorates, combined with stiff nomination signature requirements, was expected to reduce the extreme party fragmentation of the old parliament, while allowing nationwide minority interests a chance of representation. In the latter respect the formula proved of crucial value at least for the Women's Movement, but in the former it was only partly successful: thirteen parties and blocs qualified for the proportional representation contest and many others fielded local candidates. The general conclusion of the numerous well-qualified foreign observers was that both the campaign and the voting were free and fair. While certain extremist organisations directly involved in fomenting and leading the 3 October violence were barred, both far 'right' and far 'left' were represented, in the form respectively of Vladimir Zhirinovskii's Liberal Democratic Party and Gennadi Ziuganov's Communist Party of the Russian Federation. Early charges of media bias favouring the democratic parties proved to be exaggerated. The chief defects of the campaign were voter apathy and confusion, which threatened the validity of the results, and the lack-lustre and amateurish campaigning, especially by the democrats: Zhirinovskii was the only party leader who made effective use of the key media resource, the national television channels.

The plebiscite on the draft constitution was a narrow victory for Yeltsin and his democrat supporters: 54.8% of registered voters reportedly took part, of whom 58.4% approved the constitution (although later findings of confusion and possible malfeasance in vote-counting cast some doubt on the accuracy of these official figures). The election to the upper house Federation Council also yielded a result satisfactory to Yeltsin, as witness the Council's choice of the President's close supporter Vladimir Shumeiko as its speaker. The crucial lower house, the Duma, was another story. The democrats came nowhere near the majority they had confidently expected, and while centrist groups also fared poorly, both the communists and patriots polled far more strongly than anticipated. Despite this 'defeat for democracy', however, 12 December 1993 marked a great step forward in Russia's political development. For the first time in its history Russia had a legislature as well as a president chosen in fair elections by universal suffrage, and a genuine constitution endorsed (or at least not vetoed) by the electorate.

The trajectory of change

Thus ended what I have termed the transitional period between the Soviet and post-Soviet phases of Russian history, in which political life was still strongly influenced by half-reformed structures and practices originally designed to serve the Communist Party dictatorship. The possibility of a return to the old Soviet order was now scarcely credible. The final shape of post-Soviet Russia, of its political, socioeconomic and national order, remained however far from settled, and I shall close this chapter with a brief outline of how things stood and the trajectory of change in the Spring of 1994.

The political complexion of the new State Duma obviously had large implications both for policy and for legislature-executive relations. It deprived President Yeltsin of any democratic mandate to pursue the monetarist reform strategy of his Russia's Choice supporters, and threatened a new and possibly even more dangerous crisis of authority if he attempted to use his increased constitutional powers to impose it. Yet it offered even less comfort for those aspiring to a return to old-style socialism. The party spectrum in the Duma was the product of three factors: the election of half the deputies from nationwide party or bloc lists on the basis of proportional representation, the election of the other half from single-member constituencies, and the registration of deputies with Duma 'factions' (*gruppy i fraktsii*) for the purpose of parliamentary commission membership. There were some striking contrasts of party representation levels as between the proportional representation and locally elected deputies, and over half the latter were returned as independents (*bespartiinye*). By April, when all but eight deputies had registered with one or another faction, it was clear that the largest faction was Russia's Choice (75), followed by New Regional Policy (formed mainly from independents—66), Zhirinovskii's Liberal Democratic Party of Russia (64), the Agrarian Party (55), and the Communist Party of the Russian Federation (45), and there were six other factions sharing a further 131 seats. More significant, perhaps, than this 'pecking order' of individual parties was the balance of 'orientations' in the new house, which was as follows:

Democrats	35%	(Russia's Choice, Union of 12 December, Party of Unity and Concord, 'Iabloko' Bloc)
Centrists	8%	(Democratic Party of Russia, Women of Russia)
Communists	24%	(CPRF and Agrarian Party allies)
Patriots	17%	(LDPR and Russian Way Association)
Localists	15%	(New Regional Policy).

This breakdown suggests that the democrats were the most strongly represented, the communists were their main opposition, the patriots (despite the hullabaloo around Zhirinovskii) were still relatively weak, and the centrists were now weakest of all. This conclusion, however, tells only half the story, most importantly on the central issue of economic reform, for firstly, most of the localist deputies appeared to fall into the centrist category, making this orientation far stronger than the table suggests; secondly, both the Agrarian Party and (since their 1993 congress) the Communist Party of the Russian Federation favoured a managed mixed market economy rather than a command economy; and thirdly, the democratic allies of Russia's Choice did not share the latter's unambiguously monetarist positions. It seems fair to conclude, therefore, that the predominant approach within the Duma to Russia's socioeconomic future was one of moderate and pragmatic market-oriented reform, rather than either 'back to socialism' or a rapid transformation based on a single-minded emphasis on macroeconomic stabilisation.

President Yeltsin, with whatever misgivings, now moved to conform the Cabinet of Ministers to that approach. A few democrat ministers remained, but the centrist Prime Minister Viktor Chernomyrdin was in effect licensed to remake the key economic sectors of the government in his own image, free of the leading monetarists Egor Gaidar and Boris Fedorov. Whether this would lead to a sharp increase in central administrative intervention in the economy, and/or a slowing down of the privatisation programme, and how strong the inevitable inflationary pressures would prove, remained unclear. The situation consequently permitted of more than one prognosis. At best it could hold intra-parliamentary and parliamentary-executive conflict within tolerable limits, while moderating popular hardship and discontent, as private enterprise and market institutions progressively established themselves. This would create a socioeconomic environment in which the infant presidential democracy could put down firm roots. It could also take the edge off centre-regional conflict, help contain minority nationalism, facilitate cooperation within the CIS, and contribute to Russian national self-esteem and solidarity, thereby curbing nationalist extremism. A range of intermediate scenarios separated this happy prospect from the worst case, which envisaged runaway inflation, inducing a state of such social desperation and disorder as would render constitutional government impossible, and the alternatives would then be civil war, national disintegration, or an authoritarian presidency, beyond which the shape of a future Russia would be totally unpredictable.

Even, however, if a transition to capitalist democracy is achieved without such disastrous setbacks, it will be capitalist democracy with a Russian face, at least as distinctive as are the societies of, say, the United States, Germany, Japan and Italy. It will embody and transmute both elements culturally encoded over many generations, and others laid down in the over seven decades of communist rule. That this process is already observable in diverse areas of economic, social and cultural life is brought out in several of the chapters in this book.

Notes

1 Compare Zygmunt Bauman's distinction between 'systemic' and 'political' revolutions in Zygmunt Bauman, 'A Post-modern Revolution', in Janina Frentzel-Zagorska (ed.), *From a One-Party State to Democracy: Transition in Eastern Europe* (Amsterdam-Atlanta: Rodopi, 1993) pp.3-19. Further on the issues discussed here, see T.H. Rigby, *The Changing Soviet System: Mono-organisational Socialism from its Origins to Gorbachev's Restructuring* (Aldershot: Edward Elgar, 1990) pp.183-244; Adam Przeworski, *Democracy and the Market: Political and Economic Reforms in Eastern Europe and Latin America* (Cambridge: Cambridge University Press, 1991); Claus Offe, 'Capitalism by design? Democratic theory facing the triple transition in Eastern Europe', *Social Research*, vol.58, no.4, 1991, pp.866-892; Philip G. Roeder, *Red Sunset: The Failure of Soviet Politics* (Princeton: Princeton University Press, 1993); Rasma Karklins, 'Explaining Regime Change in the Soviet Union', *Europe-Asia Studies*, vol.46, no.1, 1994, pp.29-46.

2 T.H. Rigby, 'Reconceptualising the Soviet System', in Stephen White, Alex Pravda and Zvi Gitelman (eds.) *Developments in Soviet and Post-Soviet Politics* (London: Macmillan, 1992) pp.300-319 at p.313.

3 See especially John Miller, *Mikhail Gorbachev and the End of Soviet Power* (London: Macmillan, 1993). Further on this section, see Archie Brown, *The Gorbachev Factor* (Oxford: Oxford University Press, 1995).

4 T.H. Rigby, 'Smertel'na li sovetskaia bolezn'?', *Obozrenie* (Paris), no.1, October 1982, pp.9-11.

5 Compare John Miller, *Mikhail Gorbachev and the End of Soviet Power*, p.61.

6 Eugene Huskey, 'Executive-Legislative Relations', in Eugene Huskey (ed.), *Executive Power and Soviet Politics: The Rise and Decline of the Soviet State* (Armonk: M.E. Sharpe, 1992) pp.83-105 at p.90.

7 Compare L. Byzov, 'Politicheskie sily Rossii', *Argumenty i Fakty*, no.16-17, 1992, p.2 and S. Stankevich, 'Chto takoe partiinaia zhizn' segodnia', *Izvestiia*, 20 April 1992, p.2. For more details on these groups and their leaders, see Vladimir Pribylovsky, *Dictionary of Political Parties and Organizations* (Washington DC: Center for Strategic and International Studies, 1992).

8 *Izvestiia*, 6 November 1992, p.2.

9 The following paragraphs draw on my article 'One Step Back, Two Steps Forward', *Quadrant*, vol.38, no.3, March 1994, pp.21-28, in which I attempt to set these developments in a broad historical context. For an alternative perspective, see Archie Brown's chapter, above.

10 See Fred Hiatt and Margaret Shapiro, 'Yeltsin defies legal trap set by his hardline opponents', *The Washington Post*, 26 September 1993, pp.A1 and A46.

Contributors

Archie Brown is Professor of Politics and Fellow of St Antony's College at the University of Oxford, and a Fellow of the British Academy. He has held visiting professorships at Yale University, the University of Connecticut, Columbia University, and the University of Texas at Austin. He is author of *Soviet Politics and Political Science* (Macmillan: 1974) and *The Gorbachev Factor* (Oxford University Press: 1995). As editor and co-author his books include *Political Culture and Communist Studies* (Macmillan: 1984), *Political Leadership in the Soviet Union* (Macmillan: 1989), *New Thinking in Soviet Politics* (Macmillan: 1992), and *The Cambridge Encyclopedia of Russia and the former Soviet Union* (Cambridge University Press: 1994).

Stephen Fortescue is Senior Lecturer in Political Science at the University of New South Wales. He has also held appointments at the Australian National University and the Centre for Russian and East European Studies, University of Birmingham, and his publications include *The Communist Party and Soviet Science* (Macmillan: 1986) and *Science Policy in the Soviet Union* (Routledge: 1990).

Leslie Holmes is Professor of Political Science and Director of the Centre for Russian and Euro-Asian Studies at the University of Melbourne. He previously held appointments at the University of Wales and the University of Kent at Canterbury, and has held visiting appointments at St Antony's College, Oxford, and at the Russian Research Center at Harvard University. He is author of *The Policy Process in Communist States* (Sage Publications: 1981), *Politics in the Communist World* (Oxford University Press: 1986), *The End of Communist Power: Anti-Corruption Campaigns and Legitimation Crisis* (Oxford University Press: 1993) and *Post-Communism* (Polity Press: 1994).

William Maley is Senior Lecturer in Politics, University College, University of New South Wales. He has been a Visiting Professor at the Russian Diplomatic Academy, and a Visiting Fellow at the Centre for the Study of Public Policy at the University of Strathclyde. He has co-edited *The Soviet Withdrawal from Afghanistan* (Cambridge University Press: 1989) and *The Transition from Socialism: State and Civil Society in the USSR* (Longman: 1991), and co-authored *The Theory of Politics: An Australian Perspective* (Longman Cheshire: 1990), *Regime Change in Afghanistan: Foreign Intervention and the Politics of Legitimacy*

(Westview Press: 1991), *Political Order in Post-Communist Afghanistan* (Lynne Rienner: 1992), and *The Australian Political System* (Longman Cheshire, 1994).

John Miller is Reader in Politics at La Trobe University, and has held appointments at the Institute of Soviet and East European Studies at the University of Glasgow, and at the Research School of Social Sciences at the Australian National University. As well as many journal articles, he has written *Mikhail Gorbachev and the End of Soviet Power* (Macmillan: 1993), and co-edited *Gorbachev at the Helm: A New Era in Soviet Politics?* (Croom Helm: 1987).

Robert F. Miller is a Visiting Fellow in the Transformation of Communist Systems Project at the Australian National University, having previously taught at the University of Illinois at Urbana. He is author of *One Hundred Thousand Tractors: The MTS and the Development of Controls in Soviet Agriculture* (Harvard University Press: 1970) and *Soviet Foreign Policy Today* (Allen & Unwin: 1991), co-edited *Gorbachev at the Helm: A New Era in Soviet Politics?* (Croom Helm: 1987), and edited *The Developments of Civil Society in Communist Systems* (Allen & Unwin, 1992).

A.V. Obolonsky is a Professor of the Institute of State and Law of the Russian Academy of Sciences, Moscow, from which he obtained the degree of Doctor of Juridical Sciences. He has held visiting appointments at the University of Chicago, Indiana University, and the University of New South Wales, and his publications include *Chelovek i gosudarstvennoe upravlenie* (Nauka: 1987) as well as chapters in a range of books, and articles in *Izvestiia, Gosudarstvo i pravo, Obshchestvennye nauki i sovremennost', Druzhba narodov, International Minds*, and *Mind and Human Interaction*. In 1992, he appeared as an expert witness before the Russian Constitutional Court.

T.H. Rigby is Emeritus Professor of Political Science at the Australian National University. He served in the British Embassy in Moscow, and has held visiting apppintments at Oxford University, the Kennan Institute of Advanced Russian Studies, Columbia University, and Moscow State University. He is author of *Communist Party Membership in the USSR 1917-1967* (Princeton University Press: 1968), *Lenin's Government: Sovnarkom 1917-1922* (Cambridge University Press: 1979), *Political Elites in the USSR: Central leaders and local cadres from Lenin to Gorbachev* (Edward Elgar: 1990), and *The Changing Soviet System: Mono-organisational Socialism from its Origins to Gorbachev's Restructuring* (Edward Elgar: 1990).

Amin Saikal is Reader in Political Science and Director of the Centre for Middle Eastern and Central Asian Studies at the Australian National University. He has been a Visiting Fellow at Princeton University, Cambridge University, and the Institute of Development Studies of the University of Sussex. He authored *The Rise and Fall of the Shah* (Princeton University Press: 1980), edited *Refugees in the Modern World* (Australian National University: 1989) co-edited *The Soviet Withdrawal from Afghanistan* (Cambridge University Press: 1989), and co-authored *Regime Change in Afghanistan: Foreign Intervention and the Politics of Legitimacy* (Westview Press: 1991).

Peter Sawczak studied Slavic languages and literatures at Monash University, the Free University of Berlin and Harvard University. Prior to joining the Australian Department of Foreign Affairs and Trade in 1992, he taught Ukrainian literature at Monash University. His research interests include post-revolutionary and contemporary Russian and Ukrainian literature and Russian religious philosophy. He is currently attached to the Australian Embassy in Moscow.

Sergei Serebriany is a Research Fellow at the Institute for Advanced Studies in the Humanities of the Russian State University for the Humanities, Moscow, specialising in Indological studies. He was previously a Research Fellow in the Gorkii Institute of World Literature of the USSR Academy of Sciences, and has also served as Visiting Professor of Comparative Literature at the University of Illinois at Urbana. His publications include *Vid'iapati* (Nauka: 1980), as well as chapters in many books, and articles in journals such as *Vostok-Oriens* and *Voprosy literatury*.

Index